Battlefield of the mind

PSALMS
AND
PROVERBS

Battlefield
of the
mind
PSALMS
AND
PROVERBS

RENEW YOUR MIND THROUGH
THE POWER OF GOD'S WORD

AMPLIFIED VERSION

FEATURING NOTES *and* COMMENTARY BY
JOYCE MEYER

New York • Boston • Nashville

Battlefield of the Mind Bible Psalms and Proverbs

FaithWords

Hachette Book Group

1290 Avenue of the Americas, New York, NY 10104

faithwords.com

twitter.com/faithwords

First Edition: March 2017

Faith Words is a division of Hachette Book Group, Inc.
The Faith Words name and logo are trademarks of Hachette Book Group, Inc.
The publisher is not responsible for websites (or their content)
that are not owned by the publisher.

The Hachette Speakers Bureau provides a wide range of authors
for speaking events. To find out more, go to www.HachetteSpeakersBureau.com
or call (866) 376-6591.

Print book interior design by Koechel Peterson & Associates
Library of Congress Cataloging-in-Publication Data has been applied for.
ISBNs: 978-1-4789-4749-3 (imitation leather), 978-1-4789-4748-6 (ebook)

Printed in China
RRD-C 10   9   8   7   6   5

A Personal Word from Joyce Meyer

Everything in life—the decisions we make, the words we speak, and the actions we take—begins in the mind. Before we say or do anything, we think about it. The fact that our thoughts are so powerful and wield so much influence over every area of our lives is why the enemy, Satan, attacks our minds so often and so strategically.

No matter what the enemy does, he is a defeated foe. Jesus has won the victory over him, and He wants us to enjoy the victorious life He died to give us. To enforce the victory Jesus wants us to have, we need to know how to recognize and resist the enemy's attempts to use our thoughts against us.

I developed the *Battlefield of the Mind Bible*, from which this special *Battlefield of the Mind Psalms and Proverbs* edition is taken, because I have learned from personal experience that the only way to win the battle of the mind is with the Word of God. The enemy tries to influence us by telling us lies, but we can combat his tactics and overcome him with the Truth. While throughout all of God's Word, from Genesis to Revelation, we find verses and passages of Scripture that offer the insights and instruction we need to think godly thoughts, Psalms and Proverbs have throughout biblical history held a special place in the heart of believers. I like to think of these two books as the "Book of Worship" and the "Book of Wisdom." Thus together they can be thought of as speaking to the "whole" man, his emotions and his mind. I have written various types of notes and commentary on these passages to help you understand what they mean, so you can use them to win the battle Satan tries to wage against your thoughts.

Those notes include:

BOOK INTRODUCTIONS

Psalms and Proverbs both open with a book introduction summarizing how the book pertains to winning the battle of the mind. The introductions also include "Winning Thoughts" from each book, which are important points based on specific verses in the book. The introductions also include "Verses for Victory" from each book, which call your attention to specific verses or passages that are vital to developing a triumphant mind-set.

"WINNING THE BATTLES OF THE MIND" ARTICLES

Each individually titled "Winning the Battles of the Mind" article is a full page that represents my core teachings on the battlefield of the mind, the power of thoughts and words, and the importance of aligning mind-sets with God's Word. These inspiring articles are designed to not only help readers *recognize* and *fight* the battles of the mind, but to help them win. Each article closes with "A Prayer for Victory" that you can pray for yourself. You can use them to confirm your faith and affirm your trust in God, or ask for His help in specific ways as you move toward winning the battles of your thought life.

"KEYS TO A VICTORIOUS LIFE" ARTICLES

There are many keys to a life of victory in your mind. These Scripture-based articles are intended to help you recognize, understand, and apply those keys. They also explain the keys to overcoming mental challenges or conflicts and will help you think and speak according to God's Word.

POWERPOINTS

PowerPoints are brief but powerful comments tied to specific Bible verses or biblical principles that provide insight into how to think, speak, or live in order to think as God would have you think and be victorious in your thoughts.

"SPEAK GOD'S WORD" ENTRIES

Scripture confessions designed to teach you how to confess God's Word for yourself—one of the most powerful things you can do as a believer! These confessions will help you train your mind to successfully recognize and resist the enemy when he comes against your mind.

"A PRAYER TO RENEW YOUR MIND" ENTRIES

Anytime you see "A Prayer To Renew Your Mind," you can pray the specific Scripture verse or verses to which it is connected. Praying God's Word not only renews your thinking and helps establish the Word in your thoughts, it is also a highly effective way to pray.

HOW TO HAVE A REAL RELATIONSHIP WITH JESUS

The most important relationship in anyone's life is a genuine, personal relationship with Jesus Christ. At the end of this Book, you'll find a page that will lead you into this life-changing relationship with Him.

I pray that

Battlefield of the Mind: Psalms and Proverbs
will become a valuable resource in your spiritual life,
one that serves as a mighty weapon to help you win
the battle of the mind.

T H E
PSALMS

Psalms

Author: | David, Asaph, the sons of
Korah, Moses, and others
Date: | 1000 BC–300 BC

The book of Psalms includes many verses on the mind, particularly verses that call us to *remember* or *know* or *understand* something about God or about ourselves. The words *remember*, *know*, and *understand* all pertain to the mind.

The Psalms are also full of insights on winning the battle of the mind and scriptures you can confess to defeat the enemy. The writers of the Psalms often expressed their thoughts and feelings—positive or negative—to the Lord. Whenever they struggled with negative thoughts though, they eventually remembered God's goodness and faithfulness and ended up with a positive mind-set.

When you wrestle with wrong thoughts or emotions, let me encourage you to allow the Psalms to restore your hope and strengthen your faith and confidence in God.

WINNING THOUGHTS FROM PSALMS:

When you cry for help, the Lord hears (see Psalm 34:17).

When the enemy tries to oppress your mind with negative or discouraging thoughts, one way to overcome him is to praise God (see Psalm 42:5).

God will always help you in times of trouble (see Psalm 46:1).

God knows you thoroughly. He is aware of your every thought before you think it and of your every word before you speak it (see Psalm 139:1–4).

VERSES FOR VICTORY FROM PSALMS:

As for God, His way is blameless. The word of the LORD is tested [it is perfect, it is faultless]; He is a shield to all who take refuge in Him. | Psalm 18:30

Trust [rely on and have confidence] in the LORD and do good; dwell in the land and feed [securely] on His faithfulness. | Psalm 37:3

He who dwells in the shelter of the Most High will remain secure and rest in the shadow of the Almighty [whose power no enemy can withstand]. | Psalm 91:1

I will bow down [in worship] toward Your holy temple and give thanks to Your name for Your lovingkindness and Your truth; for You have magnified Your word together with Your name. | Psalm 138:2

PSALMS

The following expressions occur often in the Psalms: **Selah** may mean *Pause, Crescendo* or *Musical Interlude;* **Maskil** possibly, *Contemplative,* or *Didactic,* or *Skillful Psalm;* **Mikhtam** possibly, *Epigrammatic Poem,* or *Atonement Psalm;* **Sheol** the nether world.

BOOK ONE

Psalm 1

The Righteous and the Wicked Contrasted.

[1] BLESSED [fortunate, prosperous, and favored by God] is the man who does not walk in the counsel of the wicked [following their advice and example],
Nor stand in the path of sinners,
Nor sit [down to rest] in the seat of scoffers (ridiculers).
[2] But his delight is in the law of the LORD,
And on His law [His precepts and teachings] he [habitually] meditates day and night. [Rom 13:8–10; Gal 3:1–29; 2 Tim 3:16]
[3] And he will be like a tree *firmly* planted [and fed] by streams of water,
Which yields its fruit in its season;
Its leaf does not wither;
And in whatever he does, he prospers [and comes to maturity]. [Jer 17:7, 8]

[4] The wicked [those who live in disobedience to God's law] are not so,
But they are like the chaff [worthless and without substance] which the wind blows away.

Speak God's Word

I am like a tree firmly planted and fed by streams of water, which yields its fruit in its season; its leaf does not wither; and in whatever I do, I prosper and come to maturity.

[*adapted from* PSALM 1:3]

[5] Therefore the wicked will not stand [unpunished] in the judgment,
Nor sinners in the assembly of the righteous.
[6] For the LORD knows *and* fully approves the way of the righteous,
But the way of the wicked shall perish.

Psalm 2

The Reign of the LORD's Anointed.

[1] WHY ARE the nations in an uproar [in turmoil against God],
And why do the people devise a vain *and* hopeless plot?
[2] The kings of the earth take their stand;
And the rulers take counsel together
Against the LORD and His Anointed (the Davidic King, the Messiah, the Christ), saying, [Acts 4:25–27]
[3] "Let us break apart their [divine] bands [of restraint]
And cast away their cords [of control] from us."

[4] He who sits [enthroned] in the heavens laughs [at their rebellion];
The [Sovereign] Lord scoffs at them [and in supreme contempt He mocks them].
[5] Then He will speak to them in His [profound] anger
And terrify them with His displeasure, saying,
[6] "Yet as for Me, I have anointed *and* firmly installed My King
Upon Zion, My holy mountain."

[7] "I will declare the decree of the LORD:
He said to Me, 'You are My Son;

WINNING THE BATTLES *of the* MIND
What Goes In Comes Out

In the early days of computers, people said, "Garbage in, garbage out." That was a way of explaining that the computer only worked with the data put into it. If we wanted different results, we needed to put in different information. Most people understand that concept, but when it comes to their minds, many don't seem to get it.

If you are going to win the battle of the mind, where you focus your attention is crucial. The more you meditate on God's Word, the stronger you'll become and the more easily you'll win the victories you desire.

There is a difference between meditating on the Bible and reading the Bible. Some people like to think that whenever they read God's Word, they're absorbing the deep things of God, but often they have little idea of what they've read when they finish. Those who meditate on God's Word are those who think—and think seriously—about what they're reading. They're saying, in effect, "God, speak to me. As I ponder Your Word, reveal its depth to me."

The psalmist made it quite clear that meditating on and thinking about God's Word bring results. "But his delight is in the law of the LORD, and on His law [His precepts and teachings] he [habitually] meditates day and night. And he will be like a tree *firmly* planted [and fed] by streams of water, which yields its fruit in its season; its leaf does not wither; and in whatever he does, he prospers [and comes to maturity]" (Ps. 1:2–3).

As you ponder who God is and what He's saying to you, you'll grow. It's really that simple. If you read about and allow your mind to focus on God's love and power, that's what will operate in you. If you think about loving others, that is what you will end up doing, but if you think only about how others have hurt you and what people should be doing for you, then you will be self-focused.

Sadly, some Christians don't put much effort into studying the Word. They hear others teach and preach, and they may listen to online sermons and read the Bible occasionally, but they're not dedicated to making God's Word a major and regular part of their lives.

Be careful what you think about. The more you think about Jesus Christ and the principles He taught, the more you become like Jesus and the stronger you grow. And as you grow, you're winning the battles in your mind.

A PRAYER FOR VICTORY

Lord God, help me to think about the things that honor You. Make me hungry for more of You and teach me to meditate and focus on Your Word more and more. In Jesus' name. Amen.

KEYS *to a* Victorious
Life *Think About God's Word*

The Word of God teaches us what we should spend our time thinking about. The psalmist said he thought about or meditated on the "precepts" of God (see Ps. 119:15). That means he spent a lot of time pondering and thinking on the ways of God, His goodness, His instructions. I recommend that you spend time daily just thinking about God, how amazing He is and all the wonderful things He has promised in His Word.

It is very beneficial to think about God's Word because it reveals His will and His amazing plan for His children. The more you think about it, the easier it will be for you to do it. It is also a proven fact that when we think about good things, our joy and peace increase, but when we think about vain or useless things, we become frustrated and dissatisfied.

This day [I proclaim] I have begotten You. [2 Sam 7:14; Heb 1:5; 3:5, 6; 2 Pet 1:17, 18]

8 'Ask of Me, and I will assuredly give [You] the nations as Your inheritance, And the ends of the earth as Your possession.

9 'You shall break them with a rod of iron; You shall shatter them [in pieces] like earthenware.'" [Rev 12:5; 19:15]

POWERPOINT

In Psalm 2:7, the psalmist wrote that he would "declare the decree of the LORD." The written Word of God is His formal decree. When we declare God's Word out of our mouths, with hearts full of faith, those faith-filled words go forth to establish God's order and plan in our lives. It is very important to learn that words contain the power of life and death (see Prov. 18:21).

10 Now therefore, O kings, act wisely; Be instructed *and* take warning, O leaders (judges, rulers) of the earth.

11 Worship the LORD *and* serve Him with reverence [with awe-inspired fear and submissive wonder]; Rejoice [yet do so] with trembling.

12 Kiss (pay respect to) the Son, so that He does not become angry, and you perish in the way, For His wrath may soon be kindled *and* set aflame. How blessed [fortunate, prosperous, and favored by God] are all those who take refuge in Him!

Psalm 3

Morning Prayer of Trust in God.

A Psalm of David. When he fled from Absalom his son.

1 O LORD, how my enemies have increased! Many are rising up against me.

2 Many are saying of me, "There is no help [no salvation] for him in God." *Selah.*

3 But You, O LORD, are a shield for me,

A Prayer To Renew Your Mind

Lord, You are a shield for me, my glory and my honor, and the One who lifts my head. When I cry to You, You will answer me from Your holy mountain.

· *adapted from Psalm 3:3–4*

My glory [and my honor], and the One who lifts my head.

4 With my voice I was crying to the LORD,

And He answered me from His holy mountain. *Selah.*

5 I lay down and slept [safely];

I awakened, for the LORD sustains me.

6 I will not be intimidated *or* afraid of the ten thousands

Who have set themselves against me all around.

7 Arise, O LORD; save me, O my God!

For You have struck all my enemies on the cheek;

You have shattered the teeth of the wicked.

8 Salvation belongs to the LORD;

May Your blessing be upon Your people. *Selah.*

Psalm 4

Evening Prayer of Trust in God.

To the Chief Musician; on stringed instruments. A Psalm of David.

1 ANSWER ME when I call, O God of my righteousness!

You have freed me when I was hemmed in *and* relieved me when I was in distress;

Be gracious to me and hear [and respond to] my prayer.

2 O sons of men, how long will my honor *and* glory be [turned into] shame?

How long will you [my enemies] love worthless (vain, futile) things and seek deception *and* lies? *Selah.*

3 But know that the LORD has set apart for Himself [and dealt wonderfully with]

the godly man [the one of honorable character and moral courage—the one who does right].

The LORD hears *and* responds when I call to Him.

4 Tremble [with anger or fear], and do not sin;

Meditate in your heart upon your bed and be still [reflect on your sin and repent of your rebellion]. [Eph 4:26] *Selah.*

5 Offer righteous sacrifices;

Trust [confidently] in the LORD.

6 Many are saying, "Oh, that we might see some good!"

Lift up the light of Your face upon us, O LORD.

7 You have put joy in my heart,

More than [others know] when their wheat and new wine have yielded abundantly.

8 In peace [and with a tranquil heart] I will both lie down and sleep,

For You alone, O LORD, make me dwell in safety *and* confident trust.

POWERPOINT

Many people say they cannot sleep at night because they can't get their minds to settle down. But Psalm 4:8 says, "In peace [and with a tranquil heart] I will both lie down and sleep." When we use our mind to reason our way through a situation to figure out what to do, we rotate our mind around and around an issue until we become worn-out and confused. We can experience peace of mind and heart when we trust in God, not in our human insight and understanding. You and I can grow to the place where we are satisfied to know the One Who knows, even if we ourselves do not know.

WINNING THE BATTLES *of the* MIND
Understanding Righteousness

The Bible includes many names of God. In Psalm 4:1, David calls Him the "God of my righteousness." We find the concept of righteousness mentioned throughout the Word of God, and it's important for us to understand it.

There are two kinds of righteousness. The first kind is righteousness through right behavior; this is the one we are most familiar with. We struggle through life trying to do what is expected of us, and what society tells us is right. If we have faith in God, we also struggle trying to please Him by obeying all His commands. Most of us feel we never succeed or measure up to the standard that has been set. Those feelings of failure and being wrong or inadequate lead to guilt and condemnation, which press us down in life and cause us to live beneath the privileges we have as children of God. We spend our lives trying to get something that God's Word says we can have freely as a gift of God's grace through faith. I like to say it is like trying to get into a chair we are already seated in.

The second kind of righteousness available to us is God's righteousness. It is His gift to us at the time we receive Jesus Christ as our Savior. It comes by grace through faith. Since it is a free gift, we cannot earn it, deserve it, or pay for it. The gift of righteousness God gives us has already been paid for through the suffering, death, and resurrection of Jesus.

In this kind of righteousness, God takes our sin and gives us His righteousness, and by an act of His love and mercy, He views us as having right standing with Him through faith (see 2 Cor. 5:21). This is the great exchange! God takes our sins, puts them on Jesus, and gives us His righteousness. Someone had to pay the price for sin, and we could not. So God sent Jesus to be our substitute and pay our sin debt in full. God is the God of our righteousness, the One who sees us as righteous not because of anything we have ever done, but because of what Jesus has done for us.

Once we know we have been made right with God through faith in Jesus, the knowledge of His love and what He has done for us causes us to "want" to do what is right, and we are then doing it for the right reason. We do what is right because He loves us, and not to get Him to love us, because His love is a free gift.

A PRAYER FOR VICTORY

God of my righteousness, thank You for sending Jesus to suffer and die for my sins so I do not have to struggle to try to please You. Help me to live with a constant awareness that You see me as righteous because of Him. In His name. Amen.

Psalm 5

Prayer for Protection from the Wicked.

To the Chief Musician; on wind instruments. A Psalm of David.

¹ LISTEN TO my words, O LORD,
Consider my groaning *and* sighing.
² Heed the sound of my cry for help, my King and my God,
For to You I pray.
³ In the morning, O LORD, You will hear my voice;
In the morning I will prepare [a prayer and a sacrifice] for You and watch *and* wait [for You to speak to my heart].

⁴ For You are not a God who takes pleasure in wickedness;
No evil [person] dwells with You.
⁵ The boastful *and* the arrogant will not stand in Your sight;
You hate all who do evil.
⁶ You destroy those who tell lies;
The LORD detests *and* rejects the bloodthirsty and deceitful man.
⁷ But as for me, I will enter Your house through the abundance of Your steadfast love *and* tender mercy;

At Your holy temple I will bow [obediently] in reverence for You.

⁸ O LORD, lead me in Your righteousness because of my enemies;
Make Your way straight (direct, right) before me.
⁹ For there is nothing trustworthy *or* reliable *or* truthful in what they say;
Their heart is destruction [just a treacherous chasm, a yawning gulf of lies].
Their throat is an open grave;
They [glibly] flatter with their [silken] tongue. [Rom 3:13]
¹⁰ Hold them guilty, O God;
Let them fall by their own designs *and* councils!
Cast them out because of the abundance of their transgressions,
For they are mutinous *and* have rebelled against You.

¹¹ But let all who take refuge *and* put their trust in You rejoice,
Let them ever sing for joy;
Because You cover *and* shelter them,
Let those who love Your name be joyful *and* exult in You.

KEYS *to a* **Victorious Life** *First Thing*

David said, "In the morning, O LORD, You will hear my voice; in the morning I will prepare [a prayer and a sacrifice] for You and watch and *wait [for You to speak to my heart]" (Ps. 5:3).*

What was the first thing you said after getting up this morning? I believe we can prophesy (speak forth) and set the tone of the day by what we say at the beginning of it. Maybe you said, "I'm tired, and I dread going to work." These kinds of words often come naturally, but you can decide to live supernaturally and say what God would say. Can you imagine Him saying, "This is going to be a lousy day"? Of course not! He would say something awesome and positive, and we should too— "I have favor everywhere I go"; "Today is going to be an awesome day"; "I'm going to see the hand of God at work today!"

A Prayer To Renew Your Mind

You, O Lord, bless me and all the people who are in right standing with You; You surround me with favor as with a shield.

· *adapted from Psalm 5:12*

¹²For You, O Lᴏʀᴅ, bless the righteous man [the one who is in right standing with You];
You surround him with favor as with a shield.

Psalm 6

Prayer for Mercy in Time of Trouble.

To the Chief Musician; on stringed instruments, set [possibly] an octave below. A Psalm of David.

¹O LORD, do not rebuke *or* punish me in Your anger,
Nor discipline me in Your wrath.
²Have mercy on me *and* be gracious to me, O Lᴏʀᴅ, for I am weak (faint, frail);
Heal me, O Lᴏʀᴅ, for my bones are dismayed *and* anguished.
³My soul [as well as my body] is greatly dismayed.
But as for You, O Lᴏʀᴅ—how long [until You act on my behalf]?

⁴Return, O Lᴏʀᴅ, rescue my soul;
Save me because of Your [unfailing] steadfast love *and* mercy.
⁵For in death there is no mention of You;
In Sheol (the nether world, the place of the dead) who will praise You *and* give You thanks?

⁶I am weary with my groaning;
Every night I soak my bed with tears,
I drench my couch with my weeping.
⁷My eye grows dim with grief;
It grows old because of all my enemies.

⁸Depart from me, all you who do evil,
For the Lᴏʀᴅ has heard the voice of my weeping. [Matt 7:23; Luke 13:27]
⁹The Lᴏʀᴅ has heard my supplication [my plea for grace];

The Lᴏʀᴅ receives my prayer.
¹⁰Let all my enemies be ashamed and greatly horrified;
Let them turn back, let them suddenly be ashamed [of what they have done].

Psalm 7

The Lᴏʀᴅ Implored to Defend the Psalmist against the Wicked.

An Ode of David, [perhaps in a wild, irregular, enthusiastic strain,] which he sang to the Lᴏʀᴅ concerning the words of Cush, a Benjamite.

¹O LORD my God, in You I take refuge;
Save me and rescue me from all those who pursue me,
²So that my enemy will not tear me like a lion,
Dragging me away while there is no one to rescue [me].

³O Lᴏʀᴅ my God, if I have done this,
If there is injustice in my hands,
⁴If I have done evil to him who was at peace with me,
Or without cause robbed him who was my enemy,
⁵Let the enemy pursue me and overtake me;
And let him trample my life to the ground
And lay my honor in the dust.   *Selah.*

⁶Arise, O Lᴏʀᴅ, in Your anger;
Lift up Yourself against the rage of my enemies;
Rise up for me; You have commanded judgment *and* vindication.
⁷Let the assembly of the nations be gathered around You,
And return on high over them.
⁸The Lᴏʀᴅ judges the peoples;
Judge me, O Lᴏʀᴅ, *and* grant me justice according to my righteousness and according to the integrity within me.
⁹Oh, let the wickedness of the wicked come to an end, but establish the righteous [those in right standing with You];
For the righteous God tries the hearts and minds. [Rev 2:23]
¹⁰My shield *and* my defense depend on God,

Who saves the upright in heart.
11 God is a righteous judge,
And a God who is indignant every day.

12 If a man does not repent, God will
sharpen His sword;
He has strung *and* bent His [mighty]
bow and made it ready.
13 He has also prepared [other] deadly
weapons for Himself;
He makes His arrows fiery shafts [aimed
at the unrepentant].
14 Behold, the [wicked and irreverent] man
is pregnant with sin,
And he conceives mischief and gives
birth to lies.
15 He has dug a pit and hollowed it out,
And has fallen into the [very] pit which
he made [as a trap].
16 His mischief will return on his own head,
And his violence will come down on the
top of his head [like loose dirt].

17 I will give thanks to the LORD according
to His righteousness *and* justice,
And I will sing praise to the name of the
LORD Most High.

Psalm 8

The LORD's Glory and Man's
Dignity.

To the Chief Musician; set to a Philistine
lute [or perhaps to a particular Hittite
tune]. A Psalm of David.

1 O LORD, our Lord,
How majestic *and* glorious *and* excellent
is Your name in all the earth!
You have displayed Your splendor above
the heavens.
2 Out of the mouths of infants and
nursing babes You have established
strength
Because of Your adversaries,
That You might silence the enemy *and*
make the revengeful cease. [Matt
21:15, 16]

3 When I see *and* consider Your heavens,
the work of Your fingers,
The moon and the stars, which You have
established,
4 What is man that You are mindful of him,

8:5 Or *the angels;* Heb *Elohim.*

POWERPOINT

Have you ever wondered if you are
good enough for God to love you?
Unfortunately, many people believe God
loves them only as long as they don't
make mistakes. The psalmist asked,
"What is man that You are mindful of
him, and the son of [earthborn] man
that You care for him?" (Ps. 8:4). I
think David knew that God loved Him,
but He was still amazed that He did.
The Bible tells us that we are God's
creation, the work of His hands,
and that He loves each one of us
unconditionally, and that is amazing!

And the son of [earthborn] man that
You care for him?
5 Yet You have made him a little lower
than *God,
And You have crowned him with glory
and honor.
6 You made him to have dominion over
the works of Your hands;
You have put all things under his feet,
[1 Cor 15:27; Eph 1:22, 23; Heb 2:6–8]
7 All sheep and oxen,
And also the beasts of the field,
8 The birds of the air, and the fish of the sea,
Whatever passes through the paths of
the seas.

9 O LORD, our Lord,
How majestic *and* glorious *and* excellent
is Your name in all the earth!

Psalm 9

A Psalm of Thanksgiving
for God's Justice.

To the Chief Musician; on Muth-labben.
A Psalm of David.

1 I WILL give thanks *and* praise the
LORD, with all my heart;
I will tell aloud all Your wonders *and*
marvelous deeds.

KEYS *to a* Victorious Life *Be Glad*

Twice in Philippians 4:4 the apostle Paul tells us to rejoice. He urges us to "not be anxious or worried about anything" (Phil. 4:6), but to pray and give thanks to God in every circumstance and in everything—not after everything is working out good in our lives.

If we wait until everything is perfect before rejoicing and giving thanks, we won't ever have consistent joy. Learning to enjoy life, to "be in high spirits" even in the midst of difficult circumstances, is one way we develop spiritual maturity. Paul also writes that we "are progressively being transformed into His image from [one degree of] glory to [even more] glory" (2 Cor. 3:18). We need to learn how to enjoy the glory (the spiritual maturity) we are experiencing at each level of our development. Let's learn to pray a prayer of rejoicing and be glad in the Lord this day and every day along the way toward our goal (see Ps. 9:2).

When I first started my ministry, I depended on my circumstances for happiness. Finally the Lord showed me the doorway to happiness. He gave me a breakthrough by teaching me that fullness of joy is found in His presence—not in His presents (see Ps. 16:11)!

True joy comes from seeking God's face.

---

²I will rejoice and exult in you;
  I will sing praise to Your name, O Most
  High.

³When my enemies turn back,
  They stumble and perish before You.
⁴For You have maintained my right and
  my cause;
  You have sat on the throne judging
  righteously.
⁵You have rebuked the nations, You
  have destroyed the wicked *and*
  unrepentant;
  You have wiped out their name forever
  and ever.
⁶The enemy has been cut off *and* has
  vanished in everlasting ruins,
  You have uprooted their cities;
  The very memory of them has perished.

⁷But the Lord will remain *and* sit
  enthroned forever;
  He has prepared *and* established His
  throne for judgment. [Heb 1:11]

⁸And He will judge the world in
  righteousness;
  He will execute judgment for the
  nations with fairness (equity).
  [Acts 17:31]
⁹The Lord also will be a refuge *and* a
  stronghold for the oppressed,
  A refuge in times of trouble;
¹⁰And those who know Your name [who
  have experienced Your precious
  mercy] will put their confident trust
  in You,
  For You, O Lord, have not abandoned
  those who seek You. [Ps 42:1]

¹¹Sing praises to the Lord, who dwells in
  Zion;
  Declare among the peoples His [great
  and wondrous] deeds.
¹²For He who avenges blood [unjustly
  shed] remembers them (His people);
  He does not forget the cry of the
  afflicted *and* abused.

13 Have mercy on me *and* be gracious to
   me, O LORD;
   See how I am afflicted by those who
   hate me,
   You who lift me up from the gates of
   death,
14 That I may tell aloud all Your praises,
   That in the gates of the daughter of Zion
   (Jerusalem)
   I may rejoice in Your salvation *and* Your
   help.
15 The nations have sunk down in the pit
   which they have made;
   In the net which they hid, their own foot
   has been caught.
16 The LORD has made Himself known;
   He executes judgment;
   The wicked are trapped by the work of
   their own hands.
                Higgaion (meditation) Selah.

17 The wicked will turn to Sheol (the
   nether world, the place of the dead),
   Even all the nations who forget God.
18 For the poor will not always be
   forgotten,
   Nor the hope of the burdened perish
   forever.
19 Arise, O LORD, do not let man prevail;
   Let the nations be judged before You.
20 Put them in [reverent] fear of You,
   O LORD,
   So that the nations may know they are
   but [frail and mortal] men.   *Selah.*

Psalm 10

A Prayer for the Overthrow
of the Wicked.

1 WHY DO You stand far away,
   O LORD?
   Why do You hide [Yourself, veiling Your
   eyes] in times of trouble?
2 In pride *and* arrogance the wicked hotly
   pursue *and* persecute the afflicted;
   Let them be caught in the plots which
   they have devised.

3 For the wicked boasts *and* sings the
   praises of his heart's desire,
   And the greedy man curses and spurns
   [and even despises] the LORD.
4 The wicked, in the haughtiness of his
   face, will not seek *nor* inquire for *Him;*

POWERPOINT

Psalm 10:4 is about the thoughts of
the wicked, who think there is no God.
In contrast, the righteous know there
is a God and think about Him often.
In fact, our lives depend on spending
regular, quality time with God. Once
I learned that fellowship with Him
is vital, I gave it priority in my life. I
encourage you to do the same and to
think about Him often. God is with us
all the time, and we should not ignore
Him for hours at a time.

All his thoughts are, "There is no God
   [so there is no accountability or
   punishment]."

5 His ways prosper at all times;
   Your judgments [LORD] are on high, out
   of his sight [so he never thinks about
   them];
   As for all his enemies, he sneers at
   them.
6 He says to himself, "I will not be
   moved;
   For throughout all generations I will not
   be in adversity [for nothing bad will
   happen to me]."
7 His mouth is full of curses and deceit
   (fraud) and oppression;
   Under his tongue is mischief and
   wickedness [injustice and sin].
8 He lurks in ambush in the villages;
   In hiding places he kills the innocent;
   He lies in wait for the unfortunate [the
   unhappy, the poor, the helpless].
9 He lurks in a hiding place like a lion in
   his lair;
   He lies in wait to catch the afflicted;
   He catches the afflicted when he draws
   him into his net.
10 He crushes [his prey] and crouches;
   And the unfortunate fall by his mighty
   claws.
11 He says to himself, "God has [quite]
   forgotten;

He has hidden His face; He will never
see my deed."

¹²Arise, O LORD! O God, lift up Your hand
[in judgment];
Do not forget the suffering.
¹³Why has the wicked spurned *and* shown
disrespect to God?
He has said to himself, "You will not
require me to account."
¹⁴You have seen it, for You have noted
mischief and vexation (irritation) to
take it into Your hand.
The unfortunate commits *himself* to
You;
You are the helper of the fatherless.
¹⁵Break the arm of the wicked and the
evildoer,
Seek out his wickedness until You find
no more.

¹⁶The LORD is King forever and ever;
The nations will perish from His land.
¹⁷O LORD, You have heard the desire of
the humble *and* oppressed;
You will strengthen their heart, You will
incline Your ear to hear,
¹⁸To vindicate *and* obtain justice for the
fatherless and the oppressed,

So that man who is of the earth will no
longer terrify them.

Psalm 11

The LORD a Refuge and Defense.

To the Chief Musician.
A Psalm of David.

¹IN THE LORD I take refuge [and put my
trust];
How can you say to me, "Flee like a bird
to your mountain;
²For look, the wicked are bending the
bow;
They take aim with their arrow on the
string
To shoot [by stealth] in darkness at the
upright in heart.
³"If the foundations [of a godly society]
are destroyed,
What can the righteous do?"

⁴The LORD is in His holy temple; the
LORD's throne is in heaven.
His eyes see, His eyelids test the children
of men. [Acts 7:49; Rev 4:2]
⁵The LORD tests the righteous and the
wicked,

KEYS *to a* Victorious Life *Make Christ Your Foundation*

*A foundation is the most important part of a building. Without a solid foundation,
the building won't last long. Everything else concerning the building is built on
the foundation. If the foundation is weak or cracked, nothing built on it is safe. It
could crumble or fall apart at any time, especially if stress is placed on it by
a storm.*

*David warned, "If the foundations [of a godly society] are destroyed, what can the
righteous do?" (Ps. 11:3). The Bible encourages people to build their lives on the
solid rock of Christ, rooted securely in Him (see Matt. 7:24–27; Eph. 3:17). If you
try to build your life on what people say and think about you, on how they treat
you, on how you feel, or based on your past mistakes, you are building on sinking
sand. But if you trade that old, cracked foundation for a solid foundation, one
based on Christ and His love, nothing can shake you.*

And His soul hates the [malevolent] one who loves violence. [James 1:12]

6 Upon the wicked (godless) He will rain coals of fire;

Fire and brimstone and a dreadful scorching wind will be the portion of their cup [of doom].

7 For the LORD is [absolutely] righteous, He loves righteousness (virtue, morality, justice);

The upright shall see His face.

Psalm 12

God, a Helper against the Treacherous.

To the Chief Musician; set an octave below. A Psalm of David.

1 SAVE *AND* help *and* rescue, LORD, for godly people cease to be,

For the faithful vanish from among the sons of men.

2 They speak deceitful *and* worthless words to one another;

With flattering lips and a double heart they speak.

3 May the LORD cut off all flattering lips, The tongue that speaks great things [in boasting];

4 Who have said, "With our tongue we will prevail;

Our lips are our own; who is lord *and* master over us?"

5 "Because of the devastation of the afflicted, because of the groaning of the needy,

Now I will arise," says the LORD; "I will place him in the safety for which he longs."

6 The words *and* promises of the LORD are pure words,

Like silver refined in an earthen furnace, purified seven times.

7 You, O LORD, will preserve *and* keep them;

You will protect him from this [evil] generation forever.

8 The wicked strut about [in pompous self-importance] on every side,

As vileness is exalted *and* baseness is prized among the sons of men.

Psalm 13

Prayer for Help in Trouble.

To the Chief Musician. A Psalm of David.

1 HOW LONG, O LORD? Will You forget me forever?

How long will You hide Your face from me?

KEYS *to a* Victorious Life *Learn by Doing*

Worry is failing to trust God to take care of the various situations in our lives. When we worry, we are actually acting on the thought If I try hard enough, I can find a solution to my problem, which is the opposite of trusting God.

Most of us have spent our lives trying to take care of ourselves, and it takes time to learn how to trust God in every situation. But we learn by doing as David did. Surrounded by his enemies, David said, "But I have trusted and relied on and been confident in Your lovingkindness and faithfulness; my heart shall rejoice and delight in Your salvation" (Ps. 13:5). We have to step out in faith, and as we do, we will experience the faithfulness of God, which makes it easier to trust Him the next time.

2 How long must I take counsel in my soul,
  Having sorrow in my heart day after day?
  How long will my enemy exalt himself
  and triumph over me?

3 Consider and answer me, O Lord my
    God;
  Give light (life) to my eyes, or I will sleep
    the *sleep of* death,
4 And my enemy will say, "I have
    overcome him,"
  And my adversaries will rejoice when I
    am shaken.

5 But I have trusted *and* relied on *and*
    been confident in Your lovingkindness
    and faithfulness;
  My heart shall rejoice *and* delight in
    Your salvation.
6 I will sing to the Lord,
  Because He has dealt bountifully
    with me.

Psalm 14

Folly and Wickedness of Men.

To the Chief Musician.
A Psalm of David.

1 THE [SPIRITUALLY ignorant] fool has
    said in his heart, "There is no God."
  They are corrupt, they have committed
    repulsive *and* unspeakable deeds;
  There is no one who does good. [Rom 3:10]
2 The Lord has looked down from heaven
    upon the children of men
  To see if there are any who understand
    (act wisely),
  Who [truly] seek after God, [longing for
    His wisdom and guidance].
3 They have all turned aside, together they
    have become corrupt;
  There is no one who does good, not even
    one. [Rom 3:11, 12]

4 Have all the workers of wickedness *and*
    injustice no knowledge,
  Who eat up my people as they eat bread,
  And do not call upon the Lord?
5 There they tremble with great fear,
  For God is with the [consistently]
    righteous generation.
6 You [evildoers] shamefully plan against
    the poor,
  But the Lord is his safe refuge.

7 Oh, that the salvation of Israel would
    come out of Zion!
  When the Lord restores His captive
    people,
  Then Jacob will rejoice, Israel will be
    glad. [Rom 11:25–27]

Psalm 15

Description of a Citizen of Zion.

A Psalm of David.

1 O LORD, who may lodge [as a guest] in
    Your tent?
  Who may dwell [continually] on Your
    holy hill?
2 He who walks with integrity *and*
    strength of character, and works
    righteousness,
  And speaks *and* holds truth in his
    heart.
3 He does not slander with his tongue,
  Nor does evil to his neighbor,
  Nor takes up a reproach against his friend;
4 In his eyes an evil person is despised,
  But he honors those who fear the
    Lord [and obediently worship Him
    with awe-inspired reverence and
    submissive wonder].
  He keeps his word even to his own
    disadvantage and does not change it
    [for his own benefit];
5 He does not put out his money at
    interest [to a fellow Israelite],
  And does not take a bribe against the
    innocent.
  He who does these things will never be
    shaken. [Ex 22:25, 26]

Psalm 16

The Lord, the Psalmist's Portion
in Life and Deliverer in Death.

A Mikhtam of David [probably intended
to record memorable thoughts].

1 KEEP *AND* protect me, O God, for in
    You I have placed my trust *and* found
    refuge.
2 I said to the Lord, "You are my Lord;
  I have no good besides You."
3 As for the saints (godly people) who are
    in the land,

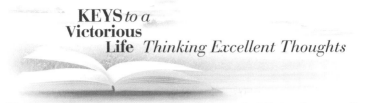

KEYS *to a* Victorious Life *Thinking Excellent Thoughts*

We can never become excellent in our actions if we don't first make a commitment to become excellent in our thoughts. The Bible teaches us to think on things that are filled with virtue and excellence, things such as believing the best at all times, things that are honorable, just, pure, lovely, and lovable (see Phil. 4:8).

What kinds of thoughts do you entertain? When you recognize that your thoughts are not good, do you take action to cast them out of your mind or do you lazily let them remain? It is impossible to become one of "the majestic and *the noble* and *the excellent ones" without first developing an excellent mind (Ps. 16:3). God has called each of us to be excellent in all that we do and to enjoy an excellent life. If you haven't done so yet, start today thinking in that direction.*

They are the majestic *and* the noble *and* the excellent ones in whom is all my delight.

⁴The sorrows [pain and suffering] of those who have chosen another *god* will be multiplied [because of their idolatry];

I will not pour out their drink offerings of blood,

Nor will I take their names upon my lips.

⁵The LORD is the portion of my inheritance, my cup [He is all I need]; You support my lot.

⁶The [boundary] lines [of the land] have fallen for me in pleasant places;

Indeed, my heritage is beautiful to me.

⁷I will bless the LORD who has counseled me;

Indeed, my heart (mind) instructs me in the night.

⁸I have set the LORD continually before me; Because He is at my right hand, I will not be shaken.

⁹Therefore my heart is glad and my glory [my innermost self] rejoices;

My body too will dwell [confidently] in safety,

¹⁰For You will not abandon me to Sheol (the nether world, the place of the dead),

Nor will You allow Your Holy One to undergo decay. [Acts 13:35]

¹¹You will show me the path of life; In Your presence is fullness of joy; In Your right hand there are pleasures forevermore. [Acts 2:25–28, 31]

Psalm 17

Prayer for Protection against Oppressors.

A Prayer of David.

¹HEAR THE just (righteous) cause, O LORD; listen to my loud [piercing] cry;

Listen to my prayer, that comes from guileless lips.

²Let my verdict of vindication come from Your presence;

A Prayer To Renew Your Mind

Thank You, Lord, that You will show me the path of life; in Your presence is fullness of joy; at Your right hand there are pleasures forevermore.

· *adapted from Psalm 16:11*

Speak God's Word

*I intend that my mouth will not transgress
and that I will not sin with my words.*

[*adapted from* PSALM 17:3]

May Your eyes look with equity *and*
  behold things that are just.
³You have tried my heart;
You have visited me in the night;
You have tested me and You find
  nothing [evil in me];
I intend that my mouth will not
  transgress.
⁴Concerning the deeds of men, by the
  word of Your lips
I have kept away from the paths of the
  violent.
⁵My steps have held closely to Your paths;
My feet have not staggered.

⁶I have called upon You, for You, O God,
  will answer me;
Incline Your ear to me, hear my speech.
⁷Wondrously show Your [marvelous and
  amazing] lovingkindness,
O Savior of those who take refuge at
  Your right hand
From those who rise up *against them.*

⁸Keep me [in Your affectionate care,
  protect me] as the apple of Your eye;
Hide me in the [protective] shadow of
  Your wings
⁹From the wicked who despoil *and* deal
  violently with me,
My deadly enemies who surround me.
¹⁰They have closed their unfeeling *heart*
  [to kindness and compassion];
With their mouths they speak proudly
  and make presumptuous claims.
¹¹They track us down *and* have now
  surrounded us in our steps;
They set their eyes to force us to the
  ground,
¹²He is like a lion eager to tear [his prey],
And like a young lion lurking in hiding
  places.

¹³Arise, O Lᴏʀᴅ, confront him, cast him
  down;
Save my soul from the wicked with Your
  sword,
¹⁴From men with Your hand, O Lᴏʀᴅ,
From men of the world [these moths
  of the night] whose portion [of
  enjoyment] is in this life—idle and
  vain,
And whose belly You fill with Your
  treasure;
They are satisfied with children,

KEYS *to a* **Victorious Life** *Filling the God-Shaped Hole*

*There is a God-shaped hole inside every one of us, and even if we had all the
money in the world, nothing we bought could fill it. The only thing that is
able to satisfy that craving is God Himself. Seek God as your first and most
vital necessity in life. Put Him first in your time, thoughts, conversation, and
actions. Love Him with all your heart and talk to Him throughout the day about
everything that takes place in your life.*

*David prayed, "As for me, I shall see Your face in righteousness; I will be [fully]
satisfied when I awake [to find myself] seeing Your likeness" (Ps. 17:15). As you
include God in all that you do, you will develop an intimacy with Him that will
satisfy your soul like nothing else in the world can do.*

And they leave what they have left [of wealth] to their children.

15 As for me, I shall see Your face in righteousness;
I will be [fully] satisfied when I awake [to find myself] seeing Your likeness.

Psalm 18

David Praises the Lord for Rescuing Him.

To the Chief Musician. A Psalm of David, the servant of the Lord, who spoke the words of this song to the Lord on the day when the Lord rescued him from the hand of all his enemies and from the hand of Saul. And he said:

1 "I LOVE You [fervently and devotedly], O Lord, my strength."

2 The Lord is my rock, my fortress, and the One who rescues me;
My God, my rock *and* strength in whom I trust *and* take refuge;
My shield, and the horn of my salvation, my high tower—my stronghold. [Heb 2:13]

3 I call upon the Lord, who is worthy to be praised;
And I am saved from my enemies. [Rev 5:12]

4 The cords of death surrounded me,
And the streams of ungodliness *and* torrents of destruction terrified me.

5 The cords of Sheol (the nether world, the place of the dead) surrounded me;
The snares of death confronted me.

Speak God's Word

The Lord is my rock, my fortress, and the One who rescues me; my God, my rock and strength in whom I trust and take refuge; my shield, and the horn of my salvation, my high tower—my stronghold. I call upon the Lord, who is worthy to be praised; and I am saved from my enemies.

| adapted from PSALM 18:2–3 |

6 In my distress [when I seemed surrounded] I called upon the Lord
And cried to my God for help;
He heard my voice from His temple,
And my cry for help came before Him, into His *very* ears.

7 Then the earth shook and quaked,
The foundations of the mountains trembled;
They were shaken because He was indignant *and* angry.

8 Smoke went up from His nostrils,
And fire from His mouth devoured;
Coals were kindled by it.

9 He bowed the heavens also and came down;
And thick darkness was under His feet.

10 And He rode upon a cherub (storm) and flew;
And He sped on the wings of the wind.

11 He made darkness His hiding place (covering); His pavilion (canopy) around Him,
The darkness of the waters, the thick clouds of the skies.

12 Out of the brightness before Him passed His thick clouds,
Hailstones and coals of fire.

13 The Lord also thundered in the heavens,
And the Most High uttered His voice,
Hailstones and coals of fire.

14 He sent out His arrows and scattered them;
And *He sent* an abundance of lightning flashes and confused *and* routed them [in defeat].

15 Then the stream beds of the waters appeared,
And the foundations of the world were laid bare
At Your rebuke, O Lord,
At the blast of the breath of Your nostrils.

16 He reached from on high, He took me;
He drew me out of many waters.

17 He rescued me from my strong enemy,
And from those who hated me, for they were too strong for me.

18 They confronted me in the day of my disaster,
But the Lord was my support.

19 He brought me out into a broad place;
   He rescued me because He was pleased
   with me *and* delighted in me.

20 The LORD dealt with me according to
   my righteousness (moral character,
   spiritual integrity);
   According to the cleanness of my hands
   He has rewarded me.

21 For I have kept the ways of the LORD,
   And have not wickedly departed from
   my God.

22 For all His ordinances were before me,
   And I did not put away His statutes
   from me.

23 I was blameless before Him,
   And I kept myself free from my sin.

24 Therefore the LORD has rewarded me
   according to my righteousness (moral
   character, spiritual integrity),
   According to the cleanness of my hands
   in His sight.

25 With the kind (merciful, faithful, loyal)
   You show Yourself kind,
   With the blameless You show Yourself
   blameless,

26 With the pure You show Yourself pure,
   And with the crooked You show Yourself
   astute.

27 For You save an afflicted *and* humble
   people,
   But bring down those [arrogant fools]
   with haughty eyes.

28 For You cause my lamp to be lighted *and*
   to shine;
   The LORD my God illumines my
   darkness.

29 For by You I can crush a troop,
   And by my God I can leap over a wall.

30 As for God, His way is blameless.
   The word of the LORD is tested [it is
   perfect, it is faultless];
   He is a shield to all who take refuge in
   Him.

31 For who is God, but the LORD?
   Or who is a rock, except our God,

32 The God who encircles me with strength
   And makes my way blameless?

33 He makes my feet like hinds' feet [able to
   stand firmly and tread safely on paths
   of testing and trouble];
   He sets me [securely] upon my high
   places.

34 He trains my hands for war,
   So that my arms can bend a bow of
   bronze.

35 You have also given me the shield of
   Your salvation,

KEYS *to a* Victorious Life *Enjoy All Kinds of People*

I once read that most of our unhappiness comes from people not being what we want them to be or doing what we want them to do, and I couldn't agree more. That being the case, how can we enjoy the day if we don't learn to enjoy all different types of people, especially the ones we may find annoying?

I have found it helpful to realize that God has created all kinds of people with many different temperaments and personalities, and I truly believe He enjoys and loves them all. Because I cannot enjoy anyone whom I am judging critically, I often remind myself that I need to value people where they are, not where I would like them to be. Being merciful in my attitude toward others actually helps me enjoy my life, and it will do the same for you (see Ps. 18:25). I urge you to accept those who are different from you and learn to enjoy them as God does.

And Your right hand upholds *and*
   sustains me;
Your gentleness [Your gracious response
   when I pray] makes me great.
36 You enlarge the path beneath me *and*
   make my steps secure,
So that my feet will not slip.

37 I pursued my enemies and overtook
   them;
And I did not turn back until they were
   consumed.
38 I shattered them so that they were not
   able to rise;
They fell [wounded] under my feet.
39 For You have encircled me with strength
   for the battle;
You have subdued under me those who
   rose up against me.
40 You have also made my enemies turn
   their backs to me [in defeat],
And I silenced *and* destroyed those who
   hated me.
41 They cried for help, but there was no one
   to save them—
Even to the LORD [they cried], but He
   did not answer them.
42 Then I beat them fine as the dust before
   the wind;
I emptied them out as the dirt of the
   streets.

43 You have rescued me from the
   contentions of the people;
You have placed me as the head of the
   nations;
A people whom I have not known
   serve me.
44 As soon as they hear me, they respond
   and obey me;
Foreigners feign obedience to me.
45 Foreigners lose heart,
And come trembling out of their
   strongholds.

46 The LORD lives, blessed be my rock;
And may the God of my salvation be
   exalted,
47 The God who avenges me,
And subdues peoples (nations)
   under me.
48 He rescues me from my enemies;
Yes, You lift me up above those who rise
   up against me;

You deliver me from the man of
   violence.
49 Therefore will I give thanks *and* praise
   You, O LORD, among the nations,
And sing praises to Your name. [Rom
   15:9]
50 He gives great triumphs to His king,
And shows steadfast love *and* mercy to
   His anointed,
To David and his descendants forever.
   [2 Sam 22:2–51]

Psalm 19

The Works and the Word of God.

To the Chief Musician.
A Psalm of David.

1 THE HEAVENS are telling of the glory
   of God;
And the expanse [of heaven] is declaring
   the work of His hands. [Rom 1:20, 21]
2 Day after day pours forth speech,
And night after night reveals knowledge.
3 There is no speech, nor are there
   [spoken] words [from the stars];
Their voice is not heard.
4 Yet their voice [in quiet evidence] has
   gone out through all the earth,
Their words to the end of the world.
In them *and* in the heavens He has made
   a tent for the sun, [Rom 10:18]
5 Which is as a bridegroom coming out of
   his chamber;
It rejoices as a strong man to run his
   course.
6 The sun's rising is from one end of the
   heavens,
And its circuit to the other end of them;
And there is nothing hidden from its
   heat.

7 The law of the LORD is perfect (flawless),
   restoring *and* refreshing the soul;
The statutes of the LORD are reliable *and*
   trustworthy, making wise the simple.
8 The precepts of the LORD are right,
   bringing joy to the heart;
The commandment of the LORD is pure,
   enlightening the eyes.
9 The fear of the LORD is clean, enduring
   forever;
The judgments of the LORD are true,
   they are righteous altogether.

A Prayer To Renew Your Mind

Let the words of my mouth and the meditation of my heart be acceptable and pleasing in Your sight, O Lord, my rock and my Redeemer.

· *adapted from Psalm 19:14*

10 They are more desirable than gold, yes, than much fine gold;
 Sweeter also than honey and the drippings of the honeycomb.
11 Moreover, by them Your servant is warned [reminded, illuminated, and instructed];
 In keeping them there is great reward.
12 Who can understand his errors *or* omissions? Acquit me of hidden (unconscious, unintended) *faults.*
13 Also keep back Your servant from presumptuous (deliberate, willful) *sins;*
 Let them not rule *and* have control over me.
 Then I will be blameless (complete), And I shall be acquitted of great transgression.

14 Let the words of my mouth and the meditation of my heart
 Be acceptable *and* pleasing in Your sight, O LORD, my [firm, immovable] rock and my Redeemer.

Psalm 20

Prayer for Victory over Enemies.

To the Chief Musician.
A Psalm of David.

1 MAY THE LORD answer you (David) in the day of trouble!
 May the name of the God of Jacob set you *securely* on high [and defend you in battle]!
2 May He send you help from the sanctuary (His dwelling place)
 And support *and* strengthen you from Zion!
3 May He remember all your meal offerings And accept your burnt offering.   *Selah.*
4 May He grant you your heart's desire And fulfill all your plans.
5 We will sing joyously over your victory, And in the name of our God we will set up our banners.
 May the LORD fulfill all your petitions.

KEYS *to a* Victorious Life *Attitude Determines Altitude*

The Bible teaches us that our words have power and that we will have what we consistently say. Along with that, our thoughts affect our moods and attitudes. In other words, our attitude in life affects our altitude in life, meaning our attitude determines how far we can go in life—how far we can go in pursuing our dreams, relationships, business, intimate relationship with God, etc.

Your thoughts and my thoughts will determine the kind of lives we will have in the future. You don't have to think about and focus on whatever falls into your head. You can think things on purpose. Sometimes it is good to just sit down and have a think session. Are the "words of my mouth and the meditation of my heart . . . acceptable and *pleasing" in the Lord's sight (Ps. 19:14)? After almost forty years of knowing these things, I still have to practice them daily. Be determined to maintain good thoughts.*

KEYS *to a* Victorious Life *Pray About Everything, Fear Nothing*

Some years ago the Lord spoke these words to me: "Pray about everything and fear nothing." During the next couple of weeks, He continued showing me different things about prayer versus fear. Many of them dealt with little areas in which fear would try to creep into my life and cause me problems. He showed me that in every case, no matter how great or important or how small or insignificant, the solution was to pray.

Sometimes we become afraid just by staring at our circumstances. The more we focus on the problem, the more fearful we become. Instead, we are to keep our eyes, thoughts, and our words focused on God. He is able to handle anything that we may ever have to face in this life.

God has promised to strengthen us, to harden us to difficulties, to hold us up and retain us "with the saving strength of His right hand" (Ps. 20:6). He also commands us to not be afraid. But remember, He is not commanding us to never feel fear, but rather to not let it control us.

The Lord is saying to you and me personally, "Do not fear, I will help you" (Isa. 41:13). But we will never experience the help of God until we place everything in His loving hands and live by faith rather than fear.

When you feel fear, don't back down or run away. Instead, pray and move forward even though you feel afraid.

---

⁶Now I know that the LORD saves His anointed;
He will answer him from His holy heaven
With the saving strength of His right hand.
⁷Some *trust* in chariots and some in horses,
But we will remember *and* trust in the name of the LORD our God.
⁸They have bowed down and fallen,
But we have risen and stood upright.
⁹O LORD, save [the king];
May the King answer us in the day we call.

REMEMBER, when you are in Christ, victory belongs to you!

Psalm 21

Praise for Help.

To the Chief Musician.
A Psalm of David.

¹O LORD the king will delight in Your strength,
And in Your salvation how greatly will he rejoice!
²You have given him his heart's desire,
And You have not withheld the request of his lips.   *Selah.*
³For You meet him with blessings of good things;
You set a crown of pure gold on his head.
⁴He asked life of You,
And You gave it to him,
Long life forever and evermore.

5 His glory is great because of Your
   victory;
 Splendor and majesty You bestow upon
   him.
6 For You make him most blessed [and a
   blessing] forever;
 You make him joyful with the joy of
   Your presence. [Gen 12:2]

7 For the king [confidently] trusts in the
   LORD,
 And through the lovingkindness
   (faithfulness, goodness) of the Most
   High he will never be shaken.
8 Your hand will reach out *and* defeat all
   your enemies;
 Your right hand will reach those who
   hate you.
9 You will make them as [if in] a blazing
   oven in the time of your anger;
 The LORD will swallow them up in His
   wrath,
 And the fire will devour them.
10 Their offspring You will destroy from
   the earth,
 And their descendants from the sons of
   men.
11 For they planned evil against You;
 They devised a [malevolent] plot
 And they will not succeed.
12 For You will make them turn their backs
   [in defeat];
 You will aim Your bowstring [of divine
   justice] at their faces.
13 Be exalted, LORD, in Your strength;
 We will sing and praise Your power.

Psalm 22

A Cry of Anguish and a Song
of Praise.

To the Chief Musician; set to [the tune
of] Aijeleth Hashshahar (The Doe
of the Dawn). A Psalm of David.

1 MY GOD, my God, why have You
   forsaken me?
 Why are You so far from helping me,
   and from the words of my groaning?
   [Matt 27:46]
2 O my God, I call out by day, but You do
   not answer;
 And by night, but I find no rest *nor*
   quiet.

3 But You are holy,
 O You who are enthroned in [the holy
   place where] the praises of Israel [are
   offered].
4 In You our fathers trusted [leaned on,
   relied on, and were confident];
 They trusted and You rescued them.
5 They cried out to You and were
   delivered;
 They trusted in You and were not
   disappointed *or* ashamed.

6 But I am [treated as] a worm
   [insignificant and powerless] and not a
   man;
 I am the scorn of men and despised by
   the people. [Matt 27:39–44]
7 All who see me laugh at me *and* mock
   me;
 They [insultingly] open their lips, they
   shake their head, *saying,* [Matt 27:43]
8 "He trusted *and* committed himself to
   the LORD, let Him save him.
 Let Him rescue him, because He
   delights in him." [Matt 27:39, 43; Mark
   15:29, 30; Luke 23:35]

9 Yet You are He who pulled me out of the
   womb;
 You made me trust when on my
   mother's breasts.
10 I was cast upon You from birth;
 From my mother's womb You have been
   my God.

11 Do not be far from me, for trouble is
   near;
 And there is no one to help.
12 Many [enemies like] bulls have
   surrounded me;
 Strong *bulls* of Bashan have encircled
   me. [Ezek 39:18; Amos 4:1]
13 They open wide their mouths against
   me,
 Like a ravening and a roaring lion.
14 I am poured out like water,
 And all my bones are out of joint.
 My heart is like wax;
 It is melted [by anguish] within me.
15 My strength is dried up like a fragment
   of clay pottery;
 And my [dry] tongue clings to my jaws;
 And You have laid me in the dust of
   death. [John 19:28]

KEYS *to a* Victorious Life *What Do You Do with Disappointment?*

Psalm 22:5 speaks of those who trusted in God "and were not disappointed or ashamed." There is nothing unusual or wrong about initial feelings of disappointment, but it is what we do from that point forward that makes all the difference in the world. Absolutely nobody gets everything they want all the time, so we need to learn how to deal properly with disappointment.

Trusting God completely, and believing that His plan is infinitely better for you than your own, will prevent you from being disappointed with God. You might feel anger toward your situation, but don't ever be angry with God. When you get angry, you naturally want to lash out at someone, but it is unwise to make God your target. He is the only One Who can help you and truly comfort you; therefore, it is much better to run to Him in your time of pain than to run away from Him.

16 For [a pack of] dogs have surrounded me;
A gang of evildoers has encircled me,
They pierced my hands and my feet. [Is 53:7; John 19:37]

17 I can count all my bones;
They look, they stare at me. [Luke 23:27, 35]

18 They divide my clothing among them
And cast lots for my garment. [John 19:23, 24]

19 But You, O LORD, do not be far from me;
O You my help, come quickly to my assistance.

20 Rescue my life from the sword,
My only *life* from the paw of the dog (the executioner).

21 Save me from the lion's mouth;
From the horns of the wild oxen You answer me.

22 I will tell of Your name to my countrymen;
In the midst of the congregation I will praise You. [John 20:17; Rom 8:29; Heb 2:12]

23 You who fear the LORD [with awe-inspired reverence], praise Him!
All you descendants of Jacob, honor Him.
Fear Him [with submissive wonder], all you descendants of Israel.

24 For He has not despised nor detested the suffering of the afflicted;
Nor has He hidden His face from him;
But when he cried to Him for help, He listened.

25 My praise will be of You in the great assembly.
I will pay my vows [made in the time of trouble] before those who [reverently] fear Him.

26 The afflicted will eat and be satisfied;
Those who [diligently] seek Him *and* require Him [as their greatest need] will praise the LORD.
May your hearts live forever!

27 All the ends of the earth will remember and turn to the LORD,
And all the families of the nations will bow down *and* worship before You,

28 For the kingship *and* the kingdom are the LORD's
And He rules over the nations.

29 All the prosperous of the earth will eat and worship;
All those who go down to the dust (the dead) will bow before Him,
Even he who cannot keep his soul alive.

30 Posterity will serve Him;

They will tell of the Lord to the next generation.
[31] They will come and declare His righteousness
To a people yet to be born—that He has done it [and that it is finished]. [John 19:30]

Psalm 23

The LORD, the Psalmist's Shepherd.

A Psalm of David.

[1] THE LORD is my Shepherd [to feed, to guide and to shield me], [Ezek 34:11–31] I shall not want.
[2] He lets me lie down in green pastures; He leads me beside the still *and* quiet waters. [Rev 7:17]
[3] He refreshes *and* restores my soul (life); He leads me in the paths of righteousness
for His name's sake.

[4] Even though I walk through the [sunless] *valley of the shadow of death, I fear no evil, for You are with me; Your rod [to protect] and Your staff [to guide], they comfort *and* console me.
[5] You prepare a table before me in the presence of my enemies.

23:4 Or *valley of deep darkness.*

You have anointed *and* refreshed my head with oil;
My cup overflows.
[6] Surely goodness and mercy *and* unfailing love shall follow me all the days of my life,
And I shall dwell forever [throughout all my days] in the house *and* in the presence of the LORD.

Psalm 24

The King of Glory Entering Zion.

A Psalm of David.

[1] THE EARTH is the LORD's, and the fullness of it,
The world, and those who dwell in it. [1 Cor 10:26]
[2] For He has founded it upon the seas

KEYS *to a* Victorious Life *Looking Ahead*

Your future has no room for your past, and I encourage you not to get stuck in a moment in your life that is over. God is a Redeemer and a Restorer. He promises to refresh and restore our souls, and He will—if we invite Him in and cooperate with His healing process in our lives.

When Psalm 23:2 says that He makes us lie down in green pastures and leads us beside still and quiet waters, it reminds me that God wants us to have peace. In order to do that, we need to stop running from the past and simply make a decision to be still, face the past, and receive healing from God. As long as we are running, something is chasing us, but if we confront it with God by our side, we can defeat it and enjoy the new life that is ours in Christ.

WINNING THE BATTLES *of the* MIND
Fear No Evil

Wouldn't life be better if we didn't have to deal with the debilitating fear that Satan tries to put on us every day, fear that is intended to keep us from having the power, love, and sound mind that God wants us to have? If you have ever struggled as I once did with anxiety, you are familiar with the worry, stress, and the feeling of heaviness that comes with it.

Many people struggle with fear that has no obvious cause or source. They wonder why they are always afraid and can't change, no matter how hard they try. Others worry constantly about what *might* happen. "What if . . ." is their favorite phrase. The endless list of possible tragedies keeps these unfortunate people bound up and miserable.

We need to learn to resist fear when it rises against us. Second Timothy 1:7 tells us, "For God did not give us a spirit of timidity *or* cowardice *or* fear, but [He has given us a spirit] of power and of love and of sound judgment *and* personal discipline [abilities that result in a calm, well-balanced mind and self-control]."

Sometimes we think of fear as an emotion, but we need to realize that fear is actually a spirit. In fact, I believe fear is one of Satan's favorite tools, and he particularly loves to torment Christians with it. At every possible opportunity, he will whisper in your ear, telling you that God has forgotten you and there is no hope.

Psalm 23:4 says, "Even though I walk through the [sunless] valley of the shadow of death, I fear no evil, for You are with me; Your rod [to protect] and Your staff [to guide], they comfort *and* console me." The psalmist David said he walked *through* the valley.

When we fear or become afraid, we can be sure that's not God at work, but one of the sly tricks of the enemy. If he can make us think that God is not going to help us, we'll start to lose the battle.

God is love. We can never say these words enough. Fear is a spirit that must be confronted head on—it will not leave on its own. We need to proclaim the Word of God and command fear to leave. So the next time fear knocks on your door, send faith to answer!

A PRAYER FOR VICTORY

Lord Jesus, there are times I feel unworthy of Your love, but You do not love me because I'm worthy; You love me because You are love. Thank You for Your reassurance that I am truly loved by You; therefore I have no reason to fear. Amen.

KEYS *to a* Victorious Life *Trust Takes Time*

How many times have you become frustrated and all upset needlessly over troublesome situations that come your way? How many years of your life have you spent saying, "Oh, I'm believing God. I'm trusting God," when, in reality, you were only worrying, talking negatively, and trying to figure out everything on your own? You may have thought you were trusting God because you were saying, "I trust God," but inside you were anxious and panicky. You were trying to learn to trust God, but you were not quite there yet. I know. I did that for many years myself.

Psalm 25:2 speaks of having unwavering trust and steadfast confidence in the Lord. We do not develop that kind of trust and confidence quickly; they are built up over a period of time. It usually takes some time to overcome an ingrained habit of worry, anxiety, or fear. That is why it is so important to "hang in there" with God. Don't quit and give up, because you gain experience and spiritual strength every round you face with courage; and each time you will find that you've become a little stronger than you were the last time. Sooner or later, if you remain steadfast and don't give up, you will be more than the devil can handle.

If you are in a time of trials, use that time to build your trust in God. Trust Him to deliver you out of the snare or to bring you through the battle successfully.

And established it upon the streams *and* the rivers.

³Who may ascend onto the mountain of the Lord?

And who may stand in His holy place?

⁴He who has clean hands and a pure heart,

Who has not lifted up his soul to what is false,

Nor has sworn [oaths] deceitfully. [Matt 5:8]

⁵He shall receive a blessing from the Lord,

And righteousness from the God of his salvation.

⁶This is the generation (description) of those who diligently seek Him *and* require Him as their greatest need,

Who seek Your face, even [as did] Jacob. [Ps 42:1]   *Selah.*

⁷Lift up your heads, O gates,
And be lifted up, ancient doors,

That the King of glory may come in.

⁸Who is the King of glory?

The Lord strong and mighty,

The Lord mighty in battle.

⁹Lift up your heads, O gates,

And lift them up, ancient doors,

That the King of glory may come in.

¹⁰Who is [He then] this King of glory?

The Lord of hosts,

He is the King of glory [who rules over all creation with His heavenly armies].
                                                      Selah.

Psalm 25

Prayer for Protection, Guidance and Pardon.

A Psalm of David.

¹TO YOU, O Lord, I lift up my soul.

²O my God, in You I [have unwavering] trust [and I rely on You with steadfast confidence],

A Prayer To Renew Your Mind

Let me know Your ways, O Lord; teach me Your paths. Guide me in Your truth and teach me, for You are the God of my salvation. For You and only You I wait expectantly all the day long.

· *adapted from Psalm 25:4–5*

Do not let me be ashamed *or* my hope in You be disappointed;
Do not let my enemies triumph over me.
³Indeed, none of those who [expectantly] wait for You will be ashamed;
Those who turn away from what is right *and* deal treacherously without cause will be ashamed (humiliated, embarrassed).

⁴Let me know Your ways, O Lord;
Teach me Your paths.
⁵Guide me in Your truth and teach me,
For You are the God of my salvation;
For You [and only You] I wait [expectantly] all the day long.
⁶Remember, O Lord, Your [tender] compassion and Your lovingkindnesses,
For they have been from of old.
⁷Do not remember the sins of my youth or my transgressions;
According to Your lovingkindness remember me,
For Your goodness' sake, O Lord.

⁸Good and upright is the Lord;
Therefore He instructs sinners in the way.
⁹He leads the humble in justice,
And He teaches the humble His way.
¹⁰All the paths of the Lord are lovingkindness *and* goodness and truth *and* faithfulness
To those who keep His covenant and His testimonies.

A Prayer To Renew Your Mind

God, You lead the humble in justice, and You teach the humble Your way.

· *adapted from Psalm 25:9*

¹¹For Your name's sake, O Lord,
Pardon my wickedness *and* my guilt, for they are great.

¹²Who is the man who fears the Lord [with awe-inspired reverence and worships Him with submissive wonder]?
He will teach him [through His word] in the way he should choose.
¹³His soul will dwell in prosperity *and* goodness,
And his descendants will inherit the land.
¹⁴The secret [of the wise counsel] of the Lord is for those who fear Him,
And He will let them know His covenant *and* reveal to them [through His word] its [deep, inner] meaning. [John 7:17; 15:15]
¹⁵My eyes are continually toward the Lord,
For He will bring my feet out of the net.

¹⁶Turn to me [Lord] and be gracious to me,
For I am alone and afflicted.
¹⁷The troubles of my heart are multiplied;
Bring me out of my distresses.
¹⁸Look upon my affliction and my trouble,
And forgive all my sins.
¹⁹Look upon my enemies, for they are many;
They hate me with cruel *and* violent hatred.
²⁰Guard my soul and rescue me;
Do not let me be ashamed *or* disappointed,
For I have taken refuge in You.
²¹Let integrity and uprightness protect me,
For I wait [expectantly] for You.
²²O God, redeem Israel,
Out of all his troubles.

Psalm 26

Protestation of Integrity and Prayer for Protection.

A Psalm of David.

¹VINDICATE ME, O Lord, for I have walked in my integrity;
I have [relied on and] trusted [confidently] in the Lord without wavering *and* I shall not slip.
²Examine me, O Lord, and try me;
Test my heart and my mind.

Speak God's Word

I walk in my integrity; I have trusted confidently in the Lord without wavering and I will not slip. I invite God to examine me and try me; test my heart and my mind. For His lovingkindness is before my eyes, and I walk faithfully in His truth.

| *adapted from* PSALM 26:1–3 |

³ For Your lovingkindness is before my eyes,
And I have walked [faithfully] in Your truth.
⁴ I do not sit with deceitful *or* unethical *or* worthless men,
Nor seek companionship with pretenders (self-righteous hypocrites).
⁵ I hate the company of evildoers,
And will not sit with the wicked.
⁶ I will wash my hands in innocence,
And I will go about Your altar, O LORD,
⁷ That I may proclaim with the voice of thanksgiving
And declare all Your wonders.

⁸ O LORD, I love the habitation of Your house
And the place where Your glory dwells.
⁹ Do not sweep my soul away with sinners,

POWERPOINT

Integrity means being honest and doing the right thing in every situation. We cannot make other people have integrity, but each of us is responsible to God and to ourselves to have integrity in our own lives. When we see wrongdoing all around us, we need to avoid the temptation to say, "Everyone else is doing it, so what's the problem?" Even if no one else in the world keeps their word or acts honorably, we need to keep our word and live with integrity because it is the right thing to do. We are to follow God, not the ways of the world.

Nor [sweep away] my life with men of bloodshed,
¹⁰ In whose hands is a wicked scheme,
And whose right hand is full of bribes.
¹¹ But as for me, I shall walk in my integrity;
Redeem me and be merciful *and* gracious to me.

KEYS *to a* Victorious Life *What Does Your Heart Say?*

Have you ever said something and thought, Where did that come from? *The truth is it came from somewhere inside of you. You had to think it at some point, or it wouldn't have come out. Proverbs 23:7 says, "For as he thinks in his heart, so is he." Whatever is in our hearts or in our minds will ultimately come out of our mouths. We can find out the true condition of our hearts by listening to ourselves.*

If you don't like what you are saying, ask God to examine you, and try you; to test your heart and your mind and to help you think as He thinks (see Ps. 26:2). And pray this prayer from Psalm 51:10: "Create in me a clean heart, O God, and renew a right and *steadfast spirit within me."*

¹² My foot stands on a level place;
In the congregations I will bless the LORD.

Psalm 27

A Psalm of Fearless Trust in God.

A Psalm of David.

¹ THE LORD is my light and my
salvation—
Whom shall I fear?
The LORD is the refuge *and* fortress of
my life—
Whom shall I dread?
² When the wicked came against me to
eat up my flesh,
My adversaries and my enemies, they
stumbled and fell.
³ Though an army encamp against me,
My heart will not fear;

A Prayer To Renew Your Mind

Lord, You are my light and my
salvation—whom shall I fear? You are
my refuge and the fortress of my life—
whom shall I dread?

· *adapted from Psalm 27:1*

Though war arise against me,
Even in this I am confident.

⁴ One thing I have asked of the LORD, and
that I will seek:
That I may dwell in the house of the
LORD [in His presence] all the days of
my life,
To gaze upon the beauty [the delightful
loveliness and majestic grandeur] of
the LORD

KEYS *to a* Victorious Life *Love Overcomes Rejection*

The psalmist writes in Psalm 27:10 of an extremely painful type of rejection—
being abandoned by a father and mother. Rejection of any kind, no matter who
rejects us, can cause depression. To be rejected means to be thrown away as
having no value or as being unwanted. We were created for acceptance, not
rejection. The emotional pain of rejection is one of the deepest kinds of pain we
can know, especially if the rejection comes from someone we love or expect to love
us, such as parents or a spouse.

If you have been depressed, it might be due to a root of rejection in your life.
Overcoming rejection is certainly not easy, but we can overcome it through the
love of Jesus Christ.

In Ephesians 3:18, Paul prayed for the church that they would "be fully capable of
comprehending with all the saints (God's people) the width and length and height
and depth of His love [fully experiencing that amazing, endless love]." He said this
experience far surpasses mere knowledge.

Watch for all the ways that God shows His love for you, and it will overcome the
rejection you may have experienced from other people. Every time God gives us
favor, He is showing us that He loves us. There are many ways He shows His love
for us all the time; we simply need to begin watching for them.

Having a deep revelation concerning God's love for us will help keep us from
depression.

And to meditate in His temple. [Ps 16:11; 18:6; 65:4; Luke 2:37]

5 For in the day of trouble He will hide me in His shelter;

In the secret place of His tent He will hide me;

He will lift me up on a rock.

6 And now my head will be lifted up above my enemies around me,

In His tent I will offer sacrifices with shouts of joy;

I will sing, yes, I will sing praises to the LORD.

7 Hear, O LORD, when I cry aloud;

Be gracious *and* compassionate to me and answer me.

8 *When You said,* "Seek My face [in prayer, require My presence as your greatest need]," my heart said to You,

"Your face, O LORD, I will seek [on the authority of Your word]."

9 Do not hide Your face from me,

Do not turn Your servant away in anger;

You have been my help;

Do not abandon me nor leave me,

O God of my salvation!

10 Although my father and my mother have abandoned me,

Yet the LORD will take me up [adopt me as His child]. [Ps 22:10]

11 Teach me Your way, O LORD,

And lead me on a level path

Because of my enemies [who lie in wait].

12 Do not give me up to the will of my adversaries,

For false witnesses have come against me;

They breathe out violence.

Speak God's Word

The Lord is my strength and my impenetrable shield; my heart trusts with unwavering confidence in Him, and I am helped; therefore my heart greatly rejoices, and with my song I shall thank Him and praise Him.

| *adapted from* PSALM 28:7 |

13 *I would have despaired* had I not believed that I would see the goodness of the LORD

In the land of the living.

14 Wait for *and* confidently expect the LORD;

Be strong and let your heart take courage;

Yes, wait for *and* confidently expect the LORD.

Psalm 28

A Prayer for Help, and Praise for Its Answer.

A Psalm of David.

1 TO YOU I call, O LORD,

My rock, do not be deaf to me,

For if You are silent to me,

I will become like those who go down to the pit (grave).

2 Hear the voice of my supplication (specific requests, humble entreaties) as I cry to You for help,

As I lift up my hands *and* heart toward Your innermost sanctuary (Holy of Holies).

3 Do not drag me away with the wicked

And with those who do evil,

Who speak peace with their neighbors,

While malice *and* mischief are in their hearts.

4 Repay them according to their work and according to the evil of their practices;

Repay them according to the deeds of their hands;

Repay them what they deserve. [2 Tim 4:14; Rev 18:6]

5 Because they have no regard for the works of the LORD

Nor the deeds of His hands,

He will tear them down and not rebuild them.

6 Blessed be the LORD,

Because He has heard the voice of my supplication.

7 The LORD is my strength and my [impenetrable] shield;

My heart trusts [with unwavering confidence] in Him, and I am helped;

Therefore my heart greatly rejoices,

And with my song I shall thank Him *and* praise Him.

KEYS *to a* Victorious Life *Love Leads to Obedience*

The more we love God, and the more we receive His love, the more we are able to obey Him promptly and reverently. We should realize that all God's commands will benefit our lives. When God tells us to not do something, He is never trying to take something away from us. Instead, He is protecting us as our "[impenetrable] shield" from something harmful (see Ps. 28:7).

Loving God means that we trust Him, and when we trust Him, we are able to trust His direction in our lives. If you are having difficulty doing something that you know God wants you to do, or not doing something you know He doesn't want you to do, remember that He loves you and is trying to help you—trust Him and obey.

⁸ The LORD is their [unyielding] strength,
And He is the fortress of salvation to His anointed.
⁹ Save Your people and bless Your inheritance;
Be their shepherd also, and carry them forever.

Psalm 29

The Voice of the LORD in the Storm.

A Psalm of David.

¹ ASCRIBE TO the LORD, O sons of the mighty,
Ascribe to the LORD glory and strength.
² Ascribe to the LORD the glory due His name;
Worship the LORD in the beauty *and* majesty of His holiness [as the creator and source of holiness].

³ The voice of the LORD is upon the waters;
The God of glory thunders;
The LORD is over many waters.
⁴ The voice of the LORD is powerful;
The voice of the LORD is full of majesty.
⁵ The voice of the LORD breaks the cedars;
Yes, the LORD breaks in pieces the cedars of Lebanon.
⁶ He makes Lebanon skip like a calf,

And Sirion (Mount Hermon) like a young, wild ox.
⁷ The voice of the LORD rakes flames of fire (lightning).
⁸ The voice of the LORD shakes the wilderness;
The LORD shakes the wilderness of Kadesh.
⁹ The voice of the LORD makes the doe labor *and* give birth
And strips the forests bare;
And in His temple all are saying, "Glory!"

¹⁰ The LORD sat *as King* at the flood;
Yes, the LORD sits as King forever.
¹¹ The LORD will give [unyielding and impenetrable] strength to His people;
The LORD will bless His people with peace.

Psalm 30

Thanksgiving for Deliverance from Death.

A Psalm; a Song at the Dedication of the House (Temple).
A Psalm of David.

¹ I WILL extol *and* praise You, O LORD, for You have lifted me up,
And have not let my enemies rejoice over me.
² O LORD my God,

Speak God's Word

God's anger is but for a moment, His favor is for my lifetime. Weeping may endure for a night, but a shout of joy comes in the morning.

| *adapted from* PSALM 30:5 |

I cried to You for help, and You have healed me.

³O LORD, You have brought my life up from Sheol (the nether world, the place of the dead);

You have kept me alive, so that I would not go down to the pit (grave).

⁴Sing to the LORD, O you His godly ones,

And give thanks at the mention of His holy *name*.

⁵For His anger is but for a moment, His favor is for a lifetime.

Weeping may endure for a night,
But a shout of joy comes in the morning.
[2 Cor 4:17]

⁶As for me, in my prosperity I said, "I shall never be moved."

⁷By Your favor *and* grace, O LORD, you have made my mountain stand strong;

You hid Your face, and I was horrified.

⁸I called to You, O LORD,

And to the Lord I made supplication (specific request).

⁹"What profit is there in my blood (death), if I go down to the pit (grave)?

Will the dust praise You? Will it declare Your faithfulness [to man]?

¹⁰"Hear, O LORD, be gracious *and* show favor to me;

O LORD, be my helper."

¹¹You have turned my mourning into dancing for me;

KEYS *to a* Victorious Life *God's Favor Lasts a Lifetime*

I have said many times that God does become angry with sin and injustice, but His nature and character are not those of an angry God.

Perhaps I can explain it this way: My father was an angry man, and he quickly punished people for every tiny infraction of his rules. Being around him made my mother, brother, and me fearful, nervous, and tense, feeling guilty and condemned for something all the time. Although we tried very hard to do what he wanted, it was impossible, because his rules were unending and changed frequently. We lived in an atmosphere of constantly awaiting punishment.

In contrast, my husband, Dave, is not an angry man. He can become angry if I do something he really does not like or if I speak to him disrespectfully, but his anger only lasts for a moment. Dave knows my personality is a bit feisty at times and that I am sorry when I behave badly, so he extends mercy to me and is always willing to forget the misdeed and return to peace.

Dealing with an angry person is very different from dealing with someone who can become angry but has no desire to stay that way. God's anger is only for a moment. His mercies are new every morning (see Lam. 3:23), and His favor lasts for a lifetime.

KEYS *to a* Victorious Life *The Importance of Joy*

Psalm 30:11 describes what our relationship with God should do for us. Are you glad? Do you have joy most of the time? Would you consider yourself a happy, joyful person in most circumstances?

At one point in my life, after being a Christian and a minister for many years, I had to answer these questions for myself, and I realized that I was mad and sad more than I was glad. I also knew that had to change.

I searched for the root of my lack of joy, and one thing I discovered was I did not truly understand the great value and importance of joy. Joy is to our lives like gasoline is to an engine. Without gasoline, the engine will not run. Without joy, I don't believe human beings run well either. Joy gives us actual physical energy; it provides the zeal and enthusiasm we need in our lives. According to Nehemiah 8:10, the joy of the Lord is our strength.

Without joy, everything is "down"—negative, dreary, flat, and tasteless. Our thoughts are negative; our attitudes are negative; our emotions are depressed; and even our heads, shoulders, and arms hang down. Jesus did not die to give us "down" lives. He is our glory and the lifter of our heads (see Ps. 3:3). He is full of joy (see John 17:13), and He wants us to be people of joy!

You have taken off my sackcloth and clothed me with joy,
12 That my soul may sing praise to You and not be silent.
O LORD my God, I will give thanks to You forever.

Psalm 31

A Psalm of Complaint and of Praise.

To the Chief Musician.
A Psalm of David.

1 IN YOU, O LORD, I have placed my trust *and* taken refuge;
Let me never be ashamed;
In Your righteousness rescue me.
2 Incline Your ear to me, deliver me quickly;
Be my rock of refuge,
And a strong fortress to save me.
3 Yes, You are my rock and my fortress;

For Your name's sake You will lead me and guide me.
4 You will draw me out of the net that they have secretly laid for me,
For You are my strength *and* my stronghold.
5 Into Your hand I commit my spirit;
You have redeemed me, O LORD, the God of truth *and* faithfulness. [Luke 23:46; Acts 7:59]

A Prayer To Renew Your Mind

Lord, You have turned my mourning into dancing; You have taken off my sackcloth and clothed me with joy, that my soul may sing praise to You and not be silent. O Lord my God, I will give thanks to You forever.

· *adapted from Psalm 30:11–12*

Speak God's Word

I will rejoice and be glad in Your steadfast love, because You have seen my affliction; You have taken note of my life's distresses.

| *adapted from* PSALM 31:7 |

A Prayer To Renew Your Mind

I trust confidently in You and Your greatness, O Lord; I say, "You are my God." My times are in Your hands.

· *adapted from Psalm 31:14–15*

6 I hate those who pay regard to vain
   (empty, worthless) idols;
   But I trust in the LORD [and rely on Him
   with unwavering confidence].
7 I will rejoice and be glad in Your
   steadfast love,
   Because You have seen my affliction;
   You have taken note of my life's
   distresses,
8 And You have not given me into the
   hand of the enemy;
   You have set my feet in a broad
   place.

9 Be gracious *and* compassionate to me,
   O LORD, for I am in trouble;
   My eye is clouded *and* weakened by
   grief, my soul and my body also.
10 For my life is spent with sorrow
   And my years with sighing;
   My strength has failed because of my
   iniquity,

And even my body has wasted away.
11 Because of all my enemies I have become
   a reproach *and* disgrace,
   Especially to my neighbors,
   And an object of dread to my
   acquaintances;
   Those who see me on the street run
   from me.
12 I am forgotten like a dead man, out of
   mind;
   I am like a broken vessel.
13 For I have heard the slander *and*
   whispering of many,
   Terror is on every side;
   While they schemed together against
   me,
   They plotted to take away my life. [Jer
   20:10]
14 But as for me, I trust [confidently] in You
   and Your greatness, O LORD;
   I said, "You are my God."

KEYS *to a* Victorious Life *Waiting on God*

When success does not come easily and we find ourselves frustrated and weary in our efforts, we need to wait for the Lord. Waiting for the Lord, as David describes in Psalm 31:24, simply means spending time with Him, being in His presence, meditating on His Word, worshiping Him, and keeping Him at the center of our lives. Waiting on God properly requires that we wait with an attitude of expectancy, believing that God is going to do something good for us.

When you wait on the Lord, you draw everything you need from Him. He is your refuge, your enabler, your joy, your peace, your righteousness, and your hope. He gives you everything you need to live in victory over any circumstance. Stay close to Him and receive the strength you need every day. Don't let anything separate you from the love of God found in Christ Jesus.

KEYS *to a* Victorious Life *Receiving God's Gift of Grace*

Jesus forgave all our sins when He died on the cross, and He paid the price for our guilt as well. When we acknowledge or admit our sin to God, telling Him everything, refusing to hide our sin, we are able to receive His gift of grace (see Ps. 32:5). Confession is good for the soul; it allows us to let go of heavy burdens caused by guilty secrets.

Feelings of guilt do not always go away instantly, but we can take God at His Word and say, "I am forgiven, and the guilt has been removed." Our feelings will eventually catch up with our decisions. We can live by the truth in God's Word and not according to the way that we feel.

15 My times are in Your hands;
  Rescue me from the hand of my enemies
    and from those who pursue *and*
    persecute me.
16 Make Your face shine upon Your
    servant;
  Save me in Your lovingkindness.
17 Let me not be put to shame, O LORD, for
    I call on You;
  Let the wicked (godless) be put to
    shame, let them be silent in Sheol (the
    nether world, the place of the dead).
18 Let the lying lips be mute,
  Which speak insolently *and* arrogantly
    against the [consistently] righteous
  With pride and contempt.

19 How great is Your goodness,
  Which You have stored up for those who
    [reverently] fear You,
  Which You have prepared for those who
    take refuge in You,
  Before the sons of man!
20 In the secret place of Your presence
    You hide them from the plots *and*
    conspiracies of man;
  You keep them secretly in a shelter
    (pavilion) from the strife of tongues.
21 Blessed be the LORD,
  For He has shown His marvelous favor
    and lovingkindness to me [when I was
    assailed] in a besieged city.

22 As for me, I said in my alarm,
  "I am cut off from Your eyes."
  Nevertheless You heard the voice of my
    supplications (specific requests)
  When I cried to You [for help].

23 O love the LORD, all you His godly ones!
  The LORD preserves the faithful [those
    with moral and spiritual integrity]
  And fully repays the [self-righteousness
    of the] arrogant.
24 Be strong and let your hearts take
    courage,
  All you who wait for *and* confidently
    expect the LORD.

Psalm 32

Blessedness of Forgiveness and of Trust in God.

A Psalm of David. A skillful song, or a didactic or reflective poem.

1 BLESSED [FORTUNATE, prosperous,
    favored by God] is he whose
    transgression is forgiven,
  And whose sin is covered.
2 Blessed is the man to whom the LORD
    does not impute wickedness,
  And in whose spirit there is no deceit.
    [Rom 4:7, 8]

³When I kept silent *about my sin*, my body wasted away

Through my groaning all the day long.
⁴For day and night Your hand [of displeasure] was heavy upon me;

My energy (vitality, strength) was drained away as with the burning heat of summer.   *Selah.*
⁵I acknowledged my sin to You,

And I did not hide my wickedness;

I said, "I will confess [all] my transgressions to the LORD";

And You forgave the guilt of my sin.

                                                   Selah.
⁶Therefore, let everyone who is godly pray to You [for forgiveness] in a time when You [are near and] may be found;

Surely when the great waters [of trial and distressing times] overflow they will not reach [the spirit in] him.
⁷You are my hiding place; You, LORD, protect me from trouble;

You surround me with songs *and* shouts of deliverance.   *Selah.*

⁸I will instruct you and teach you in the way you should go;

I will counsel you [who are willing to learn] with My eye upon you.
⁹Do not be like the horse or like the mule which have no understanding,

Whose trappings include bridle and rein to hold them in check,

Otherwise they will not come near to you.
¹⁰Many are the sorrows of the wicked,

But he who trusts in *and* relies on the LORD shall be surrounded with compassion *and* lovingkindness.
¹¹Be glad in the LORD and rejoice, you righteous [who actively seek right standing with Him];

Shout for joy, all you upright in heart.

Psalm 33

Praise to the Creator and Preserver.

¹REJOICE IN the LORD, you righteous ones;

KEYS *to a* Victorious Life *The Holy Spirit Guides Us*

Psalm 32:9 encourages us not to "be like the horse or like the mule." These animals need a "bridle and rein to hold them in check" because they have "no understanding." When we think about what this verse really means, it can help us in many ways.

A horse either follows the pull of the bridle, which controls the bit in its mouth, or it feels great pain. Our relationship with the Holy Spirit works in a similar way. He is our bridle and the bit in our mouths. He should be controlling the reins of our lives.

If we follow the promptings of the Holy Spirit, we will end up with a good life that is fruitful and enjoyable. But if we do not follow Him, we can end up in painful situations.

In the midst of life's storms, if we don't bridle our tongue, we may not reach the breakthrough God has for us or experience the fullness of His plan for our lives. But if we accept the leadership of the Holy Spirit, He will guide us in our thoughts, words, and all our actions.

Praise is becoming *and* appropriate
for those who are upright [in heart—
those with moral integrity and godly
character].

²Give thanks to the Lord with the lyre;
Sing praises to Him with the harp of ten
strings.

³Sing to Him a new song;
Play skillfully [on the strings] with a loud
and joyful sound.

⁴For the word of the Lord is right;
And all His work is done in
faithfulness.

⁵He loves righteousness and justice;
The earth is full of the lovingkindness of
the Lord.

⁶By the word of the Lord were the
heavens made,
And all their host by the breath of His
mouth. [Gen 1:1–3; Job 38:4–11; Heb
11:3; 2 Pet 3:5]

⁷He gathers the waters of the sea together
as in a wineskin;
He puts the deeps in storehouses.

⁸Let all the earth fear *and* worship the
Lord;
Let all the inhabitants of the world stand
in awe of Him.

⁹For He spoke, and it was done;
He commanded, and it stood fast.

POWERPOINT

According to Psalm 33:11, the
thoughts of God's heart, meaning His
will, stand forever. God wants to speak
to us, to share His thoughts with us.
But in order for that to happen we need
to quiet our own minds so we can hear
what He is revealing. Several years
ago God showed me that my mind was
too busy to hear anything He said.
We live in a very fast-paced and noisy
world these days, and it is important
to separate ourselves from it and have
times of being still and quiet,
waiting on God.

A Prayer To Renew Your Mind

*Thank You, Lord, that Your eye is upon
me because I fear You and worship
You with awe-inspired reverence and
obedience, and I hope confidently in
Your compassion and lovingkindness.*

· *adapted from Psalm 33:18*

¹⁰The Lord nullifies the counsel of the
nations;
He makes the thoughts *and* plans of the
people ineffective.

¹¹The counsel of the Lord stands forever,
The thoughts *and* plans of His heart
through all generations.

¹²Blessed [fortunate, prosperous, and
favored by God] is the nation whose
God is the Lord,
The people whom He has chosen as His
own inheritance. [Deut 32:8, 9]

¹³The Lord looks [down] from heaven;
He sees all the sons of man;

¹⁴From His dwelling place He looks closely
Upon all the inhabitants of the earth—

¹⁵He who fashions the hearts of them all,
Who considers *and* understands all that
they do.

¹⁶The king is not saved by the great size of
his army;
A warrior is not rescued by his great
strength.

¹⁷A horse is a false hope for victory;
Nor does it deliver anyone by its great
strength.

¹⁸Behold, the eye of the Lord is upon
those who fear Him [and worship
Him with awe-inspired reverence and
obedience],
On those who hope [confidently] in His
compassion *and* lovingkindness,

¹⁹To rescue their lives from death
And keep them alive in famine.

²⁰We wait [expectantly] for the Lord;
He is our help and our shield.

²¹For in Him our heart rejoices,
Because we trust [lean on, rely on, and
are confident] in His holy name.

²²Let Your [steadfast] lovingkindness,
O Lord, be upon us,
In proportion as we have hoped in You.

KEYS *to a* Victorious Life *Start Saying "I Trust God"*

In Psalm 34:4, the psalmist writes that God delivered him from all his fears. Fear is closely related to worry, dread, anxiety, and various other negative emotions. To win the battle of the mind, we must learn to handle fear and worry in a godly way.

I wonder how many times the words "I'm afraid . . . ," "I'm concerned that . . . ," or "I'm worried about . . ." go out into the atmosphere? Millions of people use these phrases perhaps millions of times throughout their lives. But what's the purpose? These words are not effective, and they don't help us in any way. Worry and fear don't change our circumstances; they simply change us by moving our minds away from hope and faith.

Anxiety and fear immobilize us; when we sit and worry, we are not doing anything that can help or change our situation. Fear and worry steal our peace and joy and cause stress.

Whenever you find yourself saying, "I'm worried about . . ." or "I'm afraid that . . . ," replace those negative words with "I trust God." When we say that we trust God, it releases His power to work in our lives. When you are in a battle with worry, instead of vocalizing it, study God's Word and remember His faithfulness in past situations. God will deliver you from all your fears, as Psalm 34:4 says, and you can do your part to help reach that breakthrough. Move in the right direction by eliminating "I'm worried" and "I'm afraid" from your vocabulary.

Psalm 34

The LORD, a Provider and the One Who Rescues Me.

A Psalm of David; when he pretended to be insane before Abimelech, who drove him out, and he went away.

¹I WILL bless the LORD at all times;
His praise shall continually be in my mouth.

²My soul makes its boast in the LORD;
The humble *and* downtrodden will hear it and rejoice.

³O magnify the LORD with me,
And let us lift up His name together.

⁴I sought the LORD [on the authority of His word], and He answered me,
And delivered me from all my fears. [Ps 73:25; Matt 7:7]

⁵They looked to Him and were radiant;
Their faces will never blush in shame *or* confusion.

⁶This poor man cried, and the LORD heard him
And saved him from all his troubles.

⁷The angel of the LORD encamps around those who fear Him [with awe-inspired reverence and worship Him with obedience],
And He rescues [each of] them. [2 Kin 6:8–23; Ps 18:1; 145:20]

⁸O taste and see that the LORD [our God] is good;
How blessed [fortunate, prosperous, and favored by God] is the man who takes refuge in Him. [1 Pet 2:2, 3]

⁹O [reverently] fear the LORD, you His saints (believers, holy ones);

WINNING THE BATTLES *of the* MIND
Submitting Our Mouths to God

When I first started in ministry, I knew that God had given me an ability to communicate because it was easy for me. Words are my tools. The Lord gave me the gift, and then He called me into the ministry to use that ability to work for Him. But my gift has also been my greatest problem at times. I struggled for a long time with the right use of my tongue.

Over the years, various people said things such as, "Hold your tongue," "Do you always speak first and think later?" or "Must you sound so harsh?" Had I not ignored what people were saying to me, I would have realized that God was trying to tell me something important. But I continued in my own stubborn ways, and I know I wounded people with my words. I am sorry for that, and I am grateful that God has forgiven me.

I finally realized that if God was going to use my life, I needed to obey Him concerning the proper use of my words—not just when I was in the pulpit, but all the time. God's Word says, "Keep your tongue from evil and your lips from speaking deceit" (Ps. 34:13).

I had a choice. I could continue to hurt people with my words or I could submit my mouth to God. Obviously, I wanted to be subject to the Lord, but it was still a battle.

Our words are expressions of our hearts, of what's going on inside us. If we want to know who a person really is, all we need to do is listen to their words. If we listen long enough, we learn a lot about them.

As I learned to listen to my own words, I began to learn a lot about myself. Some of the things I learned did not please me, but they also helped me realize that my words were not pleasing to God, and I wanted them to be. Once I confessed my failure to God, the victory came—not all at once and not perfectly; but God is patient, and He continues to work with us as long as we work with Him.

No matter how many problems you may have with the proper use of words, God wants to change you. It won't be easy, but you can win the battle. And the effort will be worth it.

A PRAYER FOR VICTORY

Lord, put a watch over my mouth so I will not sin against You with my tongue. Let the words of my mouth and the meditation of my heart be acceptable to You. In Jesus' name. Amen.

A Prayer To Renew Your Mind

I ask, Lord, that You would help me keep my tongue from evil and my lips from speaking deceit.

     · *adapted from Psalm 34:13*

For to those who fear Him there is no want.

¹⁰ The young lions lack [food] and grow hungry,

But they who seek the LORD will not lack any good thing.

¹¹ Come, you children, listen to me;

I will teach you to fear the LORD [with awe-inspired reverence and worship Him with obedience].

¹² Who is the man who desires life

And loves many days, that he may see good?

¹³ Keep your tongue from evil

And your lips from speaking deceit.

¹⁴ Turn away from evil and do good;

Seek peace and pursue it.

¹⁵ The eyes of the LORD are toward the righteous [those with moral courage and spiritual integrity]

And His ears are open to their cry.

¹⁶ The face of the LORD is against those who do evil,

To cut off the memory of them from the earth. [1 Pet 3:10–12]

¹⁷ When *the righteous* cry [for help], the LORD hears

And rescues them from all their distress *and* troubles.

¹⁸ The LORD is near to the heartbroken

And He saves those who are crushed in spirit (contrite in heart, truly sorry for their sin).

Speak God's Word

The eyes of the Lord are toward the righteous and His ears are open to my cry. When I cry for help, the Lord hears and rescues me from all my distress and troubles.

| adapted from PSALM 34:15, 17 |

POWERPOINT

Psalm 34:19 makes clear that "many hardships *and* perplexing circumstances" will confront people who are consistently righteous. When we are in Christ, we are righteous (see 2 Cor. 5:21), so we know we will face challenges, difficulties, and times when we won't know what to do. We may have many specific reasons to become anxious, but if we focus on our righteousness instead of our worries, we will be victorious.

¹⁹ Many hardships *and* perplexing circumstances confront the righteous,

But the LORD rescues him from them all.

²⁰ He keeps all his bones;

Not one of them is broken. [John 19:33, 36]

²¹ Evil will cause the death of the wicked,

And those who hate the righteous will be held guilty *and* will be condemned.

²² The LORD redeems the soul of His servants,

And none of those who take refuge in Him will be condemned.

Psalm 35

Prayer for Rescue from Enemies.

A Psalm of David.

¹ CONTEND, O LORD, with those who contend with me;

Fight against those who fight against me.

² Take hold of shield and buckler (small shield),

And stand up for my help.

³ Draw also the spear and javelin to meet those who pursue me.

Say to my soul, "I am your salvation."

⁴ Let those be ashamed and dishonored who seek my life;

POWERPOINT

When you are having problems, don't fall into the trap of thinking you are being punished for something you have done wrong in your life. If there is something you need to learn from your situation, be open to learning it. But remember that God is merciful, He is good, and He *wants* your needs to be met. He *wants* you to have a good job, a decent place to live, transportation to get you where you need to go, good friends, and a great spiritual life. God *wants* you to be blessed in every area of your life—spiritually, mentally, emotionally, physically, financially, and socially. In fact, when you do well in these areas, God "delights and takes pleasure" in it (see Ps. 35:27). Just be patient in your difficulties and God will come through for you.

Let those be turned back [in defeat] and humiliated who plot evil against me.

⁵ Let them be [blown away] like chaff before the wind [worthless, without substance],

With the angel of the LORD driving them on.

⁶ Let their way be dark and slippery, With the angel of the LORD pursuing *and* harassing them.

⁷ For without cause they hid their net for me;

Without cause they dug a pit [of destruction] for my life.

⁸ Let destruction come upon my enemy by surprise;

Let the net he hid for me catch him; Into that very destruction let him fall.

⁹ Then my soul shall rejoice in the LORD; It shall rejoice in His salvation.

¹⁰ All my bones will say, "LORD, who is like You,

Who rescues the afflicted from him who is too strong for him [to resist alone],

And the afflicted and the needy from him who robs him?"

¹¹ Malicious witnesses rise up; They ask me of things that I do not know.

¹² They repay me evil for good, To the sorrow of my soul.

¹³ But as for me, when they were sick, my clothing was sackcloth (mourning garment);

I humbled my soul with fasting, And I prayed with my head bowed on my chest.

¹⁴ I behaved as if grieving for my friend or my brother;

I bowed down in mourning, as one who sorrows for his mother.

¹⁵ But in my stumbling they rejoiced and gathered together [against me];

The slanderers whom I did not know gathered against me;

They slandered *and* reviled me without ceasing.

¹⁶ Like godless jesters at a feast, They gnashed at me with their teeth [in malice].

¹⁷ LORD, how long will You look on [without action]?

Rescue my life from their destructions, My only *life* from the young lions.

¹⁸ I will give You thanks in the great congregation;

I will praise You among a mighty people.

¹⁹ Do not let those who are wrongfully my enemies rejoice over me;

Nor let those who hate me without cause wink their eye [maliciously]. [John 15:24, 25]

²⁰ For they do not speak peace, But they devise deceitful words [half-truths and lies] against those who are quiet in the land.

²¹ They open their mouths wide against me; They say, "Aha, aha, our eyes have seen it!"

²² You have seen this, O LORD; do not keep silent.

O Lord, do not be far from me.

²³ Wake Yourself up, and arise to my right And to my cause, my God and my Lord.

²⁴ Judge me, O LORD my God, according to Your righteousness *and* justice;

And do not let them rejoice over me.
25 Do not let them say in their heart, "Aha,
that is what we wanted!"
Do not let them say, "We have swallowed
him up *and* destroyed him."
26 Let those be ashamed and humiliated
together who rejoice at my distress;
Let those be clothed with shame and
dishonor who magnify themselves
over me.

27 Let them shout for joy and rejoice, who
favor my vindication *and* want what is
right for me;
Let them say continually, "Let the Lord
be magnified, who delights *and* takes
pleasure in the prosperity of His
servant."
28 And my tongue shall declare Your
righteousness (justice),
And Your praise all the day long.

Psalm 36

Wickedness of Men and
Lovingkindness of God.

To the Chief Musician. *A Psalm*
of David the servant of the Lord.

1 TRANSGRESSION SPEAKS [like an
oracle] to the wicked (godless) [deep]
within his heart;
There is no fear (dread) of God before
his eyes. [Rom 3:18]
2 For he flatters *and* deceives himself in
his own eyes
Thinking that his sinfulness will not be
discovered and hated [by God].
3 The words of his mouth are wicked and
deceitful;
He has ceased to be wise *and* to do good.
4 He plans wrongdoing on his bed;
He sets himself on a path that is not good;
He does not reject *or* despise evil.

5 Your lovingkindness *and* graciousness,
O Lord, extend to the skies,
Your faithfulness [reaches] to the clouds.
6 Your righteousness is like the mountains
of God,
Your judgments are like the great deep.
O Lord, You preserve man and beast.
7 How precious is Your lovingkindness,
O God!

The children of men take refuge in the
shadow of Your wings.
8 They drink their fill of the abundance of
Your house;
And You allow them to drink from the
river of Your delights.
9 For with You is the fountain of life [the
fountain of life-giving water];
In Your light we see light. [John 4:10, 14]
10 O continue Your lovingkindness to
those who know You,
And Your righteousness (salvation) to
the upright in heart.
11 Do not let the foot of the proud [person]
overtake me,
And do not let the hand of the wicked
drive me away.
12 There those who [are perverse and] do
evil have fallen;
They have been thrust down and cannot
rise.

Psalm 37

Security of Those Who Trust
in the Lord, and Insecurity
of the Wicked.

A Psalm of David.

1 DO NOT worry because of evildoers,
Nor be envious toward wrongdoers;
2 For they will wither quickly like the grass,
And fade like the green herb.
3 Trust [rely on and have confidence] in
the Lord and do good;
Dwell in the land and feed [securely] on
His faithfulness.
4 Delight yourself in the Lord,
And He will give you the desires *and*
petitions of your heart.

A Prayer To
Renew Your Mind

*Thank You, Lord, that as I trust in You
and do good, I will dwell in the land and
feed on Your faithfulness. As I delight
myself in You, You give me the desires
and petitions of my heart. I commit my
way to You. I trust in You and believe
You will do it.*

· *adapted from Psalm 37:3–5*

KEYS *to a*
Victorious
Life *Commit It to the Lord*

God intervenes in the situations we face in life when we commit our ways to Him (see Ps. 37:5).

The more we try to take care of our own problems without asking God to help us, the more we will struggle. I was quite independent and found it difficult to humble myself and admit I needed help. However, when I finally submitted to God in these areas and found the joy of casting all my care on Him, I could not believe I had lived so long under such huge amounts of pressure.

Commit to the Lord your children, your marriage, your personal relationships, and especially anything you may be tempted to be concerned about. In order to succeed at being ourselves, we must continually be committing ourselves to God, giving to Him those things that appear to be holding us back. Only God really knows what needs to be accomplished, and He is the only One qualified to complete that work in us. The more we sincerely commit ourselves to Him, the greater the joy of letting go and trusting Him.

---

⁵Commit your way to the LORD;
  Trust in Him also and He will do it.
⁶He will make your righteousness [your
  pursuit of right standing with God]
  like the light,
  And your judgment like [the shining of]
  the noonday [sun].

⁷Be still before the LORD; wait patiently
  for Him *and* entrust yourself to Him;
  Do not fret (whine, agonize) because of
  him who prospers in his way,
  Because of the man who carries out
  wicked schemes.
⁸Cease from anger and abandon wrath;
  Do not fret; *it leads* only to evil.
⁹For those who do evil will be cut off,
  But those who wait for the LORD, they
  will inherit the land. [Is 57:13c]
¹⁰For yet a little while and the wicked one
  will be gone [forever];
  Though you look carefully where he
  used to be, he will not be [found]. [Heb
  10:36, 37; Rev 21:7, 8]
¹¹But the humble will [at last] inherit the
  land

And will delight themselves in abundant
  prosperity *and* peace. [Ps 37:29; Matt
  5:5]

¹²The wicked plots against the righteous
  And gnashes at him with his teeth.
¹³The Lord laughs at him [the wicked
  one—the one who oppresses the
  righteous],
  For He sees that his day [of defeat] is
  coming.
¹⁴The wicked have drawn the sword and
  bent their bow
  To cast down the afflicted and the needy,
  To slaughter those who are upright in
  conduct [those with personal integrity
  and godly character].

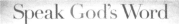

Speak God's Word

I will cease from anger and abandon wrath. I will not fret or worry—it tends to only makes things worse.

| adapted from PSALM 37:8 |

15 The sword [of the ungodly] will enter
their own heart,
And their bow will be broken.

16 Better is the little of the righteous [who
seek the will of God]
Than the abundance (riches) of many
wicked (godless). [1 Tim 6:6, 7]
17 For the arms of the wicked will be
broken,
But the LORD upholds *and* sustains the
righteous [who seek Him].
18 The LORD knows the days of the
blameless,
And their inheritance will continue
forever.
19 They will not be ashamed in the time of
evil,
And in the days of famine they will have
plenty *and* be satisfied.
20 But the wicked (ungodly) will perish,
And the enemies of the LORD will be
like the glory of the pastures *and* like
the fat of lambs [that is consumed in
smoke],
They vanish—like smoke they vanish
away.
21 The wicked borrows and does not pay
back,

But the righteous is gracious *and* kind
and gives.
22 For those blessed by God will [at last]
inherit the land,
But those cursed by Him will be cut off.
[Is 57:13c]

23 The steps of a [good and righteous] man
are directed *and* established by the
LORD,
And He delights in his way [and blesses
his path].
24 When he falls, he will not be hurled down,
Because the LORD is the One who holds
his hand *and* sustains him.
25 I have been young and now I am old,
Yet I have not seen the righteous
(those in right standing with God)
abandoned
Or his descendants pleading for bread.
26 All day long he is gracious and lends,
And his descendants are a blessing.

27 Depart from evil and do good;
And you will dwell [securely in the land]
forever.
28 For the LORD delights in justice
And does not abandon His saints
(faithful ones);
They are preserved forever,

KEYS *to a* Victorious Life *God Orders Our Steps*

If we are willing to follow God, He delights in leading us and in being involved in every area of our life. When God delights in us, He busies Himself with the steps we take (see Ps. 37:23). That is really amazing! God cares so much about us that He is concerned with everything that concerns us.

He guides us in many ways, but one of the things He guides us to do is to be merciful and deal graciously with others. He guides us to help others in any way that we can. When we follow God, we are guided away from any evil way, and He teaches us to do good. We overcome evil with good (see Rom. 12:21).

Instead of being angry with people who hurt us or treat us unfairly, we can be merciful to them and do good to them. And then God will be our Vindicator and reward us.

But the descendants of the wicked will [in time] be cut off.

29 The righteous will inherit the land
And live in it forever.
30 The mouth of the righteous proclaims wisdom,
And his tongue speaks justice *and* truth.
31 The law of his God is in his heart;
Not one of his steps will slip.
32 The wicked lies in wait for the righteous
And seeks to kill him.
33 The LORD will not leave him in his hand
Or let him be condemned when he is judged.
34 Wait for *and* expect the LORD and keep His way,
And He will exalt you to inherit the land;
[In the end] when the wicked are cut off, you will see it.

35 I have seen a wicked, violent man [with great power]
Spreading *and* flaunting himself like a cedar in its native soil,
36 Yet he passed away, and lo, he was no more;
I sought him, but he could not be found.
37 Mark the blameless man [who is spiritually complete], and behold the upright [who walks in moral integrity];
There is a [good] future for the man of peace [because a life of honor blesses one's descendants].
38 As for transgressors, they will be completely destroyed;
The future of the wicked will be cut off.
39 But the salvation of the righteous is from the LORD;
He is their refuge *and* stronghold in the time of trouble.
40 The LORD helps them and rescues them;
He rescues them from the wicked and saves them,
Because they take refuge in Him.

Psalm 38

Prayer in Time of Discipline.

A Psalm of David; to bring
to remembrance.

1 O LORD, do not rebuke me in Your wrath,
Nor discipline me in Your burning anger.

POWERPOINT

Like David, no one wants to be in dark places such as is described in Psalm 38. We all go through difficult times, but thankfully Jesus is the light of the world, and He will give us light in the dark places of our lives. We may not always know exactly what is going to happen in our situations, but we can always know that Jesus is our hope and He will help us. It is important that during our difficulties we keep a positive attitude. God is positive and He wants us to be the same way.

2 For Your arrows have sunk into me *and* penetrate deeply,
And Your hand has pressed down on me *and* greatly disciplined me.
3 There is no soundness in my flesh because of Your indignation;
There is no health in my bones because of my sin.
4 For my iniquities have gone over my head [like the waves of a flood];
As a heavy burden they weigh too much for me.
5 My wounds are loathsome and foul Because of my foolishness.
6 I am bent over and greatly bowed down;
I go about mourning all day long.
7 For my sides are filled with burning,
And there is no health in my flesh.
8 I am numb and greatly bruised [deadly cold and completely worn out];
I groan because of the disquiet *and* moaning of my heart.

9 Lord, all my desire is before You;
And my sighing is not hidden from You.
10 My heart throbs violently, my strength fails me;
And as for the light of my eyes, even that has also gone from me.
11 My loved ones and my friends stand aloof from my plague;

And my neighbors stand far away. [Luke 23:49]

12 Those who seek my life lay snares *for me,*
And those who seek to injure me
threaten mischievous things *and*
destruction;
They devise treachery all the day long.

13 But I, like a deaf man, do not hear;
I am like a mute man who does not open his mouth.

14 Yes, I am like a man who does not hear,
In whose mouth are no arguments.

15 For in You, O LORD, I hope;
You will answer, O Lord my God.

16 For I pray, "May they not rejoice over me,
Who, when my foot slips, would boast against me."

17 For I am ready to fall;
My sorrow is continually before me.

18 For I do confess my guilt *and* iniquity;
I am filled with anxiety because of my sin. [2 Cor 7:9, 10]

19 But my [numerous] enemies are vigorous and strong,
And those who hate me without cause are many.

20 They repay evil for good, they attack *and* try to kill me,
Because I follow what is good.

21 Do not abandon me, O LORD;
O my God, do not be far from me.

22 Make haste to help me,
O Lord, my Salvation.

Psalm 39

The Vanity of Life.

To the Chief Musician; for Jeduthun.
A Psalm of David.

1 I SAID, "I will guard my ways
That I may not sin with my tongue;
I will muzzle my mouth
While the wicked are in my presence."

2 I was mute and silent [before my enemies],
I refrained *even* from good,
And my distress grew worse.

3 My heart was hot within me.
While I was musing the fire burned;
Then I spoke with my tongue:

4 "LORD, let me know my [life's] end
And [to appreciate] the extent of my days;
Let me know how frail I am [how transient is my stay here].

5 "Behold, You have made my days as [short as] hand widths,
And my lifetime is as nothing in Your sight.

KEYS *to a* Victorious Life *How To Speak Right Words*

The psalmist David prayed a lot about his words. He said, "I will guard my ways that I may not sin with my tongue; I will muzzle my mouth . . ." (Ps. 39:1). "Let the words of my mouth and the meditation of my heart be acceptable and *pleasing in Your sight, O LORD, my [firm, immovable] rock and my Redeemer" (Ps. 19:14). "Set a guard, O LORD, over my mouth; keep watch over the door of my lips" (Ps. 141:3). We can see from these Scriptures that David was determined not to sin with his tongue. At the same time he relied on God for strength to follow through on his commitment.*

One of the things we should ask God for each day is to help us speak right things. Our words are very important, and they should be used for God's purposes. We should desire to be mouthpieces for God, speaking His Word faithfully.

Surely every man at his best is a mere
breath [a wisp of smoke, a vapor that
vanishes]! [Eccl 1:2]   *Selah.*
6 "Surely every man walks around like a
shadow [in a charade];
Surely they make an uproar for nothing;
Each one builds up *riches,* not knowing
who will receive them. [Eccl 2:18, 19;
1 Cor 7:31; James 4:14]

7 "And now, Lord, for what do I
expectantly wait?
My hope [my confident expectation] is
in You.
8 "Save me from all my transgressions;
Do not make me the scorn *and* reproach
of the [self-righteous, arrogant] fool.
9 "I am mute, I do not open my mouth,
Because it is You who has done it.
10 "Remove Your plague from me;
I am wasting away because of the
conflict *and* opposition of Your hand.
11 "With rebukes You discipline man for
sin;
You consume like a moth what is
precious to him;
Surely every man is a mere breath [a
wisp of smoke, a vapor that vanishes].
     Selah.

12 "Hear my prayer, O LORD, and listen to
my cry;
Do not be silent at my tears;
For I am Your temporary guest,
A sojourner like all my fathers.
13 "O look away from me, that I may smile
and again know joy
Before I depart and am no more."

Psalm 40

God Sustains His Servant.

To the Chief Musician. A Psalm
of David.

1 I WAITED patiently *and* expectantly for
the LORD;
And He inclined to me and heard my
cry.
2 He brought me up out of a horrible pit
[of tumult and of destruction], out of
the miry clay,
And He set my feet upon a rock,
steadying my footsteps *and*
establishing my path.

A Prayer To Renew Your Mind

*Lord, thank You that as I wait patiently
and expectantly for You, You incline
to me and hear my cry. When I am
discouraged or depressed, I believe You
will bring me up out of the horrible pit
and set my feet upon a rock, steadying
my footsteps and establishing my path.*

     · adapted from Psalm 40:1–2

3 He put a new song in my mouth, a song
of praise to our God;
Many will see and fear [with great
reverence]
And will trust confidently in the LORD.
[Ps 5:11]

4 Blessed [fortunate, prosperous, and
favored by God] is the man who
makes the LORD his trust,
And does not regard the proud nor those
who lapse into lies.
5 Many, O LORD my God, are the
wonderful works which You have done,
And Your thoughts toward us;
There is none to compare with You.
If I would declare and speak of *your
wonders,*
They would be too many to count.

6 Sacrifice and meal offering You do not
desire, *nor* do You delight in them;
You have opened my ears *and* given me
the capacity to hear [and obey Your
word];
Burnt offerings and sin offerings You do
not require. [Mic 6:6–8]
7 Then I said, "Behold, I come [to the
throne];
In the scroll of the book it is written
of me.
8 "I delight to do Your will, O my God;
Your law is within my heart." [Jer 31:33;
Heb 10:5–9]

9 I have proclaimed good news of
righteousness [and the joy that comes
from obedience to You] in the great
assembly;
Behold, I will not restrain my lips [from
proclaiming Your righteousness],
As You know, O LORD.

10 I have not concealed Your righteousness
within my heart;
I have proclaimed Your faithfulness and
Your salvation.
I have not concealed Your
lovingkindness and Your truth from
the great assembly. [Acts 20:20, 27]

11 Do not withhold Your compassion *and*
tender mercy from me, O LORD;
Your lovingkindness and Your truth will
continually preserve me.
12 For innumerable evils have
encompassed me;
My sins have overtaken me, so that I am
not able to see.
They are more numerous than the hairs
of my head,
And my heart has failed me.

13 Be pleased, O LORD, to save me;
O LORD, make haste to help me.
14 Let those be ashamed and humiliated
together
Who seek my life to destroy it;
Let those be turned back [in defeat] and
dishonored
Who delight in my hurt.
15 Let those be appalled *and* desolate
because of their shame
Who say to me, "Aha, aha [rejoicing in
my misfortune]!"

16 Let all who seek You rejoice and be glad
in You;
Let those who love Your salvation say
continually,
"The LORD be magnified!"
17 Even though I am afflicted and needy,
Still the Lord takes thought *and* is
mindful of me.
You are my help and my rescuer.
O my God, do not delay. [Ps 70:1–5; 1 Pet
5:7]

Psalm 41

The Psalmist in Sickness
Complains of Enemies
and False Friends.

To the Chief Musician.
A Psalm of David.

1 BLESSED [by God's grace and
compassion] is he who considers the
helpless;
The LORD will save him in the day of
trouble.
2 The LORD will protect him and keep
him alive;
And he will be called blessed in the
land;
You do not hand him over to the desire
of his enemies.

KEYS *to a* Victorious Life *God Is with You Always*

*God has promised that He will never leave you nor forsake you (see Deut. 31:8).
In the midst of sickness and the betrayal of a close friend, David said of the Lord,
"You set me in Your presence forever" (Ps. 41:12). No matter what you are going
through in life, you do not have to go through it alone. Every day with God is not
going to be a perfect day without problems. But your worst day with Jesus will
still be better than your best day without Him.*

*Say all throughout the day, "God is with me right now. Right now, God is with me.
God is with me when I go to work. God is with me when I go to the marketplace.
God is with me. He's not just with me when I go to church; God is with me all the
time. He cares about everything I do."*

³The LORD will sustain *and* strengthen him on his sickbed;

In his illness, You will restore him to health.

⁴As for me, I said, "O LORD, be gracious to me;

Heal my soul, for I have sinned against You."

⁵My enemies speak evil of me, *saying,*

"When will he die and his name perish?"

⁶And when one comes to see me, he speaks empty words,

While his heart gathers malicious gossip [against me];

When he goes away, he tells it [everywhere].

⁷All who hate me whisper together about me;

Against me they devise my hurt [imagining the worst for me], *saying,*

⁸"A wicked thing is poured out upon him *and* holds him;

And when he lies down, he will not rise up again."

⁹Even my own close friend in whom I trusted,

Who ate my bread,

Has lifted up his heel against me [betraying me]. [John 13:18]

¹⁰But You, O LORD, be gracious to me and restore me [to health],

So that I may repay them.

¹¹By this I know that You favor *and* delight in me,

Because my enemy does not shout in triumph over me.

¹²As for me, You uphold me in my integrity,

And You set me in Your presence forever.

A Prayer To Renew Your Mind

When my soul is in despair, when it has become restless and disquieted within me, I hope in You, God. I wait expectantly for You, for I shall yet praise You, the help of my countenance and my God.

· adapted from Psalm 42:11

---

¹³Blessed be the LORD, the God of Israel,

From everlasting to everlasting [from this age to the next, and forever].

Amen and Amen (so be it).

BOOK TWO

Psalm 42

Thirsting for God in Trouble and Exile.

To the Chief Musician. A skillful song, *or* a didactic *or* reflective poem, of the sons of Korah.

¹AS THE deer pants [longingly] for the water brooks,

So my soul pants [longingly] for You, O God.

²My soul (my life, my inner self) thirsts for God, for the living God.

When will I come and see the face of God? [Ps 63:1, 2; John 7:37; 1 Thess 1:9, 10]

³My tears have been my food day and night,

While they say to me all day long, "Where is your God?"

⁴These things I [vividly] remember as I pour out my soul;

How I used to go along before the great crowd of people and lead them in procession to the house of God [like a choirmaster before his singers, timing the steps to the music and the chant of the song],

With the voice of joy and thanksgiving, a great crowd keeping a festival.

⁵Why are you in despair, O my soul?

And why have you become restless *and* disturbed within me?

Hope in God *and* wait expectantly for Him, for I shall again praise Him

For the help of His presence.

⁶O my God, my soul is in despair within me [the burden more than I can bear];

Therefore I will [fervently] remember You from the land of the Jordan

And the peaks of [Mount] Hermon, from Mount Mizar.

⁷Deep calls to deep at the [thundering] sound of Your waterfalls;

All Your breakers and Your waves have rolled over me.

WINNING THE BATTLES *of the* MIND
Be Patient with Yourself

David said, "Why are you in despair, O my soul? And why have you become restless *and* disturbed within me? Hope in God *and* wait expectantly for Him, for I shall again praise Him for the help of His presence" (Ps. 42:5). Discouragement destroys hope, and without hope we give up, so naturally the enemy always tries to discourage us. The Bible repeatedly tells us not to be discouraged or dismayed. God knows we will not attain victory if we remain discouraged, so God encourages us with His Word and His presence.

When discouragement or condemnation tries to overtake you, examine your thought life. What kind of thoughts have you been thinking? Do they sound something like this?

I'm not going to make it; this is too hard. I always fail, it has always been the same; nothing ever changes. I'm sure other people don't have this much trouble getting their minds renewed. I may as well give up. I'm tired of trying. I pray, but it seems as if God doesn't hear. He probably doesn't answer my prayers because He is so disappointed in the way I act.

If this example represents your thoughts, then no wonder you get discouraged or feel condemned. Remember, you become what you think. Think discouraging thoughts, and you'll become discouraged. Think condemning thoughts, and you'll come under condemnation. Change your thinking and be set free!

Instead of thinking negatively, think like this:

Well, things are going a little slow; but, thank God, I'm making progress. I'm on the right path that will lead me to freedom. I had a rough day yesterday, I chose wrong thinking all day long, I made a mistake, but at least that is one day I won't have to repeat. This is a new day. I'm not going to give up. You love me, Lord. Your mercy is new every morning.

This is an example of how to effectively use your weapon of the Word to tear down strongholds. I recommend that you not only think right thoughts on purpose, but also go the extra mile and speak them aloud as your confession.

Remember, God is delivering you, little by little, so don't be discouraged and don't feel condemned if you make a mistake. Be patient with yourself!

A PRAYER FOR VICTORY

Lord Jesus, with Your help, I can make it. With Your help, I won't be discouraged and feel hopeless. With Your help, I can defeat every wrong thought that comes to my mind. Thank You for victory. Amen.

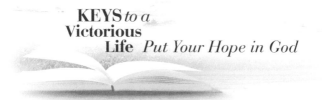

KEYS *to a* Victorious Life *Put Your Hope in God*

Does your inner man ever feel cast down? Sometimes mine does. So did David's. When he felt that way, David put his hope in God and waited expectantly for Him, praising Him as his help and his God (see Ps. 42:5).

To overcome his downcast feelings and emotions, he used songs and shouts of deliverance. That's why so many of his psalms are songs of praise to God to be sung in the midst of unsettling situations.

David knew that when he got down, his countenance went down with him. That is why he talked to himself, his soul (mind, will, and emotions), and encouraged and strengthened himself in the Lord (see 1 Sam. 30:6).

When we find ourselves in that same depressed state, we should wait expectantly for the Lord, praise Him Who is our help and our God, and encourage and strengthen ourselves in Him. When you feel discouraged, remember a victory you experienced in the past, and expect another one.

We who are righteous—in right standing with God—by believing in Jesus Christ, we who take refuge and put our trust in the Lord can sing and shout for joy! The Lord makes a covering over us and defends us. He fights our battles for us when we praise Him (see 2 Chr. 20:17, 20–21)!

You and I must realize and remember that depression is not part of our inheritance in Jesus Christ. Joy is God's will for His children.

---

8 Yet the LORD will command His
  lovingkindness in the daytime,
  And in the night His song will be with me,
  A prayer to the God of my life.

9 I will say to God my rock, "Why have
  You forgotten me?
  Why do I go mourning because of the
  oppression of the enemy?"

10 As a crushing of my bones [with a
  sword], my adversaries taunt me,
  While they say continually to me,
  "Where is your God?"

11 Why are you in despair, O my soul?
  Why have you become restless *and*
  disquieted within me?
  Hope in God *and* wait expectantly for
  Him, for I shall yet praise Him,
  The help of my countenance and
  my God.

Psalm 43

Prayer for Rescue.

1 JUDGE *AND* vindicate me, O God;
  plead my case against an ungodly
  nation.
  O rescue me from the deceitful and
  unjust man!

2 For You are the God of my strength [my
  stronghold—in whom I take refuge];
  why have You rejected me?
  Why do I go mourning because of the
  oppression of the enemy?

3 O send out Your light and Your truth, let
  them lead me;
  Let them bring me to Your holy hill
  And to Your dwelling places.

4 Then I will go to the altar of God,
  To God, my exceeding joy;

POWERPOINT

Discouragement destroys hope and disturbs our souls (see Ps. 43:5), so naturally the devil always tries to discourage us. The Bible repeatedly tells us not to be discouraged or dismayed, to not be in despair or restless or disturbed, but to hope in God. God knows that we will not come through to victory if we remain discouraged, so He always encourages us to come to Him, our "exceeding joy," and praise Him as we wait expectantly for Him (see Ps. 43:4).

With the lyre I will praise You, O God, my God!

⁵Why are you in despair, O my soul? And why are you restless *and* disturbed within me?
Hope in God *and* wait expectantly for Him, for I shall again praise Him,
The help of my [sad] countenance and my God.

Psalm 44

Former Times of Help and Present Troubles.

To the Chief Musician. *A Psalm* of the sons of Korah. A skillful song, *or* a didactic *or* reflective poem.

¹WE HAVE heard with our ears, O God, Our fathers have told us
The work You did in their days,
In the days of old.
²You drove out the [pagan] nations with Your own hand;
Then you planted *and* established them (Israel);
[It was by Your power that] You uprooted the [pagan] peoples,
Then You spread them abroad.
³For our fathers did not possess the land [of Canaan] by their own sword,
Nor did their own arm save them,

But Your right hand and Your arm and the light of Your presence,
Because You favored *and* delighted in them.

⁴You are my King, O God;
Command victories *and* deliverance for Jacob (Israel).
⁵Through You we will gore our enemies [like a bull];
Through Your name we will trample down those who rise up against us.
⁶For I will not trust in my bow,
Nor will my sword save me.
⁷But You have saved us from our enemies,
And You have put them to shame *and* humiliated those who hate us.
⁸In God we have boasted all the day long,
And we will praise *and* give thanks to Your name forever.   *Selah.*

⁹But now You have rejected us and brought us to dishonor,
And You do not go out with our armies [to lead us to victory].
¹⁰You make us turn back from the enemy,
And those who hate us have taken spoil for themselves.
¹¹You have made us like sheep to be eaten [as mutton]
And have scattered us [in exile] among the nations.
¹²You sell Your people cheaply,
And have not increased Your wealth by their sale.
¹³You have made us the reproach *and* taunt of our neighbors,
A scoffing and a derision to those around us.
¹⁴You make us a byword among the nations,
A laughingstock among the people.
¹⁵My dishonor is before me all day long,
And humiliation has covered my face,
¹⁶Because of the voice of the taunter and reviler,
Because of the presence of the enemy and the avenger.

17All this has come upon us, yet we have not forgotten You,

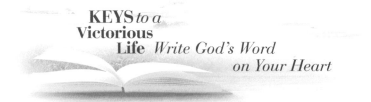

KEYS *to a* **Victorious Life** *Write God's Word on Your Heart*

In Psalm 45:1, the psalmist said his tongue was "like the pen of a skillful writer." And in Proverbs 3:1–3, the Word states we should not forget God's laws but "write them on the tablet of your heart." We see from these two Scriptures that the heart is the tablet and the tongue is the pen.

When you confess God's Word out loud with your tongue, you are effectively writing it on your heart. When you write it on your heart, it becomes more firmly established both in your heart and in the earth. God's Word is forever "settled in heaven [standing firm and unchangeable]" (Ps. 119:89), and we establish it in the earth each time we speak it. When your mouth is filled with God's Word, it is a mighty weapon against the enemy!

Nor have we been false to Your covenant [which You made with our fathers].
18 Our heart has not turned back,
Nor have our steps wandered from Your path,
19 Yet You have [distressingly] crushed us in the place of jackals
And covered us with [the deep darkness of] the shadow of death.

20 If we had forgotten the name of our God
Or stretched out our hands to a strange god,
21 Would not God discover this?
For He knows the secrets of the heart.
22 But for Your sake we are killed all the day long;
We are considered as sheep to be slaughtered. [Rom 8:35–39]
23 Awake! Why do You sleep, O Lord?
Awaken, do not reject us forever.
24 Why do You hide Your face
And forget our affliction and our oppression?
25 For our life has melted away into the dust;
Our body clings to the ground.
26 Rise up! Come be our help,
And ransom us for the sake of Your steadfast love.

Psalm 45

A Song Celebrating the King's Marriage.

To the Chief Musician; set to the [tune of] "Lilies." A Psalm of the sons of Korah. A skillful song, *or* a didactic *or* reflective poem. A Song of Love.

1 MY HEART overflows with a good theme;
I address my psalm to the King.
My tongue is like the pen of a skillful writer.
2 You are fairer than the sons of men;
Graciousness is poured upon Your lips;
Therefore God has blessed You forever.

3 Strap Your sword on *Your* thigh,
O mighty One,
In Your splendor and Your majesty!
4 And in Your majesty ride on triumphantly
For the cause of truth and humility and righteousness;
Let Your right hand guide You to awesome things.
5 Your arrows are sharp;
The peoples (nations) fall under You;
Your arrows pierce the hearts of the King's enemies.

6 Your throne, O God, is forever and ever;
The scepter of uprightness is the scepter of Your kingdom.

7 You have loved righteousness (virtue, morality, justice) and hated wickedness;
Therefore God, your God, has anointed You
Above Your companions with the oil of jubilation. [Heb 1:8, 9]

8 All Your garments are *fragrant with* myrrh, aloes *and* cassia;
From ivory palaces stringed instruments have made You glad.

9 Kings' daughters are among Your noble ladies;
At Your right hand stands the queen in gold from Ophir.

10 Hear, O daughter, consider and incline your ear [to my instruction]:
Forget your people and your father's house;

11 Then the King will desire your beauty;
Because He is your Lord, bow down *and* honor Him.

12 The daughter of Tyre will come with a gift;

> **REMEMBER**, don't wait until the battle is finished to declare your victory. Thank God in advance!

The rich among the people will seek your favor.

13 Glorious is the King's daughter within [the palace];
Her robe is interwoven with gold. [Rev 19:7, 8]

14 She will be brought to the King in embroidered garments;
The virgins, her companions who follow her,
Will be brought to You.

15 With gladness and rejoicing will they be led;
They will enter into the King's palace.

16 In place of your fathers will be your sons;
You shall make princes in all the land.

17 I will make Your name to be remembered in all generations;
Therefore the peoples will praise *and* give You thanks forever and ever.

KEYS *to a* Victorious Life *Adapting to Change*

Everything changes except God, and letting all the changes in our lives upset us won't keep them from happening. People change, circumstances change, our bodies change, and our desires and passions change. There is one certainty in life: change!

Our thoughts are the first things we need to deal with during times of change, because thoughts directly affect our emotions and determine our behavior. The psalmist said, "Therefore we will not fear, though the earth should change and though the mountains be shaken" (Ps. 46:2). When circumstances change, make the transition mentally and your emotions will be a lot easier to manage. If something changes that you are not ready for and did not choose, you will likely feel a variety of emotions about the change. By acting on God's Word and not merely reacting to the situation, you will be better able to manage your emotions instead of allowing them to control you.

Psalm 46

God the Refuge of His People.

To the Chief Musician. *A Psalm* of the sons of Korah, set to soprano voices. A Song.

[1] GOD IS our refuge and strength [mighty and impenetrable],

A very present *and* well-proved help in trouble.

[2] Therefore we will not fear, though the earth should change

And though the mountains be shaken *and* slip into the heart of the seas,

[3] Though its waters roar and foam,

Though the mountains tremble at its roaring.   *Selah.*

[4] There is a river whose streams make glad the city of God,

The holy dwelling places of the Most High.

[5] God is in the midst of her [His city], she will not be moved;

God will help her when the morning dawns.

POWERPOINT

At times we need to be quiet and reverent before the Lord, but the Bible also instructs us to dance, to play musical instruments, and to outwardly express our worship to the Lord in other ways, as we read about in Psalm 47:1. Be expressive in your praise and worship—it brings a release in your life, it honors God, and it aids in defeating the devil.

[6] The nations made an uproar, the kingdoms tottered *and* were moved;

He raised His voice, the earth melted.

[7] The LORD of hosts is with us;

The God of Jacob is our stronghold [our refuge, our high tower].   *Selah.*

[8] Come, behold the works of the LORD,

KEYS *to a* Victorious Life *Be Still and Wait*

When we encounter difficulties or need to know how to handle various situations, God will begin to give us instructions that will lead us to victory. Sometimes He will lead us to do specific things, but often He will tell us to simply stand still.

When God spoke to the people of Judah in the face of great opposition, He said, "Take your positions, stand and witness the salvation of the LORD" (2 Chr. 20:17, emphasis mine). In Psalm 46:10, God says, "Be still and know (recognize, understand) that I am God." During the battles we face in our lives, we would be wise to take some time and be still, waiting on the Lord to hear what He wants to say to us. In fact, we might even do absolutely nothing for a certain amount of time except say, "Lord, I am waiting on You. I worship You and wait for You to move against my enemies and bring forth my deliverance." However, the type of waiting that God desires is not at all passive. It is spiritually active! While we wait on God and are still in many ways, we should also be aggressively expecting Him to move on our behalf at any moment.

Who has wrought desolations *and*
wonders in the earth.
⁹ He makes wars to cease to the end of the
earth;
He breaks the bow into pieces and snaps
the spear in two;
He burns the chariots with fire.
¹⁰ "Be still and know (recognize,
understand) that I am God.
I will be exalted among the nations! I
will be exalted in the earth."
¹¹ The LORD of hosts is with us;
The God of Jacob is our stronghold [our
refuge, our high tower].   *Selah.*

Psalm 47

God the King of the Earth.

To the Chief Musician.
A Psalm of the sons of Korah.

¹ O CLAP your hands, all you people;
Shout to God with the voice of triumph
and songs of joy.
² For the LORD Most High is to be feared
[and worshiped with awe-inspired
reverence and obedience];
He is a great King over all the earth.
³ He subdues peoples under us
And nations under our feet.
⁴ He chooses our inheritance for us,
The glory *and* excellence of Jacob whom
He loves. [1 Pet 1:4, 5]   *Selah.*

POWERPOINT

The psalmist wrote frequently about
meditating on all the wonderful
works of the Lord, and he specifically
mentions thinking about God's
lovingkindness in Psalm 48:9. Never
forget this: Your mind plays an
important role in your victory. It is
the power of the Holy Spirit working
through the Word of God that brings
victory. And a large part of the work
that needs to be done is for us to line
up our thinking with God and His Word.

⁵ God has ascended amid shouting,
The LORD with the sound of a
trumpet.
⁶ Sing praises to God, sing praises;
Sing praises to our King, sing praises.
⁷ For God is the King of all the earth;
Sing praises in a skillful psalm *and* with
understanding.
⁸ God reigns over the nations;
God sits on His holy throne.
⁹ The princes of the people have gathered
together as the people of the God of
Abraham,
For the shields of the earth belong to
God;
He is highly exalted.

Psalm 48

The Beauty and Glory of Zion.

A Song; a Psalm of the sons of Korah.

¹ GREAT IS the LORD, and greatly to be
praised,
In the city of our God, His holy
mountain.
² Fair *and* beautiful in elevation, the joy of
all the earth,
Is Mount Zion [the City of David] in the
far north,
The city of the great King. [Matt 5:35]
³ God, in her palaces,
Has made Himself known as a
stronghold.

⁴ For, lo, the kings assembled themselves,
They [came and] passed by together.
⁵ They saw it, then they were amazed;
They were stricken with terror, they fled
in alarm.
⁶ Panic seized them there,
And pain, as that of a woman in
childbirth.
⁷ With the east wind
You shattered the ships of Tarshish.
⁸ As we have heard, so have we seen
In the city of the LORD of hosts, in the
city of our God:
God will establish her forever.   *Selah.*

⁹ We have thought of Your
lovingkindness, O God,
In the midst of Your temple.
¹⁰ As is Your name, O God,

So is Your praise to the ends of the earth;
Your right hand is full of righteousness
    (rightness, justice).
[11] Let Mount Zion be glad,
Let the daughters of Judah rejoice
Because of Your [righteous] judgments.
[12] Walk about Zion, go all around her;
Count her towers,
[13] Consider her ramparts,
Go through her palaces,
That you may tell the next generation
    [about her glory].
[14] For this is God,
Our God forever and ever;
He will be our guide even until death.

Psalm 49

The Folly of Trusting in Riches.

To the Chief Musician. A Psalm
of the sons of Korah.

[1] HEAR THIS, all peoples;
Listen carefully, all inhabitants of the
    world,
[2] Both low and high,
Rich and poor together:
[3] My mouth will speak wisdom,
And the meditation of my heart will be
    understanding.
[4] I will incline my ear *and* consent to a
    proverb;
On the lyre I will unfold my riddle.

[5] Why should I fear in the days of evil,
When the wickedness of those who
    would betray me surrounds me [on
    every side],
[6] Even those who trust in *and* rely on their
    wealth
And boast of the abundance of their
    riches?
[7] None of them can by any means redeem
    [either himself or] his brother,
Nor give to God a ransom for him—
[8] For the ransom of his soul is too costly,
And he should cease *trying* forever—
[9] So that he should live on eternally,
That he should never see the pit (grave)
    and undergo decay.

[10] For he sees *that even* wise men die;
The fool and the stupid alike perish
And leave their wealth to others. [Eccl
    2:12–16]

[11] Their inward thought is that their
    houses will continue forever,
And their dwelling places to all
    generations;
They have named their lands after their
    own names [ignoring God].
[12] But man, with all his [self] honor *and*
    pomp, will not endure;
He is like the beasts that perish.

[13] This is the fate of those who are foolishly
    confident,
And of those after them who approve
    [and are influenced by] their words.
                                    Selah.

[14] Like sheep they are appointed for Sheol
    (the nether world, the place of the
    dead);
Death will be their shepherd;
And the upright shall rule over them in
    the morning,
And their form *and* beauty shall be for
    Sheol to consume,
So that they have no dwelling [on earth].
[15] But God will redeem my life from the
    power of Sheol,
For He will receive me.   *Selah.*

[16] Be not afraid when [an ungodly] man
    becomes rich,
When the wealth *and* glory of his house
    are increased;
[17] For when he dies he will carry nothing
    away;
His glory will not descend after him.
[18] Though while he lives he counts himself
    happy *and* prosperous—
And though people praise you when you
    do well for yourself—
[19] He shall go to the generation of his fathers;
They shall never again see the light.
[20] A man [who is held] in honor,
Yet who lacks [spiritual] understanding
    and a teachable heart, is like the
    beasts that perish.

Psalm 50

God the Judge of the Righteous
and the Wicked.

A Psalm of Asaph

[1] THE MIGHTY One, God, the Lord, has
    spoken,

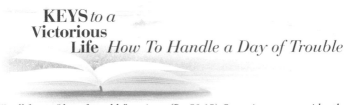

KEYS *to a* Victorious Life *How To Handle a Day of Trouble*

We all face a "day of trouble" at times (Ps. 50:15). Sometimes we consider the trouble somewhat minor, and sometimes it is very serious. When a day of trouble comes, stress always comes with it. In handling or overcoming stress, the first key is to recognize or admit we are under it. The second key is to identify and recognize the stressors that affect us most and learn how to respond to them with the right action. Another important key to relieving stress is obedience—always being willing to do anything God wants us to do.

We will have stressful circumstances come into our lives, but we can be on top of the stress, not under it. There is a big difference between being under stress and being on top of a situation! Even though we will sometimes experience stressful times, if we are obedient to God's Word and to His promptings, we can win the victory.

We all have days seemingly filled with trouble or encounter situations we don't like. But, with the power of God, we can go through them in peace. The Holy Spirit leads and guides us and often prompts us to think or do things that will relieve stress quickly.

Do you believe God is leading you into a place of victory, not into a place of defeat? Of course He is! When you feel stressed, listen to what God is saying to you and obey the promptings of the Holy Spirit, and you'll soon find yourself in a place of peace, strength, and triumph.

And summoned the earth from the rising of the sun to its setting [from east to west].

2 Out of Zion, the perfection of beauty, God has shone forth.

3 May our God come and not keep silent; Fire devours before Him, And around Him a mighty tempest rages.

4 He summons the heavens above, And the earth, to judge His people:

5 "Gather My godly ones to Me, Those who have made a covenant with Me by sacrifice."

6 And the heavens declare His righteousness, For God Himself is judge.   *Selah.*

7 "Hear, O My people, and I will speak; O Israel, I will testify against you: I am God, your God.

8 "I do not reprove you for your sacrifices; Your burnt offerings are continually before Me.

9 "I will accept no young bull from your house Nor male goat from your folds.

10 "For every beast of the forest is Mine, And the cattle on a thousand hills.

11 "I know every bird of the mountains, And everything that moves in the field is Mine.

12 "If I were hungry, I would not tell you, For the world and all it contains are Mine. [1 Cor 10:26]

13 "Shall I eat the flesh of bulls Or drink the blood of male goats?

14 "Offer to God the sacrifice of thanksgiving And pay your vows to the Most High;

15 Call on Me in the day of trouble;

WINNING THE BATTLES *of the* MIND

Dealing with Sin

T he heading under Psalm 51 reads: "A Psalm of David; when Nathan the prophet came to him after he had sinned with Bathsheba." David cried out for mercy because he had sinned with Bathsheba, and when he learned she was pregnant, he ensured that her husband would be murdered in battle.

When David realized what he had done, he was deeply repentant. Psalm 51 is a record of the prayer He cried out to God. God forgave David, but David had given God's enemies a great opportunity to blaspheme Him. We too should remember that our disobedience not only affects us, it also affects our witness to others.

Whenever we fail God, not only do we harm ourselves, we also bring dishonor to His name. Whenever we make a mistake, there are those who gleefully point their finger.

The evil one also whispers, "See how bad you are. God won't forgive you." Don't listen to those words, because there is no sin you've committed that God won't forgive. God wipes away the sin.

There's something else to learn from this: It's necessary to face the truth. God desires truth in the inner being (see Ps. 51:6).When you have sinned, what will you do about your sin? David wrote: "For I am conscious of my transgressions *and* I acknowledge them; my sin is always before me. Against You, You only, have I sinned and done that which is evil in Your sight." (Ps. 51:3–4).

It's easy for us to deceive ourselves, but God has called us to be totally, completely, and scrupulously honest in our inner being. We can't look at what others may get away with or how they justify their behavior. We can't blame others, the devil, or circumstances.

When you fail, remind yourself that the greatest king of Israel cried out to God and said, "My sin is always before me" (v. 3). Those sins, failures, or shortcomings will always be there until you admit them and confess them to the Lord. Strive to live with truth in your inner being (v. 6). You—you and God—are the only ones who know what's in your heart. Only when you are honest with yourself and with God can you know the joy of living in integrity and in truth.

A PRAYER FOR VICTORY

Holy God, please help me to desire truth in my inner being, to live in such a way that I'm as honest and as open with You as I can be. I know that the life You honor is the life You bless. In Jesus' name, I pray. Amen.

I will rescue you, and you shall honor
and glorify Me."

16But to the wicked God says:
"What right have you to recite My
statutes
Or to take My covenant on your lips?
17 "For you hate instruction *and* discipline
And cast My words behind you
[discarding them].
18 "When you see a thief, you are pleased
with him *and* condone his behavior,
And you associate with adulterers.
19 "You give your mouth to evil
And your tongue frames deceit.
20 "You sit and speak against your brother;
You slander your own mother's son.
21 "These things you have done and I kept
silent;
You thought that I was just like you.
Now I will reprimand *and* denounce you
and state *the case* in order before your
eyes.

22"Now consider this, you who forget God,

Or I will tear you in pieces, and there
will be no one to rescue [you].
23 "He who offers a sacrifice of praise *and*
thanksgiving honors Me;
And to him who orders his way rightly
[who follows the way that I show him],
I shall show the salvation of God."

Psalm 51

A Contrite Sinner's Prayer
for Pardon.

To the Chief Musician. A Psalm
of David; when Nathan the prophet
came to him after he had sinned
with Bathsheba.

1 HAVE MERCY on me, O God,
according to Your lovingkindness;
According to the greatness of
Your compassion blot out my
transgressions.
2 Wash me thoroughly from my
wickedness *and* guilt
And cleanse me from my sin.

KEYS *to a*
Victorious
Life *A Clean Heart*

*In Psalm 51:6, 10, David tells us that having a clean heart means having truth
in our innermost being, who we truly are inside. It's all about paying attention to
our thought life, because out of it comes our words, our emotions, our attitudes,
and our motives.*

*Purity and cleanness of heart is not natural to us. It is something that must be
worked into our heart by the Holy Spirit. In 1 John 3:3, we read that those whose
hope is confidently placed in God purify themselves because it is God's will, just
as He is pure.*

*There is a price to pay to have a pure and clean heart, but there is also a reward. We
will be blessed; we will see God (see Matt. 5:8)! We don't have to be afraid to make
the commitment that allows God to do a deep work in us. We may not always feel
comfortable about the truths He will bring to us, but if we will take care of our part,
holding to purity, integrity, moral courage, and godly character, God will take care of
making sure that we are blessed. He is an expert at removing worthless things out of
our hearts and lives while retaining the valuable.*

Speak God's Word

*God makes me to hear joy and gladness
and be satisfied. God hides His face from
my sins and blots out all my iniquities.*

| *adapted from* PSALM 51:8–9 |

³For I am conscious of my transgressions
    and I acknowledge them;
My sin is always before me.
⁴Against You, You only, have I sinned
    And done that which is evil in Your sight,
    So that You are justified when You speak
        [Your sentence]
    And faultless in Your judgment. [Rom 3:4]

⁵I was brought forth in [a state of]
        wickedness;
    In sin my mother conceived me [and
        from my beginning I, too, was sinful].
        [John 3:6; Rom 5:12; Eph 2:3]
⁶Behold, You desire truth in the
        innermost being,
    And in the hidden part [of my heart] You
        will make me know wisdom.
⁷Purify me with hyssop, and I will be
        clean;
    Wash me, and I will be whiter than
        snow.
⁸Make me hear joy and gladness *and* be
        satisfied;
    Let the bones which You have broken
        rejoice.
⁹Hide Your face from my sins
    And blot out all my iniquities.

¹⁰Create in me a clean heart, O God,
    And renew a right *and* steadfast spirit
        within me.
¹¹Do not cast me away from Your presence
    And do not take Your Holy Spirit
        from me.
¹²Restore to me the joy of Your salvation
    And sustain me with a willing spirit.
¹³Then I will teach transgressors Your
        ways,
    And sinners shall be converted *and*
        return to You.

¹⁴Rescue me from bloodguiltiness, O God,
        the God of my salvation;
    Then my tongue will sing joyfully of
        Your righteousness *and* Your justice.

¹⁵O Lord, open my lips,
    That my mouth may declare Your praise.
¹⁶For You do not delight in sacrifice, or
        else I would give it;
    You are not pleased with burnt offering.
        [1 Sam 15:22]
¹⁷My [only] sacrifice [acceptable] to God is
        a broken spirit;
    A broken and contrite heart [broken
        with sorrow for sin, thoroughly
        penitent], such, O God, You will not
        despise.

¹⁸By Your favor do good to Zion;
    May You rebuild the walls of Jerusalem.
¹⁹Then will You delight in the sacrifices of
        righteousness,
    In burnt offering and whole burnt
        offering;
    Then young bulls will be offered on
        Your altar.

Psalm 52

Futility of Boastful Wickedness.

To the Chief Musician. A skillful song,
    or a didactic *or* reflective poem. *A
    Psalm* of David, when Doeg the Edomite
    came and told Saul, "David has come
        to the house of Ahimelech."

¹WHY DO you boast of evil, O mighty
        man?
    The lovingkindness of God *endures* all
        day long.
²Your tongue devises destruction,
    Like a sharp razor, working deceitfully.
³You love evil more than good,
    And falsehood more than speaking what
        is right.   *Selah.*
⁴You love all words that devour,
    O deceitful tongue.

⁵But God will break you down forever;
    He will take you away and tear you away
        from your tent,
    And uproot you from the land of the
        living.   *Selah.*
⁶The righteous will see it and fear,
    And will [scoffingly] laugh, *saying,*
⁷"Look, [this is] the man who would
        not make God his strength [his
        stronghold and fortress],
    But trusted in the abundance of his riches,
    Taking refuge in his wealth."

KEYS *to a* Victorious Life *Relax While God Works*

If you know you can't fix the problem you have, why not relax while God works on it? It sounds easy, but it took many years for me to be able to do this. I know from experience that the ability to relax and accept whatever happens in life depends on our willingness to trust God completely (see Rom. 15:13).

If things don't go your way, instead of getting upset, start believing that your way was not what you needed and that God has something better in mind for you. God will give you what is best for you, even if it isn't what you think you want! "Trust [confidently] in the lovingkindness of God forever and ever" (Ps. 52:8). The minute you recognize He is in control and you put your trust in Him, your soul and body relax, and you will be able to enjoy life.

8 But as for me, I am like a green olive tree in the house of God;
I trust [confidently] in the lovingkindness of God forever and ever.
9 I will thank You forever, because You have done it, [You have rescued me and kept me safe].
I will wait on Your name, for it is good, in the presence of Your godly ones.

Psalm 53

Folly and Wickedness of Men.

To the Chief Musician; in a mournful strain. A skillful song, *or* didactic *or* reflective poem of David.

1 THE [empty-headed] fool has said in his heart, "There is no God."
They are corrupt *and* evil, and have committed repulsive injustice;
There is no one who does good.
2 God has looked down from heaven upon the children of men
To see if there is anyone who understands,
Who seeks after God [who requires Him, who longs for Him as essential to life].

3 Every one of them has turned aside *and* fallen away;
Together they have become filthy *and* corrupt;
There is no one who does good, no, not even one. [Rom 3:10–12]
4 Have workers of wickedness no knowledge *or* no understanding?
They eat up My people *as though* they ate bread

POWERPOINT

Praise and thanksgiving are two spiritual weapons available to us. They defeat the devil more quickly than any other battle plan, but they must be genuine and heartfelt, not just lip service or a method being tried to see if it works. Also, giving thanks and praise involves God's Word. We thank God and praise Him according to His Word and His goodness.

KEYS *to a* **Victorious Life** *Tell God How You Really Feel*

We can see from the opening verses in Psalm 55 that David was not hesitant when it came to telling God exactly how he felt. But he also followed up by saying he trusted God to be faithful to keep His promises. Often David would even remind God of something He had promised in His Word.

I believe it was spiritually and even physically healthy for David to express to God how he really felt. It was a way of releasing his negative feelings so they could not harm his inner man while he was waiting for God's deliverance. Sometimes we need an outlet for the pain we feel in life, and simply taking time to tell God all about it could prove very helpful. He already knows, but telling Him can be a good release for you. After telling Him all about how you feel, always follow up by telling Him you trust Him to make all things right and ask for His help to live by His Word, not by your feelings.

And have not called upon God.

⁵There they were, in great terror *and* dread, where there had been no terror *or* dread;

For God scattered the bones of him who besieged you;

You have put them to shame, because God has rejected them.

⁶Oh, that the salvation of Israel would come out of Zion!

When God restores [the fortunes of] His people,

Let Jacob rejoice, let Israel be glad.

Psalm 54

Prayer for Defense against Enemies.

To the Chief Musician; with stringed instruments. A skillful song, *or* a didactic *or* reflective poem, of David, when the Ziphites went and told Saul, "David is hiding among us."

¹SAVE ME, O God, by Your name;
And vindicate me by Your [wondrous] power.

²Hear my prayer, O God;
Listen to the words of my mouth.

³For strangers have risen against me
And violent men have sought my life;
They have not set God before them.
Selah.

⁴Behold, God is my helper *and* ally;
The Lord is the sustainer of my soul [my upholder].

⁵He will pay back the evil to my enemies;
In Your faithfulness destroy them.

⁶With a freewill offering I will sacrifice to You;

I will give thanks *and* praise Your name, O LORD, for it is good.

⁷For He has rescued me from every trouble,

And my eye has looked *with satisfaction* (triumph) on my enemies.

Psalm 55

Prayer for the Destruction of the Treacherous.

To the Chief Musician; with stringed instruments. A skillful song, *or* a didactic *or* reflective poem, of David.

¹LISTEN TO my prayer, O God,
And do not hide Yourself from my plea.

²Listen to me and answer me;
I am restless *and* distraught in my complaint and distracted

³Because of the voice of the enemy,
Because of the pressure of the wicked;
For they bring down trouble on me,
And in anger they persecute me.

⁴My heart is in anguish within me,
And the terrors of death have fallen upon me.

⁵Fear and trembling have come upon me;
Horror has overwhelmed me.

⁶And I say, "Oh, that I had wings like a dove!
I would fly away and be at rest.

⁷"I would wander far away,
I would lodge in the [peace of the] wilderness.   *Selah.*

⁸"I would hurry to my refuge [my tranquil shelter far away]
From the stormy wind *and* from the tempest."

⁹Confuse [my enemies], O Lord, divide their tongues [destroying their schemes],
For I have seen violence and strife in the city.

¹⁰Day and night they go around her walls;
Wickedness and mischief are in her midst.

¹¹Destruction is within her;
Oppression and deceit do not depart from her streets *and* market places.

¹²For it is not an enemy who taunts me—
Then I could bear it;
Nor is it one who has hated me who insolently exalts himself against me—
Then I could hide from him.

¹³But it is you, a man my equal *and* my counsel,
My companion and my familiar friend;

¹⁴We who had sweet fellowship together,
Who walked to the house of God in company.

¹⁵Let death come deceitfully upon them;
Let them go down alive to Sheol (the nether world, the place of the dead),
For evil [of every kind] is in their dwelling *and* in their hearts, in their midst.

¹⁶As for me, I shall call upon God,
And the LORD will save me.

A Prayer To Renew Your Mind

I believe, Lord, that You will redeem my life in peace from every battle that is against me.

· *adapted from Psalm 55:18*

¹⁷Evening and morning and at noon I will complain and murmur,
And He will hear my voice.

¹⁸He has redeemed my life in peace from the battle that was against me,
For there were many against me.

¹⁹God will hear and humble them,
Even He who sits enthroned from old—
                                            Selah.
Because in them there has been no change [of heart],
And they do not fear God [at all].

²⁰He [my companion] has put out his hands against those who were at peace with him;
He has broken his covenant [of friendship and loyalty].

²¹The words of his mouth were smoother than butter,
But his heart was hostile;
His words were softer than oil,
Yet they were drawn swords.

²²Cast your burden on the LORD [release it] and He will sustain *and* uphold you;
He will never allow the righteous to be shaken (slip, fall, fail). [1 Pet 5:7]

²³But You, O God, will bring down the wicked to the pit of destruction;
Men of blood and treachery will not live out half their days.
But I will [boldly and unwaveringly] trust in You.

Psalm 56

Supplication for Rescue and Grateful Trust in God.

To the Chief Musician; set to [the tune of] "Silent Dove Among Those Far Away." A Mikhtam of David. [A record of memorable thoughts] when the Philistines seized him in Gath.

¹BE GRACIOUS to me, O God, for man has trampled on me;

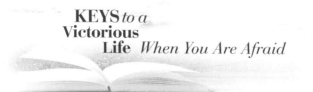

KEYS *to a* Victorious Life *When You Are Afraid*

In Psalm 56:3, David said, "When I am afraid . . ." He accepted the fact that fear is a human emotion; we all experience fear to some degree. But he added, "I will put my trust and faith in You." David lived boldly and courageously because he knew God was always with him. We can live this same way. We can choose to not live according to the fear we feel.

God taught me to use what I call the "power twins" to help me defeat the spirit of fear. They are "I pray" and "I say." When I feel fear, I begin to pray and ask for God's help, then I say, "I will not fear!" I encourage you to also use these power twins as soon as you feel fearful about anything, and you will be able to keep fear from controlling you. We can learn to manage the emotion of fear and not let it control us.

All day long the adversary oppresses *and* torments me.
² My enemies have trampled upon me all day long,
For they are many who fight proudly against me.
³ When I am afraid,
I will put my trust *and* faith in You.
⁴ In God, whose word I praise;
In God I have put my trust;
I shall not fear.
What can mere man do to me?
⁵ All day long they twist my words *and* say hurtful things;
All their thoughts are against me for evil.
⁶ They attack, they hide *and* lurk,
They watch my steps,
As they have [expectantly] waited *to take* my life.
⁷ Cast them out because of their wickedness.
In anger bring down the peoples, O God!

⁸ You have taken account of my wanderings;
Put my tears in Your bottle.
Are they not recorded in Your book?
⁹ Then my enemies will turn back in the day when I call;
This I know, that God is for me. [Rom 8:31]

¹⁰ In God, *whose* word I praise,
In the LORD, *whose* word I praise,
¹¹ In God have I put my trust *and* confident reliance; I will not be afraid.
What can man do to me?
¹² Your vows are *binding* upon me, O God;
I will give thank offerings to You.
¹³ For You have rescued my soul from death,
Yes, and my feet from stumbling,
So that I may walk before God
In the light of life.

Psalm 57

Prayer for Rescue from Persecutors.

To the Chief Musician; set to [the tune of] "Do Not Destroy." A Mikhtam of David. [A record of memorable thoughts of David] when he fled from Saul in the cave.

¹ BE GRACIOUS to me, O God, be gracious *and* merciful to me,
For my soul finds shelter *and* safety in You,
And in the shadow of Your wings I will take refuge *and* be confidently secure
Until destruction passes by.

A Prayer To Renew Your Mind

When I am afraid, I will put my trust and faith in You, God, whose word I praise. In You I have put my trust; I shall not fear. What can mere man do to me?   · adapted from Psalm 56:3–4

2 I will cry to God Most High,
  Who accomplishes *all things* on my
    behalf [for He completes my purpose
    in His plan].
3 He will send from heaven and save me;
  He calls to account him who tramples
    me down.   *Selah.*
  God will send out His lovingkindness
    and His truth.

4 My life is among lions;
  I must lie among those who breathe out
    fire—
  The sons of men whose teeth are spears
    and arrows,
  And their tongue a sharp sword.
5 Be exalted above the heavens, O God;
  Let Your glory *and* majesty be over all
    the earth.
6 They set a net for my steps;
  My very life was bowed down.
  They dug a pit before me;
  Into the midst of it they themselves have
    fallen.   *Selah.*

7 My heart is steadfast, O God, my heart is
    steadfast *and* confident!
  I will sing, yes, I will sing praises [to You]!
8 Awake, my glory!
  Awake, harp and lyre!
  I will awaken the dawn.
9 I will praise *and* give thanks to You,
    O Lord, among the people;
  I will sing praises to You among the
    nations.
10 For Your faithfulness *and*
    lovingkindness are great, reaching to
    the heavens,
  And Your truth to the clouds.

KEYS *to a* Victorious Life *A Steadfast Heart*

To have a steadfast and confident heart as described in Psalm 57:7 means that our mind is made up and we are not going to change it. If we are going to experience any kind of victory and remain positive in our lives, we must be determined to hold fast to God and His Word. If we are going to see the fulfillment of God's will, walk in or follow the leading of the Spirit, or accomplish anything worthwhile in this life, we need to set our face like flint and not waver. And we must understand that the devil is not going to roll out the red carpet for us just because we decide to get saved and serve God. He will oppose us at every turn.

Too often we are looking for something easy. But it's important to be willing to do the will of God at all costs, to stay positive and be content, and to walk in the peace of God. His will won't just happen in our lives. We are partners with God, and we must do our part. Part of what we need to do is to continue to be steadfast of heart. A steadfast heart seeks His kingdom and His righteousness first, and then God pours on all He has to give to us (see Matt. 6:33).

If you want to see God's plan fulfilled in your life, press on with "holy determination."

11 Be exalted above the heavens, O God;
Let Your glory *and* majesty be over all
the earth.

Psalm 58

Prayer for the Punishment
of the Wicked.

To the Chief Musician; set to [the tune
of] "Do Not Destroy." A Mikhtam
of David. [A record of memorable
thoughts of David.]

1 DO YOU indeed speak righteousness,
O gods (heavenly beings)?
Do you judge fairly, O sons of men? [Ps
82:1, 2]
2 No, in your heart you devise
wrongdoing;
On earth you deal out the violence of
your hands.
3 The wicked are estranged from the
womb;
These go astray from birth, speaking lies
[even twisted partial truths].
4 Their poison is like the venom of a
serpent;
They are like the deaf horned viper that
stops up its ear,
5 So that it does not listen to the voice of
charmers,
Or of the skillful enchanter casting
[cunning] spells.

6 O God, break their teeth in their mouth;
Break out the fangs of the young lions,
O LORD.
7 Let them flow away like water that runs
off;
When he aims his arrows, let them be as
headless shafts.
8 *Let them be* as a snail which melts away
(secretes slime) as it goes along,
Like the miscarriage of a woman which
never sees the sun.
9 Before your cooking pots can feel the
fire of thorns [burning under them as
fuel],
He will sweep them away with a
whirlwind, the green and the burning
ones alike.

10 The [unyieldingly] righteous will rejoice
when he sees the vengeance [of God];

He will wash his feet in the blood of the
wicked.
11 Men will say, "Surely there is a reward
for the righteous;
Surely there is a God who judges on the
earth."

Psalm 59

Prayer for Rescue from Enemies.

To the Chief Musician; set to [the tune
of] "Do Not Destroy." A Mikhtam
of David, [a record of memorable
thoughts] when Saul sent men to watch
his house in order to kill him.

1 DELIVER ME from my enemies, O my
God;
Set me *securely* on an inaccessibly high
place away from those who rise up
against me.
2 Deliver me from those who practice
wrongdoing,
And save me from bloodthirsty
men.
3 Look! They lie in wait for my life;
Fierce *and* powerful men [are uniting
together to] launch an attack against
me,
Not for my wrongdoing nor for any sin
of mine, O LORD.
4 They run and set themselves against me
though there is no guilt in me;
Stir Yourself to meet *and* help me, and
see [what they are doing]!
5 You, O LORD God of hosts, the God of
Israel,
Arise to punish all the nations;
Spare no one *and* do not be merciful to
any who treacherously plot evil. *Selah.*
6 They return at evening, they howl *and*
snarl like dogs,
And go [prowling] around the city.

A Prayer To
Renew Your Mind

*O God my strength, I will watch for
You. For You are my stronghold, my
refuge, and my protector. In Your
lovingkindness You will meet me. You
will let me look triumphantly on my
enemies.* • adapted from Psalm 59:9–10

7 Look how they belch out [insults] with
their mouths;
Swords [of sarcasm, ridicule, slander,
and lies] are in their lips,
For *they say*, "Who hears us?"
8 But You, O Lord, will laugh at them [in
scorn];
You scoff at *and* deride all the nations.

9 O [God] my strength, I will watch for
You;
For God is my stronghold [my refuge,
my protector, my high tower].
10 My God in His [steadfast]
lovingkindness will meet me;
God will let me look *triumphantly* on
my enemies [who lie in wait for me].
11 Do not kill them, or my people will
forget;
Scatter them *and* make them wander
[endlessly] back and forth by Your
power, and bring them down,
O Lord our shield!
12 For the sin of their mouths and the
words of their lips,
Let them even be trapped in their
pride,
And on account of the curses and lies
which they tell.
13 Destroy *them* in wrath, destroy *them* so
that they may be no more;
Let them know that God rules over
Jacob (Israel)
To the ends of the earth.   *Selah.*
14 They return at evening, they howl *and*
snarl like dogs,
And go [prowling] around the city.
15 They wander around for food [to devour]
And growl all night if they are not
satisfied.

16 But as for me, I will sing of Your mighty
strength *and* power;
Yes, I will sing joyfully of Your
lovingkindness in the morning;
For You have been my stronghold
And a refuge in the day of my distress.
17 To You, O [God] my strength, I will sing
praises;
For God is my stronghold [my refuge,
my protector, my high tower], the
God who shows me [steadfast]
lovingkindness.

Psalm 60

Lament over Defeat in Battle, and Prayer for Help.

To the Chief Musician; set to [the tune
of] "The Lily of the Testimony." A
Mikhtam of David [intended to record
memorable thoughts and] to teach;
when he struggled with the Arameans
of Mesopotamia and the Arameans
of Zobah, and when Joab returned
and struck twelve thousand Edomites
in the Valley of Salt.

1 O GOD, You have rejected us *and* cast
us off. You have broken [down our
defenses and scattered] us;
You have been angry; O restore us *and*
turn again to us.
2 You have made the land quake, You have
split it open;
Heal its rifts, for it shakes *and* totters.
3 You have made Your people experience
hardship;
You have given us wine to drink that
makes us stagger *and* fall.
4 You have set up a banner for those who
fear You [with awe-inspired reverence
and submissive wonder—a banner to
shield them from attack],
A banner that may be displayed because
of the truth.   *Selah.*
5 That Your beloved ones may be
rescued,
Save with Your right hand and
answer us.

6 God has spoken in His holiness [in His
promises]:
"I will rejoice, I will divide [the land of]
Shechem and measure out the Valley
of Succoth [west to east].
7 "Gilead is Mine, and Manasseh is Mine;
Ephraim is My helmet;
Judah is My scepter.
8 "Moab is My washbowl;
Over Edom I shall throw My shoe [in
triumph];
Over Philistia I raise the shout [of
victory]."
9 Who will bring me into the besieged city
[of Petra]?
Who will lead me to Edom?
10 Have You not rejected us, O God?

And will You not go out with our
  armies?
[11] Give us help against the enemy,
  For the help of man is worthless
    (ineffectual, without purpose).
[12] Through God we will have victory,
  For He will trample down our enemies.

Psalm 61

Confidence in God's Protection.

To the Chief Musician; on stringed
instruments. *A Psalm* of David.

[1] HEAR MY cry, O God;
  Listen to my prayer.
[2] From the end of the earth I call to You,
    when my heart is overwhelmed *and*
    weak;
  Lead me to the rock that is higher than
    I [a rock that is too high to reach
    without Your help].
[3] For You have been a shelter *and* a refuge
  for me,
  A strong tower against the enemy.
[4] Let me dwell in Your tent forever;
  Let me take refuge in the shelter of Your
    wings.   *Selah.*

[5] For You have heard my vows, O God;

You have given me the inheritance
  of those who fear Your name [with
  reverence].
[6] You will prolong the king's life [adding
  days upon days];
  His years will be like many generations.
[7] He will sit enthroned forever before [the
  face of] God;
  Appoint lovingkindness and truth to
    watch over *and* preserve him.
[8] So I will sing praise to Your name
  forever,
  Paying my vows day by day.

Psalm 62

God Alone a Refuge from
Treachery and Oppression.

To the Chief Musician; to Jeduthun
[Ethan, the noted musician, founder
of an official musical family].
A Psalm of David.

[1] FOR GOD alone my soul *waits* in
  silence;
  From Him comes my salvation.
[2] He alone is my rock and my salvation,
  My defense *and* my strong tower; I will
    not be shaken *or* disheartened.

KEYS *to a* **Victorious Life** *You're On Your Way*

*God's will is for us to live by faith. You may be thinking of how far you have to go
in order to be all that God wants you to be, and you feel overwhelmed. Your mind
wants to think,* This is just too much; I will never be able to do all that He asks
me to do.

*This is where faith comes in. When David's heart was "overwhelmed," he cried out
to God, "Lead me to the rock that is higher than I [a rock that is too high to reach
without Your help]" (Ps. 61:2–3). You can think,* I don't know how I am going to
do it, but I am expecting God's help. With God, all things are possible.

*Just get started and keep going day after day. Refuse to be discouraged by how
far you think you still have to go. God is pleased that you are on your way (see
Phil. 3:12).*

Speak God's Word

*For God alone my soul waits in silence;
from Him comes my salvation. He
only is my rock and my salvation, my
defense and my strong tower; I will not
be shaken or disheartened.*

[*adapted from* PSALM 62:1–2]

³How long will you attack a man
  So that you may murder him, all of
  you,
  Like a leaning wall, like a tottering
  fence?
⁴They consult only to throw him down
  from his high position [to dishonor
  him];
  They delight in lies.
  They bless with [the words of] their
  mouths,
  But inwardly they curse.   *Selah.*

⁵For God alone my soul waits in silence
  and quietly submits to Him,
  For my hope is from Him.
⁶He only is my rock and my salvation;
  My fortress *and* my defense, I will not be
  shaken *or* discouraged.
⁷On God my salvation and my glory rest;
  He is my rock of [unyielding] strength,
  my refuge is in God.
⁸Trust [confidently] in Him at all times,
  O people;
  Pour out your heart before Him.
  God is a refuge for us.   *Selah.*

⁹Men of low degree are only a breath
  (emptiness), and men of [high] rank
  are a lie (delusion).
  In the balances they go up [because they
  have no measurable weight or value];
  They are together lighter than a breath.
¹⁰Do not trust in oppression,
  And do not vainly hope in robbery;
  If riches increase, do not set your heart
  on them.

¹¹God has spoken once,
  Twice I have heard this:
  That power belongs to God.
¹²Also to You, O Lord, belong
  lovingkindness *and* compassion,

For You compensate every man
  according to [the value of] his work.
  [Jer 17:10; Rev 22:12]

Psalm 63

The Thirsting Soul Satisfied in God.

A Psalm of David; when he was
in the wilderness of Judah.

¹O GOD, You are my God; with deepest
  longing I will seek You;
  My soul [my life, my very self] thirsts for
  You, my flesh longs *and* sighs for You,
  In a dry and weary land where there is
  no water.
²So I have gazed upon You in the
  sanctuary,
  To see Your power and Your glory. [Ps
  42:1, 2]
³Because Your lovingkindness is better
  than life,
  My lips shall praise You.
⁴So will I bless You as long as I live;
  I will lift up my hands in Your name.
⁵My soul [my life, my very self] is satisfied
  as with marrow and fatness,
  And my mouth offers praises [to You]
  with joyful lips.

⁶When I remember You on my bed,
  I meditate *and* thoughtfully focus on
  You in the night watches,
⁷For You have been my help,
  And in the shadow of Your wings [where
  I am always protected] I sing for joy.
⁸My soul [my life, my very self] clings to
  You;
  Your right hand upholds me.

⁹But those who seek my life to destroy it
  Will [be destroyed and] go into
  the depths of the earth [into the
  underworld].
¹⁰They will be given over to the power of
  the sword;
  They will be a prey for foxes.
¹¹But the king will rejoice in God;
  Everyone who swears by Him [honoring
  the true God, acknowledging His
  authority and majesty] will glory,
  For the mouths of those who speak lies
  will be stopped.

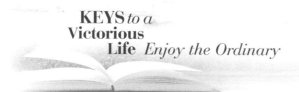

KEYS *to a* **Victorious Life** *Enjoy the Ordinary*

When David wrote Psalm 63, he was surrounded with difficulties in the wilderness of Judah, yet he could say, "My soul [my life, my very self] is satisfied as with marrow and fatness, and my mouth offers praises [to You] with joyful lips" (v. 5).

There are dozens of things pertaining to ordinary, everyday life, and you can enjoy them all if you just make a decision to do so. Things like getting dressed, driving to work, going to the grocery store, running errands, keeping things organized, and so many other activities. After all, they are the things that make up life. Begin doing them for the love of God, and realize that through the Holy Spirit you can enjoy absolutely everything you do. Joy doesn't come merely from being entertained, but from a decision to appreciate each moment you are given as a rare and precious gift from God.

Psalm 64

Prayer for Protection from Secret Enemies.

To the Chief Musician.
A Psalm of David.

¹ HEAR MY voice, O God, in my complaint;
Guard my life from the terror of the enemy.
² Hide me from the secret counsel *and* conspiracy of the ungodly,
From the scheming of those who do wrong,
³ Who have sharpened their tongues like a sword.
They aim venomous words as arrows,
⁴ To shoot from ambush at the blameless [one];
Suddenly they shoot at him, without fear.
⁵ They encourage themselves in [their pursuit of] an evil agenda;
They talk of laying snares secretly;
They say, "Who will discover us?"
⁶ They devise acts of injustice, *saying,*
"We are ready with a well-conceived plan."
For the inward thought and the heart of a man are deep (mysterious, unsearchable).

⁷ But God will shoot them with an [unexpected] arrow;
Suddenly they will be wounded.
⁸ So they will be caused to stumble;
Their own tongue is against them;
All who gaze at them will shake the head [in scorn].
⁹ Then all men will fear [God's judgment];
They will declare the work of God,
And they will consider *and* wisely acknowledge what He has done.
¹⁰ The righteous will rejoice in the LORD and take refuge in Him;
All the upright in heart will glory *and* offer praise.

Psalm 65

God's Abundant Favor to Earth and Man.

To the Chief Musician. A Psalm of David. A Song.

¹ TO YOU belongs silence [the submissive wonder of reverence], and [it bursts into] praise in Zion, O God;
And to You the vow shall be performed.
² O You who hear prayer,
To You all mankind comes.

3 Wickedness *and* guilt prevail against
    me;
  Yet as for our transgressions,
  You forgive them [removing them from
    Your sight].
4 Blessed is the one whom You choose and
    bring near
  To dwell in Your courts.
  We will be filled with the goodness of
    Your house,
  Your holy temple.

5 By awesome *and* wondrous things You
    answer us in righteousness, O God of
    our salvation,
  You who are the trust *and* hope of all the
    ends of the earth and of the farthest
    sea;
6 Who creates the mountains by His
    strength,
  Being clothed with power,
7 Who stills the roaring of the seas,
  The roaring of their waves,
  And the tumult of the peoples,
8 So they who dwell at the ends *of the earth*
    stand in awe of Your signs [the evidence
    of Your presence]. [Mark 4:36–41]
  You make the dawn and the sunset shout
    for joy.

9 You visit the earth and make it overflow
    [with water];
  You greatly enrich it;
  The stream of God is full of water;
  You provide their grain, when You have
    prepared the earth.
10 You water its furrows abundantly,
  You smooth its ridges;
  You soften it with showers,
  You bless its growth.
11 You crown the year with Your bounty,
  And Your paths overflow.
12 The pastures of the wilderness drip
    [with dew],
  And the hills are encircled with joy.
13 The meadows are clothed with flocks
  And the valleys are covered with grain;
  They shout for joy and they sing.

> **REMEMBER**, any time the enemy
> attacks your mind, the battle
> belongs to the Lord.

Psalm 66

Praise for God's Mighty Deeds and for His Answer to Prayer.

To the Chief Musician. A Song.
A Psalm.

1 SHOUT JOYFULLY to God, all the
    earth;
2 Sing of the honor *and* glory *and*
    magnificence of His name;
  Make His praise glorious.
3 Say to God, "How awesome *and* fearfully
    glorious are Your works!
  Because of the greatness of Your power
    Your enemies will pretend to be
    obedient to You.
4 "All the earth will [bow down to]
    worship You [in submissive wonder],
  And will sing praises to You;
  They will praise Your name in song."
                                    Selah.

5 Come and see the works of God,
  He is awesome in His deeds toward the
    children of men.
6 He turned the sea into dry land;
  They crossed through the river on
    foot;
  There we rejoiced in Him. [Ex 14–15]
7 Who rules by His might forever,
  His eyes keep watch on the nations;
  Do not let the rebellious exalt
    themselves.   *Selah.*

8 Bless our God, O peoples,
  And make the sound of His praise *be
    heard* abroad,
9 Who keeps us among the living,
  And does not allow our feet to slip *or*
    stumble.
10 For You have tested us, O God;
  You have refined us as silver is refined.
11 You brought us into the net;
  You laid a heavy burden [of servitude]
    on us.
12 You made men (charioteers) ride over
    our heads [in defeat];
  We went through fire and through
    water,
  Yet You brought us out into a [broad]
    place of abundance [to be refreshed].
13 I shall come into Your house with burnt
    offerings;

KEYS *to a* Victorious Life *Coming Clean*

Our prayers often remain unanswered because we regard iniquity in our heart. David said, "If I regard sin and baseness in my heart [that is, if I know it is there and do nothing about it], the Lord will not hear [me]" (Ps. 66:18). What that means, to put it plainly, is that the Lord will not hear us when we pray if we come before Him in prayer with sin hidden in our hearts.

If there is sin in our lives, we will not be able to pray boldly or with confidence. As we are praying, if we sense that we are not comfortable, we need to stop and ask God why. Ask God to reveal anything hidden. If He convicts us of something that is sinful, call it what it is—sin. God wants us to confess the sin so He may cleanse us and restore a clean conscience and then we may pray (see 1 John 1:9). There is power in truth and honesty when we come clean before the Lord and walk in the light.

Make sure your heart is pure before Him so your prayers are offered confidently and in active faith. God answers our prayers when we approach Him with boldness and with clean, pure hearts.

I shall pay You my vows,
14 Which my lips uttered
   And my mouth spoke as a promise when
   I was in distress.
15 I shall offer to You burnt offerings of fat
   lambs,
   With the [sweet] smoke of rams;
   I will offer bulls with male goats. *Selah.*

16 Come and hear, all who fear God [and
   worship Him with awe-inspired
   reverence and obedience],
   And I will tell what He has done
   for me.
17 I cried aloud to Him;
   He was highly praised with my tongue.
18 If I regard sin *and* baseness in my heart
   [that is, if I know it is there and do
   nothing about it],
   The Lord will not hear [me]; [Prov 15:29;
   28:9; Is 1:15; John 9:31; James 4:3]
19 But certainly God has heard [me];
   He has given heed to the voice of my
   prayer.
20 Blessed be God,
   Who has not turned away my prayer
   Nor His lovingkindness from me.

Psalm 67

The Nations Exhorted to Praise God.

To the Chief Musician;
on stringed instruments. A Psalm.
A Song.

1 GOD BE gracious *and* kind-hearted to
   us and bless us,
   And make His face shine [with favor] on
   us—   *Selah.*
2 That Your way may be known on earth,
   Your salvation *and* deliverance among
   all nations.
3 Let the peoples praise You, O God;
   Let all the peoples praise You.
4 Let the nations be glad and sing for
   joy,
   For You will judge the people fairly
   And guide the nations on earth. *Selah.*
5 Let the peoples praise You, O God;
   Let all the peoples praise You.
6 The earth has yielded its harvest [as
   evidence of His approval];
   God, our God, blesses us.
7 God blesses us,

And all the ends of the earth shall fear
Him [with awe-inspired reverence and
submissive wonder].

Psalm 68

The God of Sinai and
of the Sanctuary.

To the Chief Musician. A Psalm
of David. A Song.

1 LET GOD arise, and His enemies be
scattered;
Let those who hate Him flee before
Him.
2 As smoke is driven away, so drive *them*
away;
As wax melts before the fire,
So let the wicked *and* guilty perish
before [the presence of] God.
3 But let the righteous be glad; let them be
in good spirits before God,
Yes, let them rejoice with delight.
4 Sing to God, sing praises to His name;
Lift up *a song* for Him who rides
through the desert—
His name is the LORD—be in good
spirits before Him.

5 A father of the fatherless and a judge *and*
protector of the widows,
Is God in His holy habitation.
6 God makes a home for the lonely;
He leads the prisoners into prosperity,
Only the stubborn *and* rebellious dwell
in a parched land.

7 O God, when You went out before Your
people,
When You marched through the
wilderness,   *Selah.*
8 The earth trembled;
The heavens also poured down *rain* at
the presence of God;
Sinai itself trembled at the presence of
God, the God of Israel.
9 You, O God, sent abroad plentiful rain;
You confirmed Your inheritance when it
was parched *and* weary.
10 Your flock found a dwelling place in it;
O God, in Your goodness You provided
for the poor.

11 The Lord gives the command [to take
Canaan];

The women who proclaim the good
news are a great host (army);

12 "The kings of the [enemies'] armies flee,
they flee,
And the beautiful woman who remains
at home divides the spoil [left
behind]."
13 When you lie down [to rest] among the
sheepfolds,
You [Israel] are like the wings of a dove
[of victory] overlaid with silver,
Its feathers glistening with gold
[trophies taken from the enemy].
14 When the Almighty scattered [the
Canaanite] kings in the land of
Canaan,
It was snowing on Zalmon.

15 A mountain of God is the mountain of
Bashan;
A [high] mountain of many summits
is Mount Bashan [rising east of the
Jordan].
16 Why do you look with envy, mountains
with many peaks,
At the mountain [of the city of Zion]
which God has desired for His
dwelling place?
Yes, the LORD will dwell *there* forever.
17 The chariots of God are myriads,
thousands upon thousands;
The Lord is among them as He was at
Sinai, in holiness.
18 You have ascended on high, You have led
away captive *Your* captives;
You have received gifts among men,
Even from the rebellious also, that the
LORD God may dwell there. [Eph 4:8]

19 Blessed be the Lord, who bears our
burden day by day,
The God who is our salvation!   *Selah.*
20 God is to us a God of acts of salvation;
And to GOD the Lord belong escapes
from death [setting us free].
21 Surely God will shatter the head of His
enemies,
The hairy scalp of one who goes on in
his guilty ways.
22 The Lord said, "I will bring your enemies
back from Bashan;
I will bring them back from the depths
of the [Red] Sea,

POWERPOINT

According to the Amplified Bible's rendering of Psalm 68:26, to bless God is to "give thanks, gratefully praise Him." A lifestyle of gratitude requires a sacrifice of praise or thanksgiving. I would rather offer a sacrifice of my thanksgiving to God than sacrifice my joy to the enemy. Many doors are opened to the devil through complaining. When we get upset and refuse to give thanks, we end up giving up our joy. In other words, we will lose our joy to the spirit of complaining. Being thankful will help you keep your joy.

23 That your foot may crush them in blood, That the tongue of your dogs *may have* its share from your enemies."

24 They have seen Your [solemn] procession, O God, The procession of my God, my King, into the sanctuary [in holiness].
25 The singers go in front, the players of instruments last; Between them the maidens playing on tambourines.
26 Bless God in the congregations, [give thanks, gratefully praise Him], The LORD, *you who are* from [Jacob] the fountain of Israel.
27 The youngest is there, Benjamin, ruling them, The princes of Judah and their company [the southern tribes], The princes of Zebulun and the princes of Naphtali [the northern tribes].
28 Your God has commanded your strength [your power in His service and your resistance to temptation]; Show Yourself strong, O God, who acted on our behalf.
29 Because of Your temple at Jerusalem [Pagan] kings will bring gifts to You [out of respect].

30 Rebuke the beasts [living] among the reeds [in Egypt], The herd of bulls (the leaders) with the calves of the peoples; Trampling underfoot the pieces of silver; He has scattered the peoples who delight in war.
31 Princes *and* envoys shall come from Egypt; Ethiopia will quickly stretch out her hands [with the offerings of submission] to God.
32 Sing to God, O kingdoms of the earth, Sing praises to the Lord!   *Selah.*
33 To Him who rides in the highest heavens, the ancient heavens, Behold, He sends out His voice, a mighty *and* majestic voice.
34 Ascribe strength to God; His majesty is over Israel And His strength is in the skies.
35 O God, *You are* awesome *and* profoundly majestic from Your sanctuary; The God of Israel gives strength and power to His people. Blessed be God!

Psalm 69

A Cry of Distress and Imprecation on Adversaries.

To the Chief Musician; set to [the tune of] "Lilies." *A Psalm* of David.

1 SAVE ME, O God, For the waters have threatened my life [they have come up to my neck].
2 I have sunk in deep mire, where there is no foothold; I have come into deep waters, where a flood overwhelms me.
3 I am weary with my crying; my throat is parched; My eyes fail while I wait [with confident expectation] for my God.
4 Those who hate me without cause are more than the hairs of my head; Those who would destroy me are powerful, being my enemies wrongfully; I am forced to restore what I did not steal. [John 15:25]

5 O God, You know my folly;
My wrongs are not hidden from You.
6 Do not let those who wait [confidently]
for You be ashamed through me,
O Lord GOD of hosts;
Do not let those who seek You [as
necessary for life itself] be dishonored
through me, O God of Israel,
7 Because for Your sake I have borne
reproach;
Confusion *and* dishonor have covered
my face.
8 I have become estranged from my
brothers
And an alien to my mother's sons. [John
7:3–5]
9 For zeal for Your house has consumed
me,
And the [mocking] insults of those who
insult You have fallen on me. [John
2:17; Rom 15:3]
10 When I wept *and* humbled myself with
fasting,
It became my reproach.
11 When I made sackcloth my clothing [as
one in mourning],
I became a byword [a mere object of
scorn] to them.
12 They who sit in the [city's] gate talk
about me *and* mock me,
And I am the song of the drunkards.

POWERPOINT

In Psalm 69:7, the psalmist writes
about being confused. I have learned
that I am much better off doing
something positive than just wondering
all the time about everything imaginable
that could go wrong. Wondering leaves
a person in indecision, and indecision
causes confusion. Wondering,
indecision, and confusion prevent
people from receiving from God, by
faith, the answer to their prayers or their
needs. Jesus did not say, "Whatever you
ask in prayer, wonder if you will get it."
He told us to believe (see Matt. 21:22).

13 But as for me, my prayer is to You,
O LORD, at an acceptable *and*
opportune time;
O God, in the greatness of Your favor
and in the abundance of Your
lovingkindness,
Answer me with truth [that is, the
faithfulness of Your salvation].
14 Rescue me from the mire and do not let
me sink;
Let me be rescued from those who hate
me and from the deep waters.
15 Do not let the floodwater overwhelm me,
Nor the deep waters swallow me up,
Nor the pit [of Sheol] shut its mouth
over me.

16 Answer me, O LORD, for Your
lovingkindness is sweet *and* good *and*
comforting;
According to the greatness of Your
compassion, turn to me.
17 Do not hide Your face from Your servant,
For I am in distress; answer me quickly.
18 Draw near to my soul and redeem it;
Ransom me because of my enemies
[so that they do not delight in my
distress].
19 You know my reproach and my shame
and my dishonor [how I am insulted];
My adversaries are all before You [each
one fully known].

20 Reproach *and* insults have broken my
heart and I am so sick.
I looked for sympathy, but there was
none,
And for comforters, but I found none.
21 They (self-righteous hypocrites) also
gave me gall [poisonous and bitter] for
my food,
And for my thirst they gave me vinegar
to drink. [Matt 27:34, 48]

22 May their table [with all its abundance
and luxury] become a snare [to them];
And when they are in peace [secure at
their sacrificial feasts], *may it become*
a trap.
23 May their eyes be dimmed so that they
cannot see,
And make their loins shake continually
[in terror and weakness].

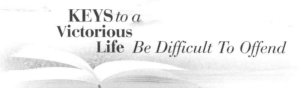

KEYS *to a* **Victorious Life** *Be Difficult To Offend*

There is no doubt—as long as we are in the world and around people, we will have opportunities to be offended. The temptation to become hurt, angry, or offended comes just as surely as any other temptation comes, but Jesus said we should pray that we will not give in to temptation (see Matt. 26:41). When David was surrounded by those who delighted in his hurt, his prayer was, "O LORD, come quickly to help me!" (Ps. 70:1).

People who want to live powerful lives can do so by becoming experts at forgiving those who offend and hurt them. When someone hurts your feelings or is rude and insensitive, quickly say, "I will not be offended." If the person is in your presence, you can say these words quietly in your heart, but later when the memory of what he or she did returns to haunt you, repeat aloud, "I will not be offended," and ask God to help you to forgive them.

---

24 Pour out Your indignation on them,
  And let [the fierceness of] Your burning
  anger overtake them.
25 May their encampment be desolate;
  May no one dwell in their tents. [Matt
  23:38; Acts 1:20]
26 For they have persecuted him whom You
  have struck,
  And they tell of the pain of those whom
  You have pierced *and* wounded.
27 Add [unforgiven] iniquity to their
  iniquity [in Your book],
  And may they not come into Your
  righteousness.
28 May they be blotted out of the book of
  life [and their lives come to an end]
  And may they not be recorded with the
  righteous (those in right standing with
  God). [Rev 3:4, 5; 20:12, 15; 21:27]

29 But I am sorrowful and in pain;
  May Your salvation, O God, set me
  [securely] on high.
30 I will praise the name of God with song
  And magnify Him with thanksgiving.
31 And it will please the LORD better than
  an ox
  Or a young bull with horns and hoofs.
32 The humble have seen it and are glad;

You who seek God [requiring Him as
  your greatest need], let your heart
  revive *and* live. [Ps 22:26; 42:1]
33 For the LORD hears the needy
  And does not despise His *who are*
  prisoners.

34 Let heaven and earth praise Him,
  The seas and everything that moves in
  them.
35 For God will save Zion and rebuild the
  cities of Judah,
  That His servants may remain there and
  possess it.
36 The descendants of His servants will
  inherit it,
  And those who love His name will dwell
  in it.

Psalm 70

Prayer for Help against Persecutors.

To the Chief Musician. *A Psalm*
of David, to bring to remembrance.

1 O GOD, *come quickly* to save me;
  O LORD, come quickly to help me!
2 Let those be ashamed and humiliated

Who seek my life;
Let them be turned back and
    humiliated
Who delight in my hurt.
³Let them be turned back because of
    their shame *and* disgrace
Who say, "Aha, aha!"

⁴May all those who seek You [as life's first
    priority] rejoice and be glad in You;
May those who love Your salvation say
    continually,
"Let God be magnified!"
⁵But I am afflicted and needy;
Come quickly to me, O God!
You are my help and my rescuer;
O LORD, do not delay.

Psalm 71

Prayer of an Old Man for Rescue.

¹IN YOU, O LORD, I have put my trust
    and confidently taken refuge;
Let me never be put to shame.
²In Your righteousness deliver me and
    rescue me;
Incline Your ear to me and save me.
³Be to me a rock of refuge *and* a
    sheltering stronghold to which I may
    continually come;
You have given the commandment to
    save me,
For You are my rock and my fortress.
⁴Rescue me, O my God, from the hand of
    the wicked (godless),
From the grasp of the unrighteous and
    ruthless man.
⁵For You are my hope;
O Lord GOD, *You are* my trust *and* the
    source of my confidence from my
    youth.
⁶Upon You have I relied *and* been
    sustained from my birth;
You are He who took me from my
    mother's womb *and* You have been my
    benefactor from that day.
My praise is continually of You.

⁷I am as a wonder to many,
For You are my strong refuge.
⁸My mouth is filled with Your praise
And with Your glory all day long.
⁹Do not cast me off *nor* send me away in
    the time of old age;

Do not abandon me when my strength
    fails *and* I am weak.
¹⁰For my enemies have spoken against me;
Those who watch for my life have
    consulted together,
¹¹Saying, "God has abandoned him;
Pursue and seize him, for there is no one
    to rescue *him*."

¹²O God, do not be far from me;
O my God, come quickly to help me!
¹³Let those who attack my life be ashamed
    and consumed;
Let them be covered with reproach and
    dishonor, who seek to injure me.
¹⁴But as for me, I will wait *and* hope
    continually,
And will praise You yet more and more.
¹⁵My mouth shall tell of Your
    righteousness
And of Your [deeds of] salvation all day
    long,
For their number is more than I know.
¹⁶I will come with the mighty acts of the
    Lord GOD [and in His strength];
I will make mention of Your
    righteousness, Yours alone.

¹⁷O God, You have taught me from my
    youth,
And I still declare Your wondrous works
    and miraculous deeds.
¹⁸And even when I am old and gray-
    headed, O God, do not abandon me,
Until I declare Your [mighty] strength to
    this generation,
Your power to all who are to come.
¹⁹Your righteousness, O God, *reaches* to
    the [height of the] heavens,
You who have done great things;
O God, who is like You, [who is Your
    equal]?
²⁰You who have shown me many troubles
    and distresses
Will revive *and* renew me again,
And will bring me up again from the
    depths of the earth.
²¹May You increase my greatness (honor)
And turn to comfort me.

²²I will also praise You with the harp,
Your truth *and* faithfulness, O my God;
To You I will sing praises with the lyre,
O Holy One of Israel.

WINNING THE BATTLES *of the* MIND
Express Your Gratitude

God tells us to praise Him continually (see Ps. 71:6, 14). Once we seriously start praising Him, our burdens and our troubles seem to weigh less heavily on us. That's part of the power of being thankful. As we give thanks to God for what's good in our lives, it helps us not to focus excessively on our problems. I believe God wants us to be grateful people, filled with gratitude not only toward God, but also toward others.

When someone does something nice for you, let that person know you appreciate them and what they did. If your bus arrived on time today, did you thank the driver? When you ate at the restaurant, did you thank the waitress for filling your coffee cup? I could go on and on, but that's my point: We need to develop an attitude of gratitude toward the people in our lives.

Another way to express gratitude is to show appreciation toward your family members, especially your spouse. I appreciate Dave, and even though we've been married a long time, I still tell him I appreciate him. He's patient with me and thoughtful. Just those few words of thanks are a great way to bless God and others.

When you express appreciation, it's good for the other person to hear the words, but remember that it also releases joy in you. You enrich both your life and another person's life, even when you show gratitude for something small or ordinary.

Another way to show your gratitude is to meditate daily on things for which you can be thankful. I have a friend who won't get out of bed in the morning until he has thanked God for at least ten things. At night he goes to sleep by focusing on at least three things that went well that day and thanking God for them.

You can also be thankful for the people who tell you the truth about yourself, even if it's not what you want to hear. I have another friend who says, "Only two people will tell you the truth about yourself: someone who's angry at you and someone who loves you very much." God uses both types of people in our lives. When you hear the truth—especially about something of which you're not aware, you can change. And after you've changed, isn't that just one more thing for which you can be thankful?

A PRAYER FOR VICTORY

God, thank You for all the good things You send into my life. Thank You for the people in my life who help me grow closer to You and become a more thankful person. In Jesus' name. Amen.

23 My lips will shout for joy when I sing
  praises to You,
And my soul, which You have redeemed.
24 My tongue also will speak of Your
  righteousness all day long;
For they are ashamed, for they are
  humiliated who seek my injury.

Psalm 72

The Reign of the Righteous King.

A Psalm of Solomon.

1 GIVE THE king [knowledge of] Your
  judgments, O God,
And [the spirit of] Your righteousness to
  the king's son [to guide all his ways].
2 May he judge Your people with
  righteousness,
And Your afflicted with justice. [1 Kin
  3:1–5]
3 The mountains will bring peace *and*
  prosperity to the people,
And the hills, in [the establishment of]
  righteousness.
4 May he bring justice to the poor among
  the people,
Save the children of the needy
And crush the oppressor,

5 Let them fear You [with awe-inspired
  reverence and worship You with
  obedience] while the sun endures,
And as long as the moon [reflects light],
  throughout all generations.
6 May he come down like rain on the
  mown grass,
Like showers that water the earth.
7 In his days may the righteous flourish,
And peace abound until the moon is no
  more. [Is 11:1–9]

8 May he also rule from sea to sea
And from the River [Euphrates] to the
  ends of the earth. [Zech 14:9]
9 The nomads of the desert will bow
  before him,
And his enemies will lick the dust.
10 The kings of Tarshish and of the islands
  will bring offerings;
The kings of Sheba and Seba will offer
  gifts.
11 Yes, all kings will bow down before him,
All nations will serve him. [Ps 138:4]

12 For he will rescue the needy when he
  cries for help,
The afflicted *and* abused also, and him
  who has no helper.
13 He will have compassion on the poor
  and needy,
And he will save the lives of the needy.
14 He will redeem their life from
  oppression *and* fraud and violence,
And their blood will be precious in His
  sight.
15 So may he live, and may the gold of
  Sheba be given to him;
And let them pray for him continually;
Let them bless *and* praise him all day
  long.

16 There will be an abundance of grain in
  the soil on the top of the mountains;
Its fruit will wave like [the cedars of]
  Lebanon,
And those of the city will flourish like
  grass of the earth.
17 May his name endure forever;
May his name continue as long as the
  sun;
And let men bless themselves by him;
Let all nations call him blessed.

18 Blessed be the LORD God, the God of
  Israel,
Who alone does wonderful things.
19 Blessed be His glorious name forever;
And may the whole earth be filled with
  His glory.
Amen and Amen.

20 The prayers of David son of Jesse are
  ended.

BOOK THREE

Psalm 73

The End of the Wicked Contrasted
with That of the Righteous.

A Psalm of Asaph.

1 TRULY GOD is good to Israel,
To those who are pure in heart.
2 But as for me, my feet came close to
  stumbling,
My steps had almost slipped.
3 For I was envious of the arrogant
As I saw the prosperity of the wicked.

⁴For there are no pains in their death,
Their body is fat *and* pampered.
⁵They are not in trouble *as other* men,
Nor are they plagued like mankind.
⁶Therefore pride is their necklace;
Violence covers them like a garment
[like a long, luxurious robe].
⁷Their eye bulges from fatness [they have
more than the heart desires];
The imaginations of their mind run riot
[with foolishness].
⁸They mock and wickedly speak of
oppression;
They speak loftily [with malice].
⁹They set their mouth against the heavens,
And their tongue swaggers through the
earth. [Rev 13:6]

¹⁰Therefore his people return to this place,
And waters of abundance [offered by the
irreverent] are [blindly] drunk by them.
¹¹They say, "How does God know?
Is there knowledge [of us] with the Most
High?"
¹²Behold, these are the ungodly,
Who always prosper *and* are at ease
[in the world]; they have increased in
wealth.
¹³Surely then in vain I have cleansed my
heart
And washed my hands in innocence.
[Mal 3:14]
¹⁴For all the day long have I been stricken,
And punished every morning.

¹⁵If I had said, "I will say this," [and
expressed my feelings],
I would have betrayed the generation of
Your children.
¹⁶When I considered how to understand
this,
It was too great an effort for me *and* too
painful
¹⁷Until I came into the sanctuary of God;
Then I understood [for I considered]
their end.
¹⁸Surely You set the wicked-minded *and*
immoral on slippery places;
You cast them down to destruction.
¹⁹How they are destroyed in a moment!
They are completely swept away by
sudden terrors!
²⁰Like a dream [which seems real] until
one awakens,

Speak God's Word

*My flesh and my heart may fail, but God is
the rock and strength of my heart and my
portion forever.*

| *adapted from* PSALM 73:26 |

O Lord, when stirred, [You observe the
wicked], You will despise their image.

²¹When my heart was embittered
And I was pierced within [as with the
fang of an adder],
²²Then I was senseless and ignorant;
I was like a beast before You.
²³Nevertheless I am continually with You;
You have taken hold of my right hand.
²⁴You will guide me with Your counsel,
And afterward receive me to honor *and*
glory.

²⁵Whom have I in heaven [but You]?
And besides You, I desire nothing on
earth.
²⁶My flesh and my heart may fail,
But God is the rock *and* strength of my
heart and my portion forever.
²⁷For behold, those who are far from You
will perish;
You have destroyed all those who are
unfaithful *and* have abandoned You.
²⁸But as for me, it is good for me to draw
near to God;
I have made the Lord GOD my refuge
and placed my trust in Him,
That I may tell of all Your works.

Psalm 74

An Appeal against the Devastation
of the Land by the Enemy.

A skillful song, *or* a didactic *or* reflective
poem, of Asaph.

¹O GOD, why have You rejected us
forever?
Why does Your anger smoke against the
sheep of Your pasture?
²Remember Your congregation, which
You have purchased of old,
Which You have redeemed to be the
tribe of Your inheritance;

Remember Mount Zion, where You have dwelt.

³Turn your footsteps [quickly] toward the perpetual ruins;

The enemy has damaged everything within the sanctuary.

⁴In the midst of Your meeting place Your enemies have roared [with their battle cry];

They have set up their own emblems for signs [of victory].

⁵It seems as if one had lifted up

An axe in a forest of trees [to set a record of destruction].

⁶And now all the carved work [of the meeting place]

They smash with hatchets and hammers.

⁷They have burned Your sanctuary to the ground;

They have profaned the dwelling place of Your name.

⁸They said in their heart, "Let us completely subdue them."

They have burned all the meeting places of God in the land.

⁹We do not see our symbols;

There is no longer any prophet [to guide us],

Nor does any among us know for how long.

¹⁰O God, how long will the adversary scoff? Is the enemy to revile Your name forever?

¹¹Why do You withdraw Your hand, even Your right hand [from judging the enemy]?

Remove Your hand from Your chest, destroy *them!*

¹²Yet God is my King of old,

Working salvation in the midst of the earth.

¹³You divided the [Red] Sea by Your strength;

You broke the heads of the sea monsters in the waters. [Ex 14:21]

¹⁴You crushed the heads of Leviathan (Egypt);

You gave him as food for the creatures of the wilderness. [Job 41:1]

¹⁵You broke open fountains and streams; You dried up ever-flowing rivers. [Ex 17:6; Num 20:11; Josh 3:13]

¹⁶The day is Yours, the night also is Yours;

You have established *and* prepared the [heavenly] light and the sun.

¹⁷You have defined *and* established all the borders of the earth [the divisions of land and sea and of the nations];

You have made summer and winter. [Acts 17:26]

¹⁸Remember this, O LORD, the enemy has scoffed,

And a foolish *and* impious people has spurned Your name.

¹⁹Oh, do not hand over the soul of your turtledove to the wild beast;

Do not forget the life of Your afflicted forever.

²⁰Consider the covenant [You made with Abraham],

For the dark places of the land are full of the habitations of violence.

²¹Let not the oppressed return dishonored; Let the afflicted and needy praise Your name.

²²Arise, O God, plead Your own cause;

Remember how the foolish man scoffs at You all day long.

²³Do not forget the [clamoring] voices of Your adversaries,

The uproar of those who rise against You, which ascends continually [to Your ears].

Psalm 75

God Abases the Proud, but Exalts the Righteous.

To the Chief Musician; set to [the tune of] "Do Not Destroy." A Psalm of Asaph. A Song.

¹WE GIVE thanks *and* praise to You, O God, we give thanks,

For Your [wonderful works declare that Your] name is near;

People declare Your wonders.

²"When I select an appointed time, I will judge with equity," [says the LORD].

³"The earth and all the inhabitants of it melt [in tumultuous times].

It is I who will steady its pillars.   *Selah.*

⁴"I said to the arrogant, 'Do not boast;' And to the wicked, 'Do not lift up the horn [of self-glorification].

KEYS *to a* Victorious Life *Be Thankful and Say So*

The Bible teaches us repeatedly to give thanks, to be thankful, and to have heartfelt gratitude (see Ps. 75:1). To help you achieve and maintain a new level of contentment in your life, I encourage you to make a list of everything for which you are thankful. It should be a long list, one that includes little things as well as big things. Why should it be long? Because we all have a lot to be thankful for if we just look for it.

The next time you have lunch or coffee with a friend, resolve to talk about the things for which you are thankful. The Bible says we are to be thankful and to say so. Meditating on what you have to be thankful for every day and verbalizing it will be amazingly helpful to you.

---

5 'Do not lift up your [defiant and aggressive] horn on high,
Do not speak with a stiff neck.' "

6 For not from the east, nor from the west,
Nor from the desert comes exaltation. [Is 14:13]

7 But God is the Judge;
He puts down one and lifts up another.

8 For a cup [of His wrath] is in the hand of the LORD, and the wine foams;
It is well mixed *and* fully spiced, and He pours out from it;
And all the wicked of the earth must drain it and drink down to its dregs. [Ps 60:3; Jer 25:15; Rev 14:9, 10; 16:19]

9 But as for me, I will declare it *and* rejoice forever;
I will sing praises to the God of Jacob.

10 All the horns of the wicked He will cut off,
But the horns of the righteous will be lifted up.

Psalm 76

The Victorious Power of the God of Jacob.

To the Chief Musician; on stringed instruments. A Psalm of Asaph. A Song.

1 GOD IS known in Judah;
His name is great in Israel.

2 His tabernacle is in Salem (Jerusalem);
His dwelling place is in Zion.

3 There He broke the flaming arrows,
The shield, the sword, and the weapons of war.   *Selah.*

4 You are glorious *and* resplendent,
More majestic than the mountains of prey.

5 The stouthearted have been stripped of their spoil,
They have slept the sleep [of death];
And none of the warriors could use his hands.

6 At Your rebuke, O God of Jacob,
Both rider and horse were cast into a dead sleep [of death]. [Ex 15:1, 21; Nah 2:13; Zech 12:4]

7 You, even You, are to be feared [with the submissive wonder of reverence];
Who may stand in Your presence when once You are angry?

8 You caused judgment to be heard from heaven;
The earth feared and was quiet

9 When God arose to [establish] judgment,
To save all the humble of the earth.   *Selah.*

10 For the wrath of man shall praise You;

With a remnant of wrath You will clothe
and arm Yourself.

11 Make vows to the LORD your God and
fulfill them;
Let all who are around Him bring gifts
to Him who is to be feared [with awe-
inspired reverence].
12 He will cut off the spirit of princes;
He is awesome *and* feared by the kings
of the earth.

Psalm 77

Comfort in Trouble from Recalling God's Mighty Deeds.

To the Chief Musician; according
to Jeduthun [one of David's three chief
musicians, founder of an official musical
family]. A Psalm of Asaph.

1 MY VOICE rises to God, and I will cry
aloud;
My voice rises to God, and He will
hear me.
2 In the day of my trouble I [desperately]
sought the Lord;
In the night my hand was stretched out
[in prayer] without weariness;
My soul refused to be comforted.

3 I remember God; then I am disquieted
and I groan;
I sigh [in prayer], and my spirit grows
faint.   *Selah.*
4 You have held my eyelids open;
I am so troubled that I cannot speak.
5 I have considered the ancient days,
The years [of prosperity] of long, long
ago.
6 I will remember my song in the night;
I will meditate with my heart,
And my spirit searches:

7 Will the Lord reject forever?
And will He never be favorable again?
8 Has His lovingkindness ceased forever?
Have His promises ended for all time?
9 Has God forgotten to be gracious?
Or has He in anger withdrawn His
compassion?   *Selah.*
10 And I said, "This is my grief,
That the right hand of the Most High
has changed [and His lovingkindness
is withheld]."

11 I will [solemnly] remember the deeds of
the LORD;
Yes, I will [wholeheartedly] remember
Your wonders of old.
12 I will meditate on all Your works

KEYS *to a* **Victorious Life** *As Your Thoughts Change, Your Life Changes*

*When we define what it means to meditate (see Ps. 77:12), we generally mean
that we choose what we want to think about and roll it over and over in our
minds until it becomes a part of us.*

*Consider this quote: "If you continue to believe as you have always believed,
you will continue to act as you have always acted. If you continue to act as you
have always acted, you will continue to get what you have always gotten. If
you want different results in your life, all you have to do is change your mind"
(Anonymous).*

*You will never do what you need to do until you think what you need to think.
God's Word will renew your mind, so love the Word, live the Word, speak the
Word, meditate on the Word—and things will begin to change (see Josh. 1:8).*

WINNING THE BATTLES *of the* MIND
Victory over Nighttime Battles

What is it about nighttime that makes us more vulnerable to the enemy's attacks? My theory is that by evening, most of us are weary and just want to drift into peaceful sleep. One of Satan's favorite times to wage the battle for our minds is when we need rest.

If we recognize that we're more susceptible to the enemy's attacks when we're tired, we can take steps to prepare to stand against him. Some people find it helpful to meditate on scriptures or to claim the promise of Isaiah 26:3: "You will keep in perfect *and* constant peace *the one* whose mind is steadfast [that is, committed and focused on You.]" These words enable us to remain vigilant even in the dark hours of night.

By arming ourselves with the Word and spending time in prayer, we can avoid getting trapped in Satan's plan when he brings to mind some troublesome event of the day and asks, "Why did you say or do that?" His trick is to cause us to focus on the problems of the day, suggesting that we must immediately settle the issue. Thus he robs us of the peaceful rest our bodies need.

The psalmist said, "In the night my hand was stretched out [in prayer] without weariness; my soul refused to be comforted" (Ps. 77:2). I experience nights like this at times and I haven't always won the battle, but I have learned some valuable lessons. One lesson I have learned is that we don't need to try and solve our problems in the middle of the night. Another lesson learned is that it is not wise to make decisions in the middle of the night. Most decisions can wait until the next day and should not take on such urgency that we believe we will not sleep unless we settle the issue *immediately*.

When Satan tries to pull that nighttime trick on you, learn to say, "I'll deal with this issue in the morning, when the sun is shining. After I've rested, I can cope." You can also say, "Lord, I surrender this to You. Give me Your rest, Your peace, and help me to make the right decision in the morning."

A PRAYER FOR VICTORY

Holy Spirit, thank You for being with me, for protecting me, and for guiding my life. When I face those dark nights and the enemy tries to attack my mind, protect me. I trust You and ask You to keep me in Your perfect peace. Amen.

And thoughtfully consider all Your
[great and wondrous] deeds.
¹³ Your way, O God, is holy [far from sin
and guilt].
What god is great like our God?
¹⁴ You are the [awesome] God who works
[powerful] wonders;
You have demonstrated Your power
among the people.
¹⁵ You have with Your [great] arm
redeemed Your people,
The sons of Jacob and Joseph.   *Selah.*

¹⁶ The waters [of the Red Sea] saw You,
O God;
The waters saw You, they were in
anguish;
The deeps also trembled.
¹⁷ The clouds poured down water;
The skies sent out a sound [of rumbling
thunder];
Your arrows (lightning) flashed here and
there.
¹⁸ The voice of Your thunder was in the
whirlwind;
The lightnings illumined the world;
The earth trembled and shook.
¹⁹ Your way [of escape for Your people] was
through the sea,
And Your paths through the great
waters,
And Your footprints were not traceable.
²⁰ You led Your people like a flock
By the hand of Moses and Aaron [to the
promised goal].

Psalm 78

God's Guidance of His People
in Spite of Their Unfaithfulness.

A skillful song, *or* a didactic *or* reflective
poem, of Asaph.

¹ LISTEN, O my people, to my teaching;
Incline your ears to the words of my
mouth [and be willing to learn].
² I will open my mouth in a parable [to
instruct using examples];
I will utter dark *and* puzzling sayings of
old [that contain important truth]—
[Matt 13:34, 35]
³ Which we have heard and known,
And our fathers have told us.

POWERPOINT

Psalm 78:8 describes the rebellious
Israelites. For them, this same cycle
of stubborn disobedience, crying out
to God to get them out of trouble,
and going right back into rebellion
when their circumstances improved is
repeated and recorded so many times
in the Old Testament that it is almost
unbelievable. Victorious living means
that we learn to give up our own ways
and be pliable and moldable
in God's hands.

⁴ We will not hide them from their
children,
But [we will] tell to the generation to
come the praiseworthy deeds of the
Lord,
And [tell of] His great might *and* power
and the wonderful works that He has
done.

⁵ For He established a testimony (a
specific precept) in Jacob
And appointed a law in Israel,
Which He commanded our fathers
That they should teach to their children
[the great facts of God's transactions
with Israel],
⁶ That the generation to come might
know them, that the children still to
be born
May arise and recount them to their
children,
⁷ That they should place their confidence
in God
And not forget the works of God,
But keep His commandments,
⁸ And not be like their fathers—
A stubborn and rebellious generation,
A generation that did not prepare its
heart to know *and* follow God,
And whose spirit was not faithful to
God.

⁹ The sons of Ephraim were armed as
archers and carrying bows,

Yet they turned back in the day of battle.
¹⁰ They did not keep the covenant of God
And refused to walk according to His law;
¹¹ And they forgot His [incredible] works
And His miraculous wonders that He had shown them.
¹² He did marvelous things in the sight of their fathers
In the land of Egypt, in the field of Zoan [where Pharaoh resided].
¹³ He divided the [Red] Sea and allowed them to pass through it,
And He made the waters stand up like [water behind] a dam. [Ex 14:22]
¹⁴ In the daytime He led them with a cloud
And all the night with a light of fire. [Ex 13:21; 14:24]
¹⁵ He split rocks in the wilderness
And gave *them* abundant [water to] drink like the ocean depths.
¹⁶ He brought streams also from the rock [at Rephidim and Kadesh]
And caused waters to run down like rivers. [Ex 17:6; Num 20:11]

¹⁷ Yet they still continued to sin against Him
By rebelling against the Most High in the desert.
¹⁸ And in their hearts they put God to the test
By asking for food according to their [selfish] appetite.
¹⁹ Then they spoke against God;
They said, "Can God prepare [food for] a table in the wilderness?
²⁰ "Behold, He struck the rock so that waters gushed out
And the streams overflowed;
Can He give bread also?
Or will He provide meat for His people?"

²¹ Therefore, when the LORD heard, He was full of wrath;
A fire was kindled against Jacob,
And His anger mounted up against Israel,
²² Because they did not believe in God [they did not rely on Him, they did not adhere to Him],
And they did not trust in His salvation (His power to save).

²³ Yet He commanded the clouds from above
And opened the doors of heaven;
²⁴ And He rained down manna upon them to eat
And gave them the grain of heaven. [Ex 16:14; John 6:31]
²⁵ Man ate the bread of angels;
God sent them provision in abundance.
²⁶ He caused the east wind to blow in the heavens
And by His [unlimited] power He guided the south wind.
²⁷ He rained meat upon them like the dust,
And winged birds (quail) like the sand of the seas. [Num 11:31]
²⁸ And He let them fall in the midst of their camp,
Around their tents.
²⁹ So they ate and were well filled,
He gave them what they craved.
³⁰ Before they had satisfied their desire,
And while their food was in their mouths, [Num 11:33]
³¹ The wrath of God rose against them
And killed some of the strongest of them,
And subdued the choice young men of Israel.
³² In spite of all this they still sinned,
For they did not believe in His wonderful *and* extraordinary works.
³³ Therefore He consumed their days like a breath [in emptiness and futility]
And their years in sudden terror.

³⁴ When He killed [some of] them, then those remaining sought Him,
And they returned [to Him] and searched diligently for God [for a time].
³⁵ And they remembered that God was their rock,
And the Most High God their Redeemer.
³⁶ Nevertheless they flattered Him with their mouths
And lied to Him with their tongues.
³⁷ For their heart was not steadfast toward Him,
Nor were they faithful to His covenant. [Acts 8:21]
³⁸ But He, the source of compassion *and* lovingkindness, forgave their wickedness and did not destroy them;

Many times He restrained His anger
And did not stir up all His wrath.

39 For He [graciously] remembered that
   they were mere [human] flesh,
   A wind that goes and does not return.

40 How often they rebelled against Him in
   the wilderness
   And grieved Him in the desert!

41 Again and again they tempted God,
   And distressed the Holy One of Israel.

42 They did not remember [the miracles
   worked by] His [powerful] hand,
   Nor the day when He redeemed them
   from the enemy,

43 How He worked His miracles in Egypt
   And His wonders in the field of Zoan
   [where Pharaoh resided],

44 And turned their rivers into blood,
   And their streams, so that they could
   not drink.

45 He sent among them swarms of flies
   which devoured them,
   And frogs which destroyed them.

46 He also gave their crops to the
   grasshopper,
   And the fruit of their labor to the locust.

47 He destroyed their vines with [great]
   hailstones
   And their sycamore trees with frost.

48 He gave over their cattle also to the
   hailstones,
   And their flocks *and* herds to
   thunderbolts. [Ex 9:18–21]

49 He sent upon them His burning anger,
   [Ex 12:23]
   His fury and indignation and distress,
   A band of angels of destruction [among
   them].

50 He leveled a path for His anger [to give it
   free run];
   He did not spare their souls from death,
   But turned over their lives to the plague.

51 He killed all the firstborn in Egypt,
   The first and best of their strength in
   the tents [of the land of the sons of]
   Ham.

52 But God led His own people forward like
   sheep
   And guided them in the wilderness like
   [a good shepherd with] a flock.

53 He led them safely, so that they did not
   fear;

But the sea engulfed their enemies. [Ex
14:27, 28]

54 So He brought them to His holy land,
   To this mountain [Zion] which His right
   hand had acquired.

55 He also drove out the nations before the
   sons of Israel
   And allotted *their land* as an
   inheritance, measured out *and*
   partitioned;
   And He had the tribes of Israel dwell in
   their tents [the tents of those who had
   been dispossessed].

56 Yet they tempted and rebelled against
   the Most High God
   And did not keep His testimonies (laws).

57 They turned back and acted unfaithfully
   like their fathers;
   They were twisted like a warped bow
   [that will not respond to the archer's
   aim].

58 For they provoked Him to [righteous]
   anger with their high places [devoted
   to idol worship]
   And moved Him to jealousy with their
   carved images [by denying Him the
   love, worship, and obedience that is
   rightfully and uniquely His].

59 When God heard this, He was filled
   with [righteous] wrath;
   And utterly rejected Israel, [greatly
   hating her ways],

60 So that He abandoned the tabernacle at
   Shiloh,
   The tent in which He had dwelled
   among men,

61 And gave up His strength *and* power
   (the ark of the covenant) into captivity,
   And His glory into the hand of the
   enemy (the Philistines). [1 Sam 4:21]

62 He also handed His people over to the
   sword,
   And was infuriated with His inheritance
   (Israel). [1 Sam 4:10]

63 The fire [of war] devoured His young
   men,
   And His [bereaved] virgins had no
   wedding songs.

64 His priests [Hophni and Phinehas] fell
   by the sword,
   And His widows could not weep. [1 Sam
   4:11, 19, 20]

65 Then the Lord awakened as from sleep,
Like a [mighty] warrior who awakens
from the sleep of wine [fully conscious
of his power].
66 He drove His enemies backward;
He subjected them to lasting shame *and*
dishonor.
67 Moreover, He rejected the tent of Joseph,
And did not choose the tribe of Ephraim
[in which the tabernacle stood].
68 But He chose the tribe of Judah [as
Israel's leader],
Mount Zion, which He loved [to replace
Shiloh as His capital].
69 And He built His sanctuary [exalted]
like the heights [of the heavens],
Like the earth which He has established
forever.
70 He also chose David His servant
And took him from the sheepfolds;
[1 Sam 16:11, 12]
71 From tending the ewes with nursing
young He brought him
To shepherd Jacob His people,
And Israel His inheritance. [2 Sam 7:7, 8]
72 So David shepherded them according to
the integrity of his heart;
And guided them with his skillful
hands.

Psalm 79

A Lament over the Destruction
of Jerusalem, and Prayer for Help.

A Psalm of Asaph.

1 O GOD, the nations have invaded [the
land of Your people] Your inheritance;
They have defiled Your sacred temple;
They have laid Jerusalem in ruins.
2 They have given the dead bodies of Your
servants as food to the birds of the
heavens,
The flesh of Your godly ones to the
beasts of the earth.
3 They have poured out their blood like
water all around Jerusalem,
And there was no one to bury them.
4 We have become an object of taunting
to our neighbors [because of our
humiliation],
A derision and mockery to those who
encircle us.

5 How long, O LORD? Will You be angry
forever?
Will Your jealousy [which cannot endure
a divided allegiance] burn like fire?
6 Pour out Your wrath on the [Gentile]
nations that do not know You,
And on the kingdoms that do not call on
Your name. [2 Thess 1:8]
7 For they have devoured Jacob
And made his pasture desolate.

8 O do not remember against us the sins
and guilt of our forefathers.
Let Your compassion *and* mercy come
quickly to meet us,
For we have been brought very low.
9 Help us, O God of our salvation, for the
glory of Your name;
Rescue us, forgive us our sins for Your
name's sake.
10 Why should the [Gentile] nations say,
"Where is their God?"
Let there be known [without delay]
among the nations in our sight [and to
this generation],
Your vengeance for the blood of Your
servants which has been poured out.
11 Let the groaning *and* sighing of the
prisoner come before You;
According to the greatness of Your power
keep safe those who are doomed to die.
12 And return into the lap of our neighbors
sevenfold
The taunts with which they have
taunted You, O Lord.
13 So we Your people, the sheep of Your
pasture,
Will give You thanks forever;
We will declare *and* publish Your praise
from generation to generation.

Psalm 80

God Implored to Rescue His People
from Their Calamities.

To the Chief Musician; set to [the tune
of] "Lilies, a Testimony." A Psalm
of Asaph.

1 HEAR US O Shepherd of Israel,
You who lead Joseph like a flock;
You who sit enthroned above the
cherubim [of the ark of the covenant],
shine forth!

POWERPOINT

God is always able to restore us (see Ps. 80:7). When you fall, as we all do, that doesn't mean you are a failure.

It simply means that you don't do everything right. Along with strengths we also have weaknesses. Let Jesus Christ be strong in your weaknesses; let Him shine His face on you with favor and approval on your weak days.

Do not receive condemnation. Your victory will come, but it may take time.

2 Before Ephraim and Benjamin and Manasseh, stir up Your power
And come to save us!
3 Restore us, O God;
Cause Your face to shine on us [with favor and approval], and we will be saved.

4 O LORD God of hosts,
How long will You be angry with the prayers of Your people?
5 You have fed them the bread of tears,
And You have made them drink [bitter] tears in abundance.
6 You make us an object of contention to our neighbors,
And our enemies laugh [at our suffering] among themselves.
7 Restore us, O God of hosts;
And cause Your face to shine on us [with favor and approval], and we will be saved.

8 You uprooted a vine (Israel) from Egypt;
You drove out the [Canaanite] nations and planted the vine [in Canaan].
9 You cleared away *the ground* before it,
And it took deep root and filled the land.
10 The mountains were covered with its shadow,
And its branches were like the cedars of God.
11 Israel sent out its branches to the [Mediterranean] Sea,
And its branches to the [Euphrates] River. [1 Kin 4:21]

12 Why have You broken down its walls *and* hedges,
So that all who pass by pick its fruit?
13 A boar from the woods eats it away,
And the insects of the field feed on it.

14 Turn again [in favor to us], O God of hosts;
Look down from heaven and see, and take care of this vine,
15 Even the stock which Your right hand has planted,
And [look down on] the son that You have reared *and* strengthened for Yourself.
16 It is burned with fire, it is cut down;
They perish at the rebuke of Your [angry] appearance.
17 Let Your hand be upon the man of Your right hand,
Upon the son of man whom You have made strong for Yourself.
18 Then we shall not turn back from You;
Revive us and we will call on Your name.
19 Restore us, O LORD God of hosts;
Cause Your face to shine on us [in favor and approval], and we shall be saved.

Psalm 81

God's Goodness and Israel's Waywardness.

To the Chief Musician; set to the Philistine lute. *A Psalm* of Asaph.

1 SING ALOUD to God our strength;
Shout for joy to the God of Jacob (Israel).
2 Raise a song, sound the timbrel,
The sweet sounding lyre with the harp.
3 Blow the trumpet at the New Moon,
At the full moon, on our feast day.
4 For this is a statute for Israel,
An ordinance of the God of Jacob.
5 He established it for a testimony in Joseph
When He went throughout the land of Egypt.
I heard the language [of One whom] I did not know, *saying,*

6 "I removed the burden from his shoulder;
His hands were freed from the basket.
7 "You called in [the time of] trouble and I rescued you;

KEYS *to a* Victorious Life *Take Time for God*

We all have the same amount of time each day, but some people find time regularly to spend with God while others do not. I have found that when we say we "don't have time to spend with God," it's simply an excuse.

The truth is that we make time for what is most important to us. At this moment, you are as close to God as you want to be. What you sow, you will reap. If you want a bigger harvest, you can simply sow more seed. If you want a closer relationship with God, spend more time with Him. God has said, "Open your mouth wide and I will fill it . . . . I would feed Israel with the finest of the wheat; and with honey from the rock I would satisfy you" (Ps. 81:10, 16). He wants you to find great peace and joy in His presence.

I answered you in the secret place of thunder;

I tested you at the waters of Meribah. [Num 20:3, 13, 24]   *Selah.*

8 "Hear, O My people, and I will admonish you—

O Israel, if you would listen to Me!

9 "Let there be no strange god among you, Nor shall you worship any foreign god.

10 "I am the LORD your God, Who brought you up from the land of Egypt.

Open your mouth wide and I will fill it.

11 "But My people would not listen to My voice,

And Israel did not [consent to] obey Me.

12 "So I gave them up to the stubbornness of their heart,

To walk in [the path of] their own counsel. [Acts 7:42, 43; 14:16; Rom 1:24, 26]

13 "Oh, that My people would listen to Me, That Israel would walk in My ways!

14 "Then I would quickly subdue *and* humble their enemies

And turn My hand against their adversaries.

15 Those who hate the LORD would pretend obedience to Him *and* cringe before Him,

And their time *of punishment* would be forever.

16 "But I would feed Israel with the finest of the wheat;

And with honey from the rock I would satisfy you."

Psalm 82

Unjust Judgments Rebuked.

A Psalm of Asaph.

1 GOD STANDS in the divine assembly; He judges among the gods (divine beings).

2 How long will you judge unjustly And show partiality to the wicked?   *Selah.*

3 Vindicate the weak and fatherless; Do justice *and* maintain the rights of the afflicted and destitute.

4 Rescue the weak and needy; Rescue them from the hand of the wicked.

5 The rulers do not know nor do they understand;

They walk on in the darkness [of complacent satisfaction];

All the foundations of the earth [the fundamental principles of the administration of justice] are shaken.

6 I said, "You are gods;
Indeed, all of you are sons of the Most
High. [Gen 6:1–4; John 10:34–36;
Rom 13:1, 2]
7 "Nevertheless you will die like men
And fall like any one of the princes."
8 Arise, O God, judge the earth!
For to You belong all the nations. [Matt
28:18–20; Rev 11:15]

Psalm 83

God Implored to Confound
His Enemies.

A Song. A Psalm of Asaph.

1 DO NOT keep silent, O God;
Do not hold Your peace or be still,
O God.
2 For behold, Your enemies are in tumult,
And those who hate You have raised
their heads [in hatred of You]. [Acts
4:25, 26]
3 They concoct crafty schemes against
Your people,
And conspire together against Your
hidden *and* precious ones.
4 They have said, "Come, and let us wipe
them out as a nation;
Let the name of Israel be remembered
no more."
5 For they have conspired together with
one mind;
Against You they make a covenant—
6 The tents of Edom and the Ishmaelites,
Of Moab and the Hagrites,
7 Gebal and Ammon and Amalek,
Philistia with the inhabitants of Tyre.
8 Assyria also has joined with them;
They have helped the children of Lot
[the Ammonites and the Moabites]
and have been an arm [of strength] to
them.   *Selah.*

9 Deal with them as [You did] with
Midian,
As with Sisera and Jabin at the brook of
Kishon, [Judg 4:12–24]
10 Who were destroyed at En-dor,
Who became like dung for the earth.
11 Make their nobles like Oreb and Zeeb
And all their princes like Zebah and
Zalmunna, [Judg 7:23–25; 8:10–21]
12 Who said, "Let us possess for ourselves

The pastures of God."

13 O my God, make them like whirling
dust,
Like chaff before the wind [worthless
and without substance].
14 Like fire consumes the forest,
And like the flame sets the mountains
on fire,
15 So pursue them with Your tempest
And terrify them with [the violence of]
Your storm.
16 Fill their faces with shame *and* disgrace,
That they may [persistently] seek Your
name, O Lord.
17 Let them be ashamed and dismayed
forever;
Yes, let them be humiliated and perish,
18 That they may know that You alone,
whose name is the Lord,
Are the Most High over all the earth.

Psalm 84

Longing for the Temple Worship.

To the Chief Musician; set to a
Philistine lute. A Psalm of the sons
of Korah.

1 HOW LOVELY are Your dwelling
places,
O Lord of hosts!
2 My soul (my life, my inner self) longs for
and greatly desires the courts of the
Lord;
My heart and my flesh sing for joy to the
living God.
3 The bird has found a house,
And the swallow a nest for herself,
where she may lay her young—
Even Your altars, O Lord of hosts,
My King and my God.
4 Blessed *and* greatly favored are those
who dwell in Your house *and* Your
presence;
They will be singing Your praises all the
day long.   *Selah.*

5 Blessed *and* greatly favored is the man
whose strength is in You,
In whose heart are the highways *to Zion.*
6 Passing through the Valley of Weeping
(Baca), they make it a place of springs;
The early rain also covers it with
blessings.

A Prayer To Renew Your Mind

Thank You, Lord God, that You are a sun and shield; You bestow grace and favor and honor; no good thing will You withhold from me, because I walk uprightly.   · *adapted from Psalm 84:11*

⁷ They go from strength to strength
   [increasing in victorious power];
   Each of them appears before God in Zion.

⁸ O LORD God of hosts, hear my prayer;
   Listen, O God of Jacob!   *Selah.*
⁹ See our shield, O God,
   And look at the face of Your anointed
   [the king as Your representative].
¹⁰ For a day in Your courts is better than a
   thousand [anywhere else];
   I would rather stand [as a doorkeeper] at
   the threshold of the house of my God
   Than to live [at ease] in the tents of
   wickedness.
¹¹ For the LORD God is a sun and shield;
   The LORD bestows grace *and* favor and
   honor;
   No good thing will He withhold from
   those who walk uprightly.

¹² O LORD of hosts,
   How blessed *and* greatly favored is the
   man who trusts in You [believing in
   You, relying on You, and committing
   himself to You with confident hope
   and expectation].

Psalm 85

Prayer for God's Mercy upon the Nation.

To the Chief Musician. A Psalm
of the sons of Korah.

¹ O LORD, You have [at last] shown favor
   to Your land [of Canaan];
   You have restored [from Babylon] the
   captives of Jacob (Israel).
² You have forgiven the wickedness of
   Your people;
   You have covered all their sin.   *Selah.*
³ You have withdrawn all Your wrath,
   You have turned away from Your
   burning anger.

⁴ Restore us, O God of our salvation,
   And cause Your indignation toward us
   to cease.
⁵ Will You be angry with us forever?
   Will You prolong Your anger to all
   generations?

KEYS *to a* Victorious Life *God Wants To Bless You*

Being able to maintain a good attitude during times of suffering is a virtue, and it is very important, but continual suffering is not God's will for anybody. The apostle Paul said he had times of being abased and times of abounding (see Phil. 4:12). We will go through difficulties in this life, but we can, and should, expect God's deliverance along with a return to the abundant life.

The psalmist said, "The LORD bestows grace and *favor and honor; no good thing will He withhold from those who walk uprightly" (Ps. 84:11). During times when we don't get what we want when we want it, God has a good reason. Perhaps the timing isn't right, or we are not mature enough to handle it yet, or He has something better in mind, but it is never because He doesn't want us to be blessed. That thought simply isn't consistent with who He is.*

POWERPOINT

If you have no idea what God's will for you is at this point, you can start thinking, *Well, I don't know God's plan, but I know that He loves me. Whatever He does will be good, and I'll be blessed.*

Practice being positive in every situation, as the psalmist was when he said, "I will hear [with expectant hope] what God the LORD will say" (Ps. 85:8). Even if whatever is taking place in your life at the moment does not seem so good, expect God to speak to you and to bring good out of it, as He has promised in His Word.

6 Will You not revive us *and* bring us to life again,

That Your people may rejoice in You?
7 Show us Your lovingkindness, O LORD, And grant us Your salvation.

8 I will hear [with expectant hope] what God the LORD will say,

For He will speak peace to His people, to His godly ones—

But let them not turn again to folly.
9 Surely His salvation is near to those who [reverently] fear Him [and obey Him with submissive wonder],

That glory [the manifest presence of God] may dwell in our land.
10 Steadfast love and truth *and* faithfulness meet together;

Righteousness and peace kiss each other.
11 Truth springs from the earth,

And righteousness looks down from heaven.

A Prayer To Renew Your Mind

Teach me Your way, O Lord, I will walk and live in Your truth; direct my heart to fear Your name with awe-inspired reverence and submissive wonder.

· *adapted from Psalm 86:11*

12 Indeed, the LORD will give what is good,

And our land will yield its produce.
13 Righteousness will go before Him

And will make His footsteps into a way [in which to walk].

Psalm 86

A Psalm of Supplication and Trust.

A Prayer of David.

1 INCLINE YOUR ear, O LORD, and answer me,

For I am distressed and needy [I long for Your help].
2 Protect my life (soul), for I am godly *and* faithful;

O You my God, save Your servant, who trusts in You [believing in You and relying on You, confidently committing everything to You].
3 Be gracious *and* merciful to me, O Lord,

For to You I cry out all the day long.
4 Make Your servant rejoice,

For to You, O Lord, I lift up my soul [all that I am—in prayer].
5 For You, O Lord, are good, and ready to forgive [our sins, sending them away, completely letting them go forever and ever];

And abundant in lovingkindness *and* overflowing in mercy to all those who call upon You.
6 Hear, O LORD, my prayer;

And listen attentively to the voice of my supplications (specific requests)!
7 In the day of my trouble I will call upon You,

For You will answer me.
8 There is no one like You among the gods, O Lord,

Nor are there any works [of wonder and majesty] like Yours.
9 All nations whom You have made shall come and kneel down in worship before You, O Lord,

And they shall glorify Your name.
10 For You are great and do wondrous works!

You alone are God.

11 Teach me Your way, O LORD,

I will walk *and* live in Your truth;

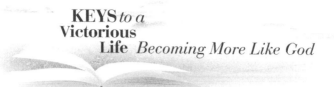

KEYS *to a* Victorious Life *Becoming More Like God*

Ephesians 5:1 teaches us to be imitators of God. So however God is, that is the way we should desire to be. God sees the desires of our hearts and will help us become more and more like He is in our behavior.

God's nature is joyful, not sad or depressed, and He is strong; therefore, we should imitate Him. He is also merciful and gracious, slow to anger and abounding in lovingkindness (see Ps. 86:15). If you become angry with people over an injustice, one way to get over the anger is to imitate God and choose to give them mercy. You can choose to forgive them even if you don't think they deserve it, just as God forgives us when we don't deserve it.

You and I can become more and more like God because His power and character are in us (see 2 Pet. 1:3–4). Begin to imitate God in your life, doing what you believe He would do in situations, instead of what you feel like doing.

Direct my heart to fear Your name
[with awe-inspired reverence and
submissive wonder]. [Ps 5:11; 69:36]
12 I will give thanks *and* praise You,
O Lord my God, with all my heart;
And will glorify Your name forevermore.
13 For great is Your lovingkindness *and*
graciousness toward me;
And You have rescued my life from the
depths of Sheol [from death].

14 O God, arrogant *and* insolent men have
risen up against me;
A band of violent men have sought my
life,
And they have not set You before
them.
15 But You, O Lord, are a God [who
protects and is] merciful and gracious,
Slow to anger and abounding in
lovingkindness and truth.
16 Turn to me, and be gracious to me;
Grant Your strength [Your might and
the power to resist temptation] to
Your servant,
And save the son of Your handmaid.
17 Show me a sign of [Your] goodwill,
That those who hate me may see it and
be ashamed,

Because You, O Lord, helped and
comforted me.

Psalm 87

The Privileges of Citizenship in Zion.

A Psalm of the sons of Korah. A Song.

1 HIS FOUNDATION is on the holy
mountain.
2 The Lord loves the gates of Zion
More than all the dwellings of Jacob
(Israel).
3 Glorious things are spoken of you,
O city of God [Jerusalem].   *Selah.*
4 "I will mention Rahab (Egypt) and
Babylon among those who know Me—
Behold, Philistia and Tyre with Ethiopia
(Cush)—
'This one was born there.'"
5 But of Zion it will be said, "This one and
that one were born in her,"
And the Most High Himself will
establish her.
6 The Lord will count, when He registers
the peoples,
"This one was born there."   *Selah.*

7 The singers as well as the players of
  flutes *will say,*
  "All my springs *and* sources of joy are in
  you [Jerusalem, city of God]."

Psalm 88

A Petition to Be Saved from Death.

A Song. A Psalm of the sons of Korah.
To the Chief Musician; set to chant
mournfully. A didactic *or* reflective
poem of Heman the Ezrahite.

1 O LORD, the God of my salvation,
  I have cried out [for help] by day and in
  the night before You. [Luke 18:7]
2 Let my prayer come before You *and*
  enter into Your presence;
  Incline Your ear to my cry!
3 For my soul is full of troubles,
  And my life draws near the grave (Sheol,
  the place of the dead).
4 I am counted among those who go down
  to the pit (grave);
  I am like a man who has no strength [a
  mere shadow],
5 Cast away [from the living] *and*
  abandoned among the dead,
  Like the slain who lie in a [nameless]
  grave,
  Whom You no longer remember,
  And they are cut off from Your hand.
6 You have laid me in the lowest pit,
  In dark places, in the depths.
7 Your wrath has rested heavily upon me,
  And You have afflicted me with all Your
  waves. [Ps 42:7]   *Selah.*
8 You have put my friends far from me;
  You have made me an object of loathing
  to them.
  I am shut up and I cannot go out.
9 My eye grows dim with sorrow.
  O LORD, I have called on You every
  day;
  I have spread out my hands to You [in
  prayer].

10 Will You perform wonders for the dead?
   Shall the departed spirits arise and
   praise You?   *Selah.*
11 Will Your lovingkindness be declared in
   the grave
   Or Your faithfulness in Abaddon (the
   underworld)?

12 Will Your wonders be known in the
   darkness?
   And Your righteousness in the land of
   forgetfulness [where the dead forget
   and are forgotten]?
13 But I have cried out to You, O LORD, for
   help;
   And in the morning my prayer will come
   to You.
14 O LORD, why do You reject me?
   Why do You hide Your face from me?
   [Matt 27:46]
15 I was afflicted and close to death from
   my youth on;
   I suffer Your terrors; I am overcome.
16 Your fierce wrath has swept over me;
   Your terrors have destroyed me.
17 They have surrounded me like flood
   waters all day long;
   They have completely encompassed me.
18 Lover and friend You have placed far
   from me;
   My familiar friends are in darkness.

Psalm 89

The LORD's Covenant with David,
and Israel's Afflictions.

A skillful song, *or* a didactic *or* reflective
poem, of Ethan the Ezrahite.

1 I WILL sing of the goodness *and*
  lovingkindness of the LORD forever;
  With my mouth I will make known
  Your faithfulness from generation to
  generation.
2 For I have said, "Goodness *and*
  lovingkindness will be built up forever;
  In the heavens [unchangeable and
  majestic] You will establish Your
  faithfulness."
3 [God has said] "I have made a covenant
  with My chosen one;
  I have sworn to David My servant,
4 I will establish your seed forever
  And I will build up your throne for all
  generations." [Is 9:7; Jer 33:14–26;
  Luke 1:32, 33; Gal 3:16]   *Selah.*

5 The heavens (angels) praise Your
  wonders, O LORD,
  Your faithfulness also in the assembly of
  the holy ones.

POWERPOINT

Perhaps like me, you have known people who were not faithful. But I have also known the faithfulness of God. Indeed, God is not like people, and His faithfulness surrounds Him (see Ps. 89:8). God promises to not ever leave you or forsake you, but to be with you until the very end (see Matt. 28:20). He is with you in your times of need, and He is planning to provide for all your needs (see Heb. 13:5). God is with you when you're going through trials, and He is planning your breakthrough (see 1 Cor. 10:13). When all others forsake you, God will stand by you (see 2 Tim. 4:16–17).

⁶ For who in the heavens can be compared to the LORD?
Who among the divine beings is like the LORD,
⁷ A God greatly feared *and* reverently worshiped in the council of the holy [angelic] ones,
And awesome above all those who are around Him?
⁸ O LORD God of hosts, who is like You, O mighty LORD?
Your faithfulness surrounds You [as an intrinsic, unchangeable part of Your very being].
⁹ You rule the swelling of the sea;
When its waves rise, You still them. [Ps 65:7; 107:29; Mark 4:39]
¹⁰ You have crushed Rahab (Egypt) like one who is slain;
You have scattered Your enemies with Your mighty arm.

¹¹ The heavens are Yours, the earth also is Yours;
The world and all that is in it, You have founded *and* established them. [Gen 1:3]
¹² The north and the south, You have created them;

Mount Tabor and Mount Hermon shout for joy at Your name.
¹³ You have a strong arm;
Mighty is Your hand, Your right hand is exalted.
¹⁴ Righteousness and justice are the foundation of Your throne;
Lovingkindness and truth go before You.
¹⁵ Blessed *and* happy are the people who know the joyful sound [of the trumpet's blast]!
They walk, O LORD, in the light *and* favor of Your countenance!
¹⁶ In Your name they rejoice all the day, And in Your righteousness they are exalted.
¹⁷ For You are the glory of their strength [their proud adornment],
And by Your favor our horn is exalted.
¹⁸ For our shield belongs to the LORD, And our king to the Holy One of Israel.

¹⁹ Once You spoke in a vision to Your godly ones,
And said, "I have given help to one who is mighty [giving him the power to be a champion for Israel];
I have exalted one chosen from the people.
²⁰ "I have found David My servant;
With My holy oil I have anointed him, [Acts 13:22]
²¹ With whom My hand shall be established *and* steadfast;
My arm also shall strengthen him.
²² "The enemy will not outwit him,
Nor will the wicked man afflict *or* humiliate him.
²³ "I will crush his adversaries before him, And strike those who hate him.
²⁴ "My faithfulness and My steadfast lovingkindness shall be with him,
And in My name shall his horn be exalted [great power and prosperity shall be conferred upon him].
²⁵ "I will also set his hand on the [Mediterranean] sea,
And his right hand on the rivers [the tributaries of the Euphrates].
²⁶ "He will cry to Me, 'You are my Father, My God, and the rock of my salvation.'
²⁷ "I will also make him My firstborn (preeminent),

KEYS *to a* Victorious Life *God Justifies and Vindicates*

The psalmist said of the Lord, "Righteousness and justice are the foundation of Your throne" (Ps. 89:14). Justice is one of God's amazing and admirable character traits. He brings justice as we wait on Him and trust Him to be our Vindicator when we have been hurt or offended or wronged. In the face of cruel accusations, Job said so powerfully, "I know that my Redeemer and Vindicator lives, and at the last He will take His stand upon the earth" (Job 19:25).

God simply asks us to pray and forgive—and He does the rest. He makes even our pain work out for our good (see Rom. 8:28). He justifies, vindicates, and recompenses us. He pays us back for our pain if we follow His commands to forgive our enemies, and He even gives us double for our trouble (see Isa. 61:7; Job 42:10). Refuse to live in unforgiveness, and trust God to reward you for any mistreatment you have endured.

The highest of the kings of the earth. [Rev 1:5]

28 "My lovingkindness I will keep for him forevermore,

And My covenant will be confirmed to him.

29 "His descendants I will establish forever,

And his throne [will endure] as the days of heaven. [Is 9:7; Jer 33:14–26; Gal 3:16]

30 "If his children turn away from My law

And do not walk in My ordinances,

31 If they break My statutes

And do not keep My commandments,

32 Then I will punish their transgression with the rod [of discipline],

And [correct] their wickedness with stripes. [2 Sam 7:14]

33 "Nevertheless, I will not break off My lovingkindness from him,

Nor allow My faithfulness to fail.

34 "My covenant I will not violate,

Nor will I alter the utterance of My lips.

35 "Once [for all] I have sworn by My holiness, [My vow which cannot be violated];

I will not lie to David.

36 "His descendants shall endure forever

And his throne [will continue] as the sun before Me. [Is 9:7; Jer 33:14–26; Gal 3:16]

37 "It shall be established forever like the moon,

And the witness in the heavens is ever faithful." [Rev 1:5; 3:14]   *Selah.*

38 But [in apparent contradiction of all this] You [the faithful LORD] have cast off and rejected;

You have been full of wrath against Your anointed.

39 You have spurned *and* repudiated the covenant with Your servant;

You have profaned his crown [by casting it] in the dust.

40 You have broken down all his [city] walls;

You have brought his strongholds to ruin.

41 All who pass along the road rob him;

He has become the scorn of his neighbors.

42 You have exalted the right hand of his foes;

You have made all his enemies rejoice.

43 Also, You have turned back the edge of his sword

And have not made him [strong enough] to stand in battle.

44 You have put an end to his splendor
And have hurled his throne to the
ground.
45 You have shortened the days of his youth;
You have covered him with shame.*Selah.*

46 How long, O LORD?
Will You hide Yourself forever?
Will Your wrath burn like fire?
47 Remember how fleeting my lifetime is;
For what vanity, [for what emptiness, for
what futility, for what wisp of smoke]
You have created all the sons of men!
48 What man can live and not see death?
Can he rescue his soul from the
[powerful] hand of Sheol (the nether
world, the place of the dead)?   *Selah.*

49 O Lord, where are Your former
lovingkindnesses [so abundant in the
days of David and Solomon],
Which You swore to David in Your
faithfulness?
50 Remember, O Lord, the reproach of
Your servants [scorned, insulted, and
disgraced];
How I bear in my heart the reproach of
all the many peoples,
51 With which Your enemies have taunted,
O LORD,
With which they have mocked the
footsteps of Your anointed.

52 Blessed be the LORD forevermore!
Amen and Amen.

BOOK FOUR

Psalm 90

God's Eternity and Man's
Transitoriness.

A Prayer of Moses the man of God.

1 LORD, YOU have been our dwelling
place [our refuge, our sanctuary, our
stability] in all generations.
2 Before the mountains were born
Or before You had given birth to the
earth and the world,
Even from everlasting to everlasting,
You are [the eternal] God.

3 You turn man back to dust,

And say, "Return [to the earth],
O children of [mortal] men!"
4 For a thousand years in Your sight
Are like yesterday when it is past,
Or as a watch in the night. [2 Pet 3:8]
5 You have swept them away like a flood,
they fall asleep [forgotten as soon as
they are gone];
In the morning they are like grass which
grows anew—
6 In the morning it flourishes and springs
up;
In the evening it wilts and withers away.

7 For we have been consumed by Your
anger
And by Your wrath we have been
terrified.
8 You have placed our wickedness before
you,
Our secret *sins* [which we tried to
conceal, You have placed] in the
[revealing] light of Your presence.
9 For all our days pass away in Your wrath;
We have finished our years like a
whispered sigh. [Num 14:26–35]
10 The days of our life are seventy years—
Or even, if because of strength, eighty
years;
Yet their pride [in additional years] is
only labor and sorrow,
For it is soon gone and we fly away.
11 Who understands the power of Your
anger? [Who connects this brevity of
life among us with Your judgment of
sin?]
And Your wrath, [who connects it] with
the [reverent] fear that is due You?
12 So teach us to number our days,
That we may cultivate *and* bring to You
a heart of wisdom.

13 Turn, O LORD [from Your fierce anger];
how long will it be?
Be compassionate toward Your
servants—revoke Your sentence.
14 O satisfy us with Your lovingkindness
in the morning [now, before we grow
older],
That we may rejoice and be glad all our
days.
15 Make us glad in proportion to the days
You have afflicted us,
And the years we have suffered evil.

16 Let Your work [the signs of Your power]
  be revealed to Your servants
And Your [glorious] majesty to their
  children.
17 And let the [gracious] favor of the Lord
  our God be on us;
Confirm for us the work of our hands—
Yes, confirm the work of our hands.

Psalm 91

Security of the One Who Trusts in the LORD.

1 HE WHO dwells in the shelter of the
  Most High
Will remain secure *and* rest in the
  shadow of the Almighty [whose power
  no enemy can withstand].
2 I will say of the LORD, "He is my refuge
  and my fortress,

My God, in whom I trust [with great
  confidence, and on whom I rely]!"
3 For He will save you from the trap of the
  fowler,
And from the deadly pestilence.
4 He will cover you *and* completely
  protect you with His pinions,
And under His wings you will find
  refuge;
His faithfulness is a shield and a wall.

5 You will not be afraid of the terror of
  night,
Nor of the arrow that flies by day,
6 Nor of the pestilence that stalks in
  darkness,
Nor of the destruction (sudden death)
  that lays waste at noon.
7 A thousand may fall at your side
And ten thousand at your right hand,

KEYS *to a* Victorious Life *The Shelter of the Most High*

Psalm 91:1 says that God has a place of shelter where we may dwell in peace and safety. The shelter is the place of rest in God, a place of peace and comfort in Him. This secret place is a "spiritual place" where worry is vanquished and peace reigns. It is the shelter of God's presence. When we spend time praying and seeking God, dwelling in His presence, we are in the secret place, or shelter, of the Most High.

When you and I dwell in Christ or dwell in "the shelter of the Most High" (Ps. 91:1), we do not just visit there occasionally; we take up permanent residence in the shadow of the Almighty.

The shelter of the Most High is a hiding place, a private place, a place of refuge. It is our shelter when we are hurting, overwhelmed, or feeling faint. It is our dwelling place where we are secure and find rest beneath the shadow of the Almighty whose power no enemy can withstand. We experience the sheltering of God against our enemy when we are mistreated or persecuted, when we are in great need, or when we feel we just cannot take it anymore.

We can be firmly planted in God. We can know the source of our help in every situation and in every circumstance. We can have our own secret place of peace and security. We can rely on God and trust Him completely.

God invites us to take refuge under the protective shadow of His wings, and He wants us to remain there always.

POWERPOINT

In the Psalms, David frequently makes statements such as, "I will say of the LORD, 'He is my refuge and my fortress, my God, in whom I trust [with great confidence, and on whom I rely]!'" (Ps. 91:2). Perhaps we should regularly ask ourselves, "What am I saying about the Lord?" We need to *say* right things, not just think them. A person may think, *I believe good things about the Lord,* but it's important to also speak those things. People often claim to believe something, yet everything they say indicates they believe the opposite! Words have power, so when we have right beliefs about God, we need to be sure to speak them.

But danger will not come near you.
8 You will only [be a spectator as you] look on with your eyes
And witness the [divine] repayment of the wicked [as you watch safely from the shelter of the Most High].
9 Because you have made the LORD, [who is] my refuge,
Even the Most High, your dwelling place, [Ps 91:1, 14]
10 No evil will befall you,
Nor will any plague come near your tent.

Speak God's Word

I dwell in the shelter of the Most High and remain secure and rest under the shadow of the Almighty whose power no enemy can withstand. He will cover me and completely protect me with His pinions, and under His wings I will find refuge; His faithfulness is a shield and a wall.

| adapted from PSALM 91:1, 4 |

11 For He will command His angels in regard to you,
To protect *and* defend *and* guard you in all your ways [of obedience and service].
12 They will lift you up in their hands,
So that you do not [even] strike your foot against a stone. [Luke 4:10, 11; Heb 1:14]
13 You will tread upon the lion and cobra;
The young lion and the serpent you will trample underfoot. [Luke 10:19]

14 "Because he set his love on Me, therefore I will save him;
I will set him [securely] on high, because he knows My name [he confidently trusts and relies on Me, knowing I will never abandon him, no, never].
15 "He will call upon Me, and I will answer him;
I will be with him in trouble;
I will rescue him and honor him.
16 "With a long life I will satisfy him
And I will let him see My salvation."

Psalm 92

Praise for the LORD's Goodness.

A Psalm.
A Song for the Sabbath day.

1 IT IS a good *and* delightful thing to give thanks to the LORD,
To sing praises to Your name, O Most High,
2 To declare Your lovingkindness in the morning
And Your faithfulness by night,
3 With an instrument of ten strings and with the harp,
With a solemn sound on the lyre.
4 For You, O LORD, have made me glad by Your works;
At the works of Your hands I joyfully sing.

5 How great are Your works, O LORD!
Your thoughts are very deep [beyond man's understanding].
6 A senseless man [in his crude and uncultivated state] knows nothing,
Nor does a [self-righteous] fool understand this:
7 That though the wicked sprout up like grass

WINNING THE BATTLES *of the* MIND
God's Angelic Protection

Psalm 91:9–13 shows us clearly that the Lord promises angelic protection and deliverance to those who serve Him and are walking in obedience to Him. Verse 13 says, "You will tread upon the lion and cobra; the young lion and the serpent you will trample underfoot." Jesus makes a similar statement to His disciples in Luke 10:19 when He says: "Listen carefully: I have given you authority [that you now possess] to tread on serpents and scorpions, and [the ability to exercise authority] over all the power of the enemy (Satan); and nothing will [in any way] harm you." These words describe our place in God. As believers, we are in a position of power and authority over the enemy and his demons and his deceptive ways. We are also in a position of favor and influence with God.

Saying we have angelic protection does not mean we will never experience any trial or affliction. It means we are protected from whatever the enemy ultimately plans for us as long as we keep our trust in God and believe and speak of Him in accordance with His Word.

One important thing we learn about this angelic protection and our deliverance is that we don't always experience an immediate breakthrough, so we need to be patient. The Lord promises in Psalm 91:15 that when we call on Him, He will answer us and be with us in our troubles; He will strengthen us and accompany us through our difficulties to victory, deliverance, and honor. It took many years for me to see the following pattern: God is with me in my trials and troubles, then He begins to deliver me out of them, and afterward He honors me. This is a progression, and we will develop peace and joy in the Lord as we go through it. Going through things with God helps us to develop a more intimate relationship with Him.

Psalm 91:14–16 assures us that we have been given His precious promises because of our personal knowledge of God and of His mercy, love, and kindness, and because we trust and rely on Him, knowing He will never leave us or forsake us. These promises include the fact that He will be with us, answer us, deliver us, and honor us with long and abundant life. These assurances give us great peace and enable us to live without worry.

A PRAYER FOR VICTORY

Thank You, God, for the assurance of Your angelic protection and for Your promises to be with me, to answer me, deliver me, and honor me with long and abundant life. In Jesus' name. Amen.

KEYS *to a* **Victorious Life** *Happy Thoughts, Happy Words, Happy Life*

The more we speak about something, the more we will have of it. For example, if you talk about the people and things you don't like, you will dislike them even more, but talking about the people and things you love will increase the ability to love in your life.

Very few people learn this blessed lesson: Love the life you have and never compare yourself, or what you have, to anyone else and you will "flourish" and be vital and fresh [rich in trust and love and contentment]" (Ps. 92:14). Learn to love everything except evil. If you dislike something, change it if you can, but if you cannot then trust God and stay happy. If you don't like your job, you can look for a different one. If you don't like your neighborhood, you can move. If you don't like the weather, realize you can't change it and change your attitude toward it.

The more you are filled with loving thoughts and the more you speak loving words, the happier you will be.

And all evildoers flourish,
They will be destroyed forever.
⁸But You, Lord, are on high forever.
⁹For behold, Your enemies, O Lord,
For behold, Your enemies will perish;
All who do evil will be scattered.

¹⁰But my horn [my emblem of strength and power] You have exalted like that of a wild ox;
I am anointed with fresh oil [for Your service].
¹¹My eye has looked on my foes;
My ears hear of the evildoers who rise up against me.
¹²The righteous will flourish like the date palm [long-lived, upright and useful];
They will grow like a cedar in Lebanon [majestic and stable].
¹³Planted in the house of the Lord,
They will flourish in the courts of our God.
¹⁴[Growing in grace] they will still thrive *and* bear fruit *and* prosper in old age;
They will flourish *and* be vital and fresh [rich in trust and love and contentment];

¹⁵[They are living memorials] to declare that the Lord is upright *and* faithful [to His promises];
He is my rock, and there is no unrighteousness in Him. [Rom 9:14]

Psalm 93

The Majesty of the Lord.

¹THE LORD reigns, He is clothed with majesty *and* splendor;
The Lord has clothed and encircled Himself with strength;
the world is firmly established, it cannot be moved.
²Your throne is established from of old;
You are from everlasting.

³The floods have lifted up, O Lord,
The floods have lifted up their voice;
The floods lift up their pounding waves.
⁴More than the sounds of many waters,
More than the mighty breakers of the sea,
The Lord on high is mighty.
⁵Your precepts are fully confirmed *and* completely reliable;

Holiness adorns Your house,
O Lᴏʀᴅ, forever.

Psalm 94

The Lᴏʀᴅ Implored to Avenge His People.

¹O LORD God, You to whom vengeance belongs,
O God, You to whom vengeance belongs, shine forth [in judgment]!
²Rise up, O Judge of the earth;
Give to the proud a fitting compensation.
³O Lᴏʀᴅ, how long will the wicked,
How long will the wicked rejoice in triumph?
⁴They pour out *words,* speaking arrogant things;
All who do evil boast proudly. [Jude 14, 15]
⁵They crush Your people, O Lᴏʀᴅ,
And afflict *and* abuse Your heritage.
⁶They kill the widow and the alien
And murder the fatherless.
⁷Yet they say, "The Lᴏʀᴅ does not see,
Nor does the God of Jacob (Israel) notice it."

⁸Consider thoughtfully, you senseless (stupid ones) among the people;
And you [dull-minded] fools, when will you become wise *and* understand?
⁹He who made the ear, does He not hear?
He who formed the eye, does He not see?
¹⁰He who instructs the nations,
Does He not rebuke *and* punish,
He who teaches man knowledge?
¹¹The Lᴏʀᴅ knows the thoughts of man,
That they are a mere breath (vain, empty, futile). [1 Cor 3:20]

¹²Blessed [with wisdom and prosperity] is the man whom You discipline *and* instruct, O Lᴏʀᴅ,

And whom You teach from Your law,
¹³That You may grant him [power to calm himself and find] peace in the days of adversity,
Until the pit is dug for the wicked *and* ungodly.
¹⁴For the Lᴏʀᴅ will not abandon His people,
Nor will He abandon His inheritance.
¹⁵For judgment will again be righteous,
And all the upright in heart will follow it.
¹⁶Who will stand up for me against the evildoers?
Who will take a stand for me against those who do wickedness?

¹⁷If the Lᴏʀᴅ had not been my help,
I would soon have dwelt in [the land of] silence.
¹⁸If I say, "My foot has slipped,"
Your compassion *and* lovingkindness,
O Lᴏʀᴅ, will hold me up.
¹⁹When my anxious thoughts multiply within me,
Your comforts delight me.
²⁰Can a throne of destruction be allied with You,
One which frames *and* devises mischief by decree [under the sacred name of law]?
²¹They band themselves together against the life of the righteous
And condemn the innocent to death.

WINNING THE BATTLES *of the* MIND
Finding Peace in Adversity

We all have a tipping point in our lives when we recognize we are under so much pressure that we are on the verge of losing our peace and are about to start behaving badly. The psalmist asked the Lord to grant His people "[power to calm himself and find] peace in the days of adversity" (Ps. 94:13). Here are some steps that will hopefully help the process:

Step 1—When we feel overwhelmed, we usually start talking to anyone who will listen. We will never regain control unless we stop talking and regroup!

Step 2—Be realistic about what is really happening. Is the problem really as bad as you are imagining it to be? Are you worrying about things that have not even happened yet and may never happen?

Step 3—As you begin to calm down, ask yourself if any of the things you feel overloaded with can be put off until later or perhaps handed off to someone else. Is help available if you ask for it? If you truly want change within your circumstances, you will need to be willing to make some changes yourself.

Step 4—Think about what you are thinking about that is frustrating you and stop thinking about it. Cast your care on God and let Him show you what He can do. Keep saying, "God, I let this go. I trust You!" until you feel yourself calming down.

Step 5—We can manage our emotions and learn to live beyond our feelings. Being the master or mistress of yourself under God's leadership is entirely possible, but it will not happen as long as you let raw emotion rule. We cannot prevent feelings from coming, but we are totally capable of using self-control even in the midst of the wildest emotion.

Step 6—Resist the devil at his onset! The root source of all lack of peace is the devil, not people or even circumstances. It is the devil's working through the people or the circumstance. The devil has set you up to be upset, and the sooner you take action and resist him, the easier it will be.

A PRAYER FOR VICTORY

God of all peace, I thank You for granting me the power to calm myself and find peace in the midst of troubling situations. Give me the wisdom I need to manage my emotions and resist the enemy's attacks to get me to be upset. In Jesus' name. Amen.

KEYS *to a* Victorious Life *First Response*

When we worry, we are focusing on our problems. When we are anxious about things, we talk about them incessantly. Why? Because what is in our heart eventually comes out of our mouth (see Matt. 12:34). The more we think and talk about our problems, the larger they become. Rather than meditating on the problems, we can meditate on the faithfulness of God and remind ourselves there is no need to worry. The psalmist said, "When my anxious thoughts multiply within me, Your comforts delight me" (Ps. 94:19).

I have heard many people say, "I just can't help it, I am a worrier." The truth is that people often choose to worry because they do not know how to trust God. We become good at worrying because we practice at it; therefore, we can become good at trusting God if we practice. Let your first response in any situation be to trust God.

22 But the LORD has become my high tower *and* defense,

And my God the rock of my refuge.

23 He has turned back their own wickedness upon them

And will destroy them by means of their own evil;

The LORD our God will wipe them out.

Psalm 95

Praise to the LORD, and Warning against Unbelief.

1 O COME, let us sing joyfully to the LORD;

Let us shout joyfully to the rock of our salvation.

2 Let us come before His presence with a song of thanksgiving;

Let us shout joyfully to Him with songs.

3 For the LORD is a great God

And a great King above all gods,

4 In whose hand are the depths of the earth;

The peaks of the mountains are His also.

5 The sea is His, for He made it [by His command];

And His hands formed the dry land. [Gen 1:9]

6 O come, let us worship and bow down,

Let us kneel before the LORD our Maker [in reverent praise and prayer].

7 For He is our God

And we are the people of His pasture and the sheep of His hand.

Today, if you will hear His voice, [Heb 3:7–11]

8 Do not harden your hearts *and* become spiritually dull as at Meribah [the place of strife],

And as at Massah [the place of testing] in the wilderness, [Ex 17:1–7; Num 20:1–13; Deut 6:16]

9 "When your fathers tested Me,

They tried Me, even though they had seen My work [of miracles].

10 "For forty years I was grieved *and* disgusted with that generation,

And I said, 'They are a people who err in their heart,

Speak God's Word

Today, if I hear God's voice, I will not harden my heart or become spiritually dull.

| *adapted from* PSALM 95:7–8 |

KEYS *to a* Victorious Life *Live in the Now*

Psalm 95:7 says, "Today, if you will hear His voice." We need to understand that God wants us to focus on each day as it comes and to learn how to be "now" people.

The choices we make today will determine whether we will enjoy every moment in our lives or waste them by being anxious or upset. Sometimes we end up missing part of today because we are too concerned about tomorrow. We need to keep our minds focused on what God wants us to be doing now.

For years, this has been my definition of anxiety: "Anxiety is caused by trying to mentally or emotionally get into things that are not here yet (the future) or things that have already been (the past)." We often spend our mental time in the past or in the future, instead of living in the moment we have now. When we don't truly give ourselves to what we are doing at the moment, we become prone to anxiety. If we live in the now, we will find the Lord there with us. Regardless of the situations life brings our way, God has promised never to leave us or forsake us but to always be with us and help us (see Heb. 13:5; Matt. 28:20). Don't waste your precious "now" worrying about yesterday or tomorrow. Live today!

And they do not acknowledge *or* regard
My ways.'
11 "Therefore I swore [an oath] in My wrath,
'They absolutely shall not enter My rest
[the land of promise].'" [Heb 4:3–11]

Psalm 96

A Call to Worship the LORD the Righteous Judge.

1 O SING to the LORD a new song;
Sing to the LORD, all the earth!
2 Sing to the LORD, bless His name;
Proclaim good news of His salvation
from day to day.
3 Declare His glory among the nations,
His marvelous works *and* wonderful
deeds among all the peoples.
4 For great is the LORD and greatly to be
praised;
He is to be feared above all gods. [Deut
6:5; Rev 14:7]
5 For all the gods of the peoples are
[worthless, lifeless] idols,
But the LORD made the heavens.

6 Splendor and majesty are before Him;
Strength and beauty are in His
sanctuary.

7 Ascribe to the LORD, O families of the
peoples,
Ascribe to the LORD glory and strength.
8 Ascribe to the LORD the glory of His
name;
Bring an offering and come into His
courts.
9 Worship the LORD in the splendor of
holiness;
Tremble [in submissive wonder] before
Him, all the earth.
10 Say among the nations, "The LORD
reigns;
Indeed, the world is firmly *and* securely
established, it shall not be moved;
He will judge *and* rule the people with
fairness." [Rev 11:15; 19:6]

11 Let the heavens be glad, and let the earth
rejoice;
Let the sea roar, and all the things it
contains;

¹²Let the field be exultant, and all that is
   in it.
Then all the trees of the forest will sing
   for joy
¹³Before the LORD, for He is coming,
For He is coming to judge the earth.
He will judge the world with
   righteousness
And the peoples in His faithfulness.
   [1 Chr 16:23–33; Rev 19:11]

Psalm 97

The LORD's Power and Dominion.

¹THE LORD reigns, let the earth rejoice;
Let the many islands *and* coastlands be
   glad.
²Clouds and thick darkness surround
   Him [as at Sinai];
Righteousness and justice are the
   foundation of His throne. [Ex 19:9]
³Fire goes before Him
And burns up His adversaries on all
   sides.
⁴His lightnings have illuminated the
   world;
The earth has seen and trembled.
⁵The mountains melted like wax at the
   presence of the LORD,
At the presence of the Lord of the whole
   earth.
⁶The heavens declare His righteousness,
And all the peoples see His glory *and*
   brilliance.

⁷Let all those be [deeply] ashamed who
   serve carved images,
Who boast in idols.
Worship Him, all you gods! [Heb 1:6]
⁸Zion heard this and was glad,
And the daughters (cities) of Judah
   rejoiced [in relief]
Because of Your judgments, O LORD.

A Prayer To Renew Your Mind

*Thank You, Lord, that light is sown like
seed for the righteous and illuminates
our path. And irrepressible joy is spread
for the upright in heart who delight in
Your favor and protection.*

· *adapted from Psalm 97:11*

⁹For You are the LORD Most High over all
   the earth;
You are exalted far above all gods.

¹⁰You who love the LORD, hate evil;
He protects the souls of His godly ones
   (believers),
He rescues them from the hand of the
   wicked. [Rom 8:13–17]
¹¹Light is sown [like seed] for the
   righteous *and* illuminates their path,
And [irrepressible] joy [is spread] for the
   upright in heart [who delight in His
   favor and protection].
¹²Rejoice in the LORD, you righteous ones
   [those whose moral and spiritual
   integrity places them in right standing
   with God],
And praise *and* give thanks at the
   remembrance of His holy name.

Psalm 98

A Call to Praise the LORD for His Righteousness.

A Psalm.

¹O SING to the LORD a new song,
For He has done marvelous *and*
   wonderful things;
His right hand and His holy arm have
   gained the victory for Him.
²The LORD has made known His salvation;
He has [openly] revealed His
   righteousness in the sight of the
   nations. [Luke 2:30, 31]
³He has [graciously] remembered His
   lovingkindness and His faithfulness to
   the house of Israel;
All the ends of the earth have witnessed
   the salvation of our God. [Acts 13:47;
   28:28]

⁴Shout joyfully to the LORD, all the earth;
Shout [in jubilation] and sing for joy and
   sing praises.
⁵Sing praises to the LORD with the lyre,
With the lyre and the sound of melody.
⁶With trumpets and the sound of the horn
Shout with joy before the King, the LORD.

⁷Let the sea thunder *and* roar, and all the
   things it contains,
The world and those who dwell in it.
⁸Let the rivers clap their hands;

KEYS *to a*
Victorious
Life *Your Thoughts Reveal Themselves*

Your thought life is directly related to your attitude. In other words, what you think secretly in your heart is expressed in your words, facial expressions, and attitudes. Would you rather be around people who have negative attitudes or around people with humble attitudes, thankful attitudes, positive attitudes, and responsible attitudes?

Let me encourage you to take an attitude inventory. If your attitude were a song, would it be "Make the World Go Away," "Raindrops Keep Falling on My Head," "I Did It My Way," or "Oh, What a Beautiful Morning"?

The psalmist's attitude was, "O sing to the LORD a new song, for He has done marvelous and *wonderful things" (Ps. 98:1). Fresh, new ways of thinking will produce a fresh, new attitude that will enable you to sing to the Lord a new song.*

Let the mountains sing together for joy
   and delight
⁹ Before the LORD, for He is coming to
   judge the earth;
He will judge the world with
   righteousness
And the peoples with fairness.

Psalm 99

Praise to the LORD for His Fidelity to Israel.

¹ THE LORD reigns, let the peoples
   tremble [with submissive wonder]!
He sits enthroned above the cherubim,
   let the earth shake!
² The LORD is great in Zion,
And He is exalted *and* magnified above
   all the peoples.
³ Let them [reverently] praise Your great
   and awesome name;
Holy is He. [Rev 15:4]
⁴ The strength of the King loves justice
   and righteous judgment;
You have established fairness;
You have executed justice and
   righteousness in Jacob (Israel).
⁵ Exalt the LORD our God
And worship at His footstool;

Holy is He.

⁶ Moses and Aaron were among His priests,
And Samuel was among those who
   called on His name;
They called upon the LORD and He
   answered them.
⁷ He spoke to them in the pillar of cloud;

POWERPOINT

Here is a powerful thought to think:
I believe God. I believe He is working in me no matter what I may feel or how the situation may look. I recommend that you purposely think right thoughts and that you also go the extra mile and speak them out loud as your confession—"call upon the Lord" as Moses, Aaron, and Samuel did (see Ps. 99:6). Remember that God is delivering you, little by little, so don't be discouraged. Be patient with yourself.

They kept His testimonies
And the statutes that He gave them.
  [Ps 105:9, 10]
8 You answered them, O LORD our God;
You were a forgiving God to them,
And yet an avenger of their *evil* practices.
9 Exalt the LORD our God
And worship at His holy hill [Zion, the
  temple mount],
For the LORD our God is holy.

Psalm 100

All Men Exhorted to Praise God.

A Psalm of Thanksgiving.

1 SHOUT JOYFULLY to the LORD, all the
  earth.
2 Serve the LORD with gladness *and* delight;
Come before His presence with joyful
  singing.
3 Know *and* fully recognize with gratitude
  that the LORD Himself is God;

It is He who has made us, not we
  ourselves [and we are His].
We are His people and the sheep of His
  pasture. [Eph 2:10]

4 Enter His gates with a song of
  thanksgiving
And His courts with praise.
Be thankful to Him, bless *and* praise His
  name.
5 For the LORD is good;
His mercy *and* lovingkindness are
  everlasting,
His faithfulness [endures] to all
  generations.

Psalm 101

The Psalmist's Profession of Uprightness.

A Psalm of David.

1 I WILL sing of [steadfast]
  lovingkindness and justice;

KEYS *to a* Victorious Life *Look for Something To Be Thankful For*

Prayer often goes unanswered because of an ungrateful heart. There are people who are grumblers, murmurers, faultfinders, and complainers. We must be careful not to be like that. We need to be the kind of people who are thankful for what God is doing. Complaining and being ungrateful are major hindrances to answered prayers.

If we want to see God at work in our spouse, our children, our finances, our circumstances, our job, we can start by being grateful for what we already have.

The Holy Spirit once impressed on me the idea that when people pray and ask God for things but don't have a thankful heart, it's a clear indication that they're not ready for something else because they won't be thankful for that either. The devil's whole plan is to keep us dissatisfied with something all the time. Being ungrateful is a symptom of a lack of spiritual maturity.

God wants us to grow in maturity and become more like His Son, Jesus. God's answer to ingratitude is a life filled with thanksgiving and praise.

Look for something today to be thankful for and offer up a prayer of praise and thanksgiving (see Ps. 100:4).

KEYS *to a* **Victorious Life** *A Humble Heart*

God hates pride, and it is something we need to be quick to recognize in our thoughts, words, and attitudes. Every human will have to confront pride at various times in life. Pride makes us think we are better than others; it causes us to judge and criticize; and it makes us unwilling to listen to and respect the ideas and opinions of others. These are just a few of the problems pride creates.

God's Word teaches us that God helps the humble (see 1 Pet. 5:5), but He is unable to help those who are proud because they don't' think they need help. They are independent, but God wants us to be totally dependent on Him.

If we want to follow God's advice and humble ourselves under His mighty hand (see 1 Pet. 5:6), we need to learn to say, "Apart from Jesus I can do nothing" (see John 15:5). Ask God to work in your life in such a way that you develop the same humble attitude that Jesus has.

To You, O Lord, I will sing praises.
²I will behave wisely *and* follow the way of integrity.
When will You come to me?
I will walk in my house in integrity *and* with a blameless heart.
³I will set no worthless *or* wicked thing before my eyes.
I hate the practice of those who fall away [from the right path];
It will not grasp hold of me.
⁴A perverse heart shall depart from me;
I will not tolerate evil.
⁵Whoever secretly slanders his neighbor, him I will silence;
The one who has a haughty look and a proud (arrogant) heart I will not tolerate.
⁶My eyes will be on the faithful (honorable) of the land, that they may dwell with me;
He who walks blamelessly is the one who will minister to *and* serve me.
⁷He who practices deceit will not dwell in my house;
He who tells lies *and* half-truths will not continue [to remain] in my presence.

⁸Morning after morning I will destroy all the wicked in the land,
That I may cut off from the city of the Lord all those who do evil.

Psalm 102

Prayer of an Afflicted Man for Mercy on Himself and on Zion.

A Prayer of the afflicted; when he is overwhelmed and pours out his complaint to God.

¹HEAR MY prayer, O Lord,
And let my cry for help come to You!
²Do not hide Your face from me in the day of my distress!
Incline Your ear to me;
In the day when I call, answer me quickly.
³For my days have vanished in smoke,
And my bones have been scorched like a hearth.
⁴My heart has been struck like grass and withered,
Indeed, [absorbed by my heartache] I forget to eat my food.
⁵Because of the sound of my groaning [in suffering and trouble]

My bones cling to my flesh.

⁶ I am like a [mournful] vulture of the wilderness;
I am like a [desolate] owl of the wasteland.

⁷ I am sleepless *and* lie awake [mourning],
I have become like a lonely bird on a housetop.

⁸ My enemies taunt me all day long;
Those who ridicule me use my *name* as a curse.

⁹ For I have eaten ashes like bread,
And have mingled my drink with tears [Is 44:20]

¹⁰ Because of Your indignation and Your wrath,
For You have lifted me up and thrown me away.

¹¹ My days are like an evening shadow that lengthens *and* vanishes [with the sun];
And as for me, I wither away like grass.

¹² But You, O LORD, are enthroned forever [ruling eternally as sovereign];
And [the fame and glory of] Your name [endures] to all generations.

¹³ You will arise and have compassion on Zion,

POWERPOINT

Those who are afflicted and going through very difficult situations can expect God to bring deliverance to them. He will never allow more to come to us than we can bear, and He always provides a way out of temptation (see 1 Cor. 10:13). You can be confident that at the exact right moment God will arise and have mercy and compassion on you. Whenever you experience a difficult or a trying time, be encouraged that God sees your situation. Know that as long as you put your trust in Him, you will definitely see victory. Stay in faith and be patient. God won't be late.

For it is time to be gracious *and* show favor to her;
Yes, the appointed time [the moment designated] has come. [Ps 12:5; 119:126]

¹⁴ For Your servants find [melancholy] pleasure in the stones [of her ruins]
And feel pity for her dust.

¹⁵ So the nations will fear the name of the LORD,
And all the kings of the earth [will recognize] Your glory. [Ps 96:9]

¹⁶ For the LORD has built up Zion;
He has appeared in His glory *and* brilliance;

¹⁷ He has regarded the prayer of the destitute,
And has not despised their prayer.

¹⁸ Let this be recorded for the generation to come,
That a people yet to be created will praise the LORD.

¹⁹ For He looked down from His holy height [of His sanctuary],
From heaven the LORD gazed on the earth,

²⁰ To hear the sighing of the prisoner,
To set free those who were doomed to death,

²¹ So that people may declare the name of the LORD in Zion
And His praise in Jerusalem,

²² When the peoples are gathered together,
And the kingdoms, to serve the LORD.

²³ He has exhausted my strength [humbling me with sorrow] in the way;
He has shortened my days.

²⁴ I said, "O my God, do not take me away in the midst of my days;
Your years are [eternal] throughout all generations.

²⁵ "At the beginning You founded the earth;
The heavens are the work of Your hands.

²⁶ "Even they will perish, but You endure;
Yes, all of them will wear out like a garment.
Like clothing You will change them and they shall be changed.

²⁷ "But You remain the same,

And Your years will never end. [Heb 1:10–12]

28 "The children of Your servants will continue,
And their descendants will be established before You."

Psalm 103

Praise for the LORD's Mercies.

A Psalm of David.

1 BLESS *AND* affectionately praise the LORD, O my soul,
And all that is [deep] within me, *bless* His holy name.
2 Bless *and* affectionately praise the LORD, O my soul,
And do not forget any of His benefits;
3 Who forgives all your sins,
Who heals all your diseases;
4 Who redeems your life from the pit,
Who crowns you [lavishly] with lovingkindness and tender mercy;
5 Who satisfies your years with good things,
So that your youth is renewed like the [soaring] eagle. [Is 40:31]

6 The LORD executes righteousness
And justice for all the oppressed.
7 He made known His ways [of righteousness and justice] to Moses,
His acts to the children of Israel.
8 The LORD is merciful and gracious,
Slow to anger and abounding in compassion *and* lovingkindness. [James 5:11]

Speak God's Word

I bless and praise the Lord, and I do not forget any of His benefits. He forgives all my sins; He heals all my diseases; He redeems my life from the pit. He crowns me with lovingkindness and tender mercy. He satisfies my years with good things, so that my youth is renewed like the eagle.

| adapted from PSALM 103:2–5 |

POWERPOINT

Psalm 103:14 reminds us that God understands our weaknesses. He knows we will at times succumb to temptations and wrong behavior, but He is also a compassionate, loving Father Who stands ready to forgive everything. The very fact that we cannot do everything right is the reason God sent Jesus to pay the price for our redemption.

9 He will not always strive *with us,*
Nor will He keep *His anger* forever.
10 He has not dealt with us according to our sins [as we deserve],
Nor rewarded us [with punishment] according to our wickedness.
11 For as the heavens are high above the earth,
So great is His lovingkindness toward those who fear *and* worship Him [with awe-filled respect and deepest reverence].
12 As far as the east is from the west,
So far has He removed our transgressions from us.
13 Just as a father loves his children,
So the LORD loves those who fear *and* worship Him [with awe-filled respect and deepest reverence].
14 For He knows our [mortal] frame;
He remembers that we are [merely] dust.
15 As for man, his days are like grass;
Like a flower of the field, so he flourishes.
16 For the wind passes over it and it is no more,
And its place knows it no longer.
17 But the lovingkindness of the LORD is from everlasting to everlasting on those who [reverently] fear Him,
And His righteousness to children's children, [Deut 10:12]
18 To those who honor *and* keep His covenant,

WINNING THE BATTLES *of the* MIND

Don't Let Your Thoughts Drain Your Energy

I believe God gives each of us abilities and corresponding energy to help us fulfill our destiny. If you are lacking energy, it may be due to faulty thinking in some area of your life. Negative thoughts—fear, bitterness, guilt, discouragement, resentment, unforgiveness, and others—always steal energy.

Some of the most energy-draining kinds of thoughts are those about past mistakes, failures, and sins, which produce guilt and condemnation. The enemy loves to fill our minds with thoughts of past failures that we cannot do anything about. But we can choose which way we think. We can think about the past and what we have lost or we can think about the future and the opportunities in front of us. We can think about our sins, or we can think about God's grace manifested by His sending Jesus to pay for our sins and remove them "as far as the east is from the west" (Ps. 103:12).

We cannot pay for our sins with feelings of guilt, because Jesus already paid for our sins when He died on the cross. His sacrifice is good for all time (see Heb. 9:28; 10:10). There is nothing we can add to what Jesus has done. We can only humbly and gratefully accept the complete forgiveness He offers and refuse the guilt.

People who love God often suffer terribly with guilty thoughts and feelings over every tiny thing they do wrong. For years I was one of those people, but learning to line up my thinking with God's Word has set me free. When I sin, I am quick to repent and receive forgiveness. When guilt comes, I simply think or sometimes say, "I am forgiven completely and there is no guilt or condemnation for those who are in Christ" (see Rom. 8:1). The mind is the battlefield, and if we want victory and enjoyment in life, we need to be willing to learn how to control and properly manage our thoughts.

God did not design us to continually feel bad about ourselves. We are not built for guilt! God loves us and wants us to keep our hearts light and free. Thoughts that produce guilt or condemnation should immediately be resisted in Jesus' name.

A PRAYER FOR VICTORY

Lord Jesus, because of Your suffering and death, I am forgiven completely and I have no guilt or condemnation for past failures and sins. Thank You that I can bring my thoughts into obedience to You and live in the freedom of Your grace and power. Amen.

And remember to do His commandments [imprinting His word on their hearts].

19 The LORD has established His throne in the heavens,
And His sovereignty rules over all [the universe].
20 Bless the LORD, you His angels,
You mighty ones who do His commandments,
Obeying the voice of His word!
21 Bless the LORD, all you His hosts,
You who serve Him and do His will.
22 Bless the LORD, all you works of His, in all places of His dominion;
Bless *and* affectionately praise the LORD, O my soul!

Psalm 104

The LORD's Care over All His Works.

1 BLESS *AND* affectionately praise the LORD, O my soul!
O LORD my God, You are very great;
You are clothed with splendor and majesty,
2 [You are the One] who covers Yourself with light as with a garment,
Who stretches out the heavens like a tent curtain,
3 Who lays the beams of His upper chambers in the waters [above the firmament],
Who makes the clouds His chariot,
Who walks on the wings of the wind,
4 Who makes winds His messengers,
Flames of fire His ministers.
[Heb 1:7]

5 He established the earth on its foundations,
So that it will not be moved forever and ever. [Job 38:4, 6]
6 You covered it with the deep as with a garment;
The waters were standing above the mountains. [Gen 1:2; 2 Pet 3:5]
7 At Your rebuke they fled;
At the sound of Your thunder they hurried away.
8 The mountains rose, the valleys sank down

To the place which You established for them.
9 You set a boundary [for the waters] that they may not cross over,
So that they will not return to cover the earth.

10 You send springs into the valleys;
Their waters flow among the mountains.
11 They give drink to every beast of the field;
The wild donkeys quench their thirst there.
12 Beside them the birds of the heavens have their nests;
They lift up their voices *and* sing among the branches. [Matt 13:32]
13 He waters the mountains from His upper chambers;
The earth is satisfied with the fruit of His works.

14 He causes grass to grow for the cattle,
And all that the earth produces for cultivation by man,
So that he may bring food from the earth—
15 And wine which makes the heart of man glad,
So that he may make his face glisten with oil,
And bread to sustain *and* strengthen man's heart.
16 The trees of the LORD drink their fill,
The cedars of Lebanon which He has planted,
17 Where the birds make their nests;
As for the stork, the fir trees are her house.

18 The high mountains are for the wild goats;
The rocks are a refuge for the shephanim.
19 He made the moon for the seasons;
The sun knows the [exact] place of its setting.
20 You [O LORD] make darkness and it becomes night,
In which prowls about every wild beast of the forest.
21 The young lions roar after their prey
And seek their food from God.
22 When the sun arises, they withdraw
And lie down in their dens.

KEYS *to a* Victorious Life *Old Things Have Passed Away*

As "a new creation" in Christ, you don't have to allow the old things that happened to you to keep affecting you. The old things have passed away. You're a new person with a new life in Christ (see 2 Cor. 5:17). You can begin to have your mind renewed by studying God's Word and learning about His good plan for you. Good things are going to happen to you, and you can start believing that you will be "filled and *satisfied with good [things]" (Ps. 104:28).*

Even if your reality is filled with negatives, you can still have a positive attitude toward it. In every situation, trust God and know that He loves you. Believe that He works good out of all things (see Rom. 8:28).

Rejoice! It's a new day, a day for good things!

---

²³ Man goes out to his work
  And remains at his labor until evening.

²⁴ O LORD, how many *and* varied are Your works!
  In wisdom You have made them all;
  The earth is full of Your riches *and* Your creatures.

²⁵ There is the sea, great and broad,
  In which are swarms without number,
  Creatures both small and great.

²⁶ There the ships [of the sea] sail,
  And Leviathan [the sea monster], which You have formed to play there.

²⁷ They all wait for You
  To give them their food in its appointed season.

²⁸ You give it to them, they gather it up;
  You open Your hand, they are filled *and* satisfied with good [things].

²⁹ You hide Your face, they are dismayed;
  You take away their breath, they die
  And return to their dust.

³⁰ You send out Your Spirit, they are created;
  You renew the face of the ground.

³¹ May the glory of the LORD endure forever;
  May the LORD rejoice *and* be glad in His works—

³² He looks at the earth, and it trembles;

He touches the mountains, and they smoke.

³³ I will sing to the LORD as long as I live;
  I will sing praise to my God while I have my being.

³⁴ May my meditation be sweet *and* pleasing to Him;
  As for me, I will rejoice *and* be glad in the LORD.

³⁵ Let sinners be consumed from the earth,
  And let the wicked be no more.
  Bless *and* affectionately praise the LORD, O my soul.
  Praise the LORD! (Hallelujah!)

Psalm 105

The LORD's Wonderful Works in Behalf of Israel.

¹ O GIVE thanks to the LORD, call upon His name;
  Make known His deeds among the people.

² Sing to Him, sing praises to Him;
  Speak of all His wonderful acts *and* devoutly praise them.

³ Glory in His holy name;
  Let the hearts of those who seek *and* require the LORD [as their most essential need] rejoice.

KEYS *to a* Victorious Life *Be Full of God*

Does God want us to be full of ourselves? No! According to Ephesians 3:19, we are supposed to be full of God! We are to get our minds off of ourselves and fill them instead with the "fullness of God." Let your mind and mouth and your entire body be "completely filled and flooded with God Himself!" We can do this by thinking about Him, talking about Him, and letting our actions glorify Him.

I encourage you to follow David's instruction in Psalm 105:4: "Seek and deeply long for the LORD and His strength [His power, His might]; seek and deeply long for His face and His presence continually." The one thing that David wanted was God!

---

⁴ Seek *and* deeply long for the LORD and His strength [His power, His might];
Seek *and* deeply long for His face *and* His presence continually.
⁵ Remember [with awe and gratitude] the wonderful things which He has done,
His amazing deeds and the judgments uttered by His mouth [on His enemies, as in Egypt], [Ps 78:43–51]
⁶ O you offspring of Abraham, His servant,
O you sons of Jacob, His chosen ones!
⁷ He is the LORD our God;
His judgments are in all the earth.

8 He has remembered His covenant forever,
The word which He commanded *and* established to a thousand generations,
⁹ *The covenant* which He made with Abraham,
And His sworn oath to Isaac, [Luke 1:72, 73]
¹⁰ Which He confirmed to Jacob as a statute,
To Israel as an everlasting covenant,
¹¹ Saying, "To you I will give the land of Canaan
As the measured portion of your inheritance."
¹² When there were only a few men in number,
Very few [in fact], and strangers in it;

¹³ And they wandered from one nation to another,
From one kingdom to another people,
¹⁴ He allowed no man to oppress them;
He rebuked kings for their sakes, *saying,* [Gen 12:17; 20:3–7]
¹⁵ "Do not touch My anointed ones,
And do My prophets no harm." [1 Chr 16:8–22]

16 And He called for a famine upon the land [of Egypt];
He cut off every source of bread. [Gen 41:54]
¹⁷ He sent a man before them,
Joseph, who was sold as a slave. [Gen 45:5; 50:20, 21]
¹⁸ His feet they hurt with shackles;
He was put in chains of iron,
¹⁹ Until the time that his word [of prophecy regarding his brothers] came true,
The word of the LORD tested *and* refined him.
²⁰ The king sent and released him,
The ruler of the peoples [of Egypt], and set him free.
²¹ He made Joseph lord of his house
And ruler of all his possessions, [Gen 41:40]
²² To imprison his princes at his will,
That he might teach his elders wisdom.
²³ Israel also came into Egypt;

Thus Jacob sojourned in the land of Ham. [Gen 46:6]

24 There the LORD greatly increased [the number of] His people,
And made them more powerful than their enemies.

25 He turned the heart [of the Egyptians] to hate His people,
To deal craftily with His servants.

26 He sent Moses His servant,
And Aaron, whom He had chosen.

27 They exhibited His wondrous signs among them,
Great miracles in the land of Ham (Egypt).

28 He sent [thick, oppressive] darkness and made *the land* dark;
And Moses and Aaron did not rebel against His words. [Ex 10:22; Ps 99:7]

29 He turned Egypt's waters into blood
And caused their fish to die. [Ex 7:20, 21]

30 Their land swarmed with frogs,
Even in the chambers of their kings. [Ex 8:6]

31 He spoke, and there came swarms of flies
And gnats in all their territory. [Ex 8:17, 24]

32 He gave them hail for rain,
With flaming fire in their land. [Ex 9:23, 25]

33 He struck their vines also and their fig trees,
And shattered the [ice-laden] trees of their territory. [Ps 78:47]

34 He spoke, and the [migratory] locusts came,
And the young locusts, even without number, [Ex 10:4, 13, 14]

35 And ate up all the vegetation in their land,
And devoured the fruit of their ground.

36 He also struck down all the firstborn in their land,
The first fruits *and* chief substance of all their strength. [Ex 12:29; Ps 78:51]

37 He brought the sons of Israel out [of Egypt] with silver and gold,
And among their tribes there was not one who stumbled. [Ex 12:35]

38 Egypt was glad when they departed,
For the dread *and* fear of them had fallen on the Egyptians. [Ex 12:33]

39 The LORD spread a cloud as a covering [by day],
And a fire to illumine the night. [Ex 13:21]

40 The Israelites asked, and He brought quail,
And satisfied them with the bread of heaven. [Ex 16:12–15]

41 He opened the rock and water flowed out;
It ran in the dry places like a river. [Ex 17:6; Num 20:11]

42 For He remembered His holy word
To Abraham His servant; [Gen 15:14]

43 He brought out His people with joy,
And His chosen ones with a joyful shout,

44 He gave them the lands of the nations [of Canaan),
So that they would possess *the fruits of* those peoples' labor, [Deut 6:10, 11]

45 So that they might observe His precepts
And keep His laws [obediently accepting and honoring and valuing them].
Praise the LORD! (Hallelujah!)

Psalm 106

Israel's Rebelliousness and the LORD's Deliverances.

1 PRAISE THE LORD! (Hallelujah!)
Oh give thanks to the LORD, for He is good;
For His mercy *and* lovingkindness endure forever! [1 Chr 16:34]

2 Who can put into words the mighty deeds of the LORD?
Or who can proclaim all His praise [that is due Him]?

3 Blessed are those who observe justice [by honoring God's precepts],
Who practice righteousness at all times.

4 Remember me, O LORD, when You favor Your people.
Visit me with Your salvation [when You rescue them],

5 That I may see the prosperity of Your chosen ones,
That I may rejoice in the gladness of Your nation,
That I may glory with Your inheritance.

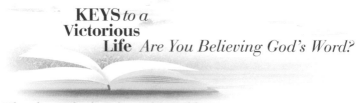

KEYS *to a* Victorious Life *Are You Believing God's Word?*

When the people of Israel were delivered from Egypt, they "believed in [the validity of] His words; they sang His praise. But they quickly forgot His works . . . did not believe His word nor *rely on it, but they sulked* and *complained" (Ps. 106:12–13, 24–25).*

When you feel frustrated or upset or have lost your peace and your joy, ask yourself this: Am I believing God's Word? The only way to be free from struggling with these negative feelings or losses is to believe the Word and obey whatever Jesus puts in your heart to do (see Heb. 4:3). Believing God's Word delivers you from struggling so you can rest in the promises of God.

If your thoughts have become negative and you are full of doubt, the reason may be that you have stopped believing God's Word and trusting Him. As soon as you start believing God's Word, your joy will return and you will be at ease once again (see Rom. 15:13).

---

⁶ We have sinned like our fathers;
    We have committed iniquity, we have
        behaved wickedly. [Lev 26:40–42]
⁷ Our fathers in Egypt did not understand
        nor appreciate Your miracles;
    They did not remember the abundance
        of Your mercies *nor* imprint Your
        lovingkindnesses on their hearts,
    But they were rebellious at the sea, at the
        Red Sea. [Ex 14:21]
⁸ Nevertheless He saved them for His
        name's sake,
    That He might make His [supreme]
        power known.
⁹ He rebuked the Red Sea, and it dried up;
    And He led them through the depths as
        through a pasture. [Ex 14:21]
¹⁰ So He saved them from the hand of the
        one that hated them,
    And redeemed them from the hand of
        the [Egyptian] enemy. [Ex 14:30]
¹¹ And the waters covered their
        adversaries;
    Not one of them was left. [Ex 14:27, 28;
        15:5]
¹² Then Israel believed in [the validity of]
        His words;
    They sang His praise.

¹³ But they quickly forgot His works;
    They did not [patiently] wait for His
        counsel *and* purpose [to be revealed
        regarding them],
¹⁴ But lusted intensely in the wilderness
    And tempted God [with their insistent
        desires] in the desert. [Num 11:4]
¹⁵ So He gave them their request,
    But sent a wasting disease among them.
        [Ps 78:29–31]
¹⁶ They envied Moses in the camp,
    And Aaron [the high priest], the holy
        one of the Lᴏʀᴅ, [Num 16:1–32]
¹⁷ Therefore the earth opened and
        swallowed Dathan,
    And engulfed the company of Abiram.
        [Num 16:31, 32]
¹⁸ And a fire broke out in their company;
    The flame consumed the wicked. [Num
        16:35, 46]
¹⁹ They made a calf in Horeb (Sinai)
    And worshiped a cast image. [Ex 32:4]
²⁰ Thus they exchanged [the true God who
        was] their glory
    For the image of an ox that eats grass.
²¹ They forgot God their Savior,

Who had done such great things in
Egypt,
22 Wonders in the land of Ham,
Awesome things at the Red Sea.
23 Therefore He said He would destroy
them,
[And He would have done so] had not
Moses, His chosen one, stepped into
the gap before Him,
To turn away His wrath from destroying
them. [Ex 32:10, 11, 32]
24 Then they despised the pleasant land [of
Canaan];
They did not believe in His word *nor* rely
on it,
25 But they sulked *and* complained in their
tents;
They did not listen to the voice of the
Lord.
26 Therefore He lifted up His hand
[swearing] to them,
That He would cause them to fall in the
wilderness,
27 And that He would cast out their
descendants among the nations
And scatter them in the lands [of the
earth].

28 They joined themselves also to [the idol]
Baal of Peor,
And ate sacrifices offered to the dead.
29 Thus they provoked Him to anger with
their practices,
And a plague broke out among them.
30 Then Phinehas [the priest] stood up and
interceded,
And so the plague was halted. [Num
25:7, 8]
31 And that was credited to him for
righteousness,
To all generations forever.

32 They provoked Him to anger at the
waters of Meribah,
So that it went hard with Moses on their
account; [Num 20:3–13]
33 Because they were rebellious against His
Spirit,
Moses spoke recklessly with his lips.

34 They did not destroy the [pagan] peoples
[in Canaan],
As the Lord commanded them,

35 But they mingled with the [idolatrous]
nations
And learned their ways,
36 And served their idols,
Which became a [dreadful] snare to
them.
37 They even sacrificed their sons and their
daughters to demons [Deut 32:17;
2 Kin 16:3]
38 And shed innocent blood,
Even the blood of their sons and of their
daughters,
Whom they sacrificed to the idols of
Canaan;
And the land was polluted with their
blood.
39 In this way they became unclean in their
practices;
They played the prostitute in their own
deeds [by giving their worship, which
belongs to God alone, to other "gods"].

40 Therefore the anger of the Lord was
kindled against His people
And He detested His own inheritance.
[Deut 32:17]
41 He gave them into the hands of the
nations,
And those who hated them ruled over
them.
42 Their enemies also oppressed them,
And they were subdued under the
[powerful] hand of their enemies.
43 Many times He rescued them;
But they were rebellious in their counsel,
And sank down in their wickedness.

44 Nevertheless He looked
[sympathetically] at their distress
When He heard their cry;
45 And He remembered His covenant for
their sake,
And relented [rescinding their sentence]
according to the greatness of His
lovingkindness [when they cried out
to Him],
46 He also made them *objects* of
compassion
Among those who had carried them
away captive. [2 Kin 25:27–30]

47 Save us, O Lord our God,
And gather us from among the nations,

That we may give thanks to Your holy name
And glory in praising You.
[48] Blessed be the LORD, the God of Israel,
From everlasting even to everlasting.
And let all the people say, "Amen."
Praise the LORD! (Hallelujah!) [1 Chr 16:35, 36]

BOOK FIVE

Psalm 107

The LORD Rescues People from Many Troubles.

[1] O GIVE thanks to the LORD, for He is good;
For His compassion *and* lovingkindness endure forever!
[2] Let the redeemed of the LORD say so,
Whom He has redeemed from the hand of the adversary,
[3] And gathered them from the lands,
From the east and from the west,
From the north and from the south.

[4] They wandered in the wilderness in a [solitary] desert region;
And did not find a way to an inhabited city.
[5] Hungry and thirsty,
They fainted.
[6] Then they cried out to the LORD in their trouble,
And He rescued them from their distresses.
[7] He led them by the straight way,
To an inhabited city [where they could establish their homes].
[8] Let them give thanks to the LORD for His lovingkindness,

KEYS *to a* Victorious Life *Speak the Word*

When you realize that the enemy is trying to distract you, you can either allow him to beat you up with worry and negative thoughts or you can stand up to him. One way to stand against him is to open your mouth and begin to confess your authority in Christ (see Ps. 107:2).

Sometimes while I am preparing to speak at a church or seminar, negative thoughts begin to occur to me. When that happens, I encourage myself with my own mouth and say out loud, "Everything is going to be all right."

Satan places anxious and worried thoughts in our minds, sometimes actually bombarding our minds with them. He hopes we will receive them and begin speaking them. If we do, he then has material to actually create in our lives the very circumstances he has been giving us anxious thoughts about.

Once we recognize anxious thoughts, we can take authority over them, asking for God's help and being determined to live the good life God wants us to live.

Let me encourage you not to be the devil's mouthpiece. Don't speak the lies he puts into your mind. Find out what God's Word promises you and begin to declare His Word, which is "living and active and *full of power . . . sharper than any two-edged sword" (Heb. 4:12). As we speak the Word with our mouths in faith, we wield a mighty sword that penetrates and exposes the enemy's tactics and lies.*

WINNING THE BATTLES *of the* MIND
Confession and Possession

What do you say about yourself and about your life? When I hear people make comments about themselves that remind me of statements I used to make about myself, it makes me sad to hear them. They say such things as, "I never get anything right" or "I am addicted to sweets" or "I worry all the time" or "My problems are overwhelming." People who speak this way are saying what they really think. The problem is, what they are saying does not agree with God's Word.

Psalm 107:2 says that those of us who are redeemed should "say so." You and I are "the redeemed of the LORD." We are not hoping or waiting to be redeemed; Jesus has already paid the price for our redemption. It is ours, and we need to learn to agree with it.

If we truly live by faith and believe God's promises, our confession needs to change so that our words line up with our beliefs. You can start "saying so" by declaring by faith, "I am redeemed from sin, guilt, and condemnation." "I am redeemed from bondage to food." "I am redeemed from anger, bitterness, and resentment." "I am redeemed from worry, anxiety, and fear." "I am redeemed from envy and jealousy." Because these statements are true, you can also declare, "I am free to love God, to love myself, and to love other people" and "Even when I face challenges, I can do whatever I need to do in life through Christ Who gives me strength" (see Phil. 4:13).

We can begin speaking by faith because we believe God's Word is true, and in God's perfect timing, we will see His promises manifested in our lives. In God's kingdom, we first believe and then we receive. I said thousands of times by faith, "God loves me" before I ever truly felt His love.

We choose to believe what God says and then we say the same thing by faith. The result is that our confession of God's promises releases our faith and causes us to possess them experientially.

God's principle of faith is the exact opposite of what the world teaches. The world says, "Don't believe anything you can't see, smell, taste, or touch." God's Word says "we walk by faith, not by sight" (2 Cor. 5:7).

A PRAYER FOR VICTORY

Lord, I pray that I will grow more and more in faith as I study Your Word and that my confession of your Word will help to renew my mind.
In Jesus' name. Amen.

Speak God's Word

I give thanks to the Lord for His loving-kindness and for His wonderful acts. He satisfies the parched throat, and fills the hungry appetite with what is good.

| *adapted from* PSALM 107:8–9 |

And for His wonderful acts to the children of men!

⁹ For He satisfies the parched throat,
And fills the hungry appetite with what is good.

¹⁰ Some dwelt in darkness and in the deep (deathly) darkness,
Prisoners [bound] in misery and chains, [Luke 1:79]

¹¹ Because they had rebelled against the precepts of God
And spurned the counsel of the Most High.

¹² Therefore He humbled their heart with hard labor;
They stumbled and there was no one to help.

¹³ Then they cried out to the LORD in their trouble,
And He saved them from their distresses.

¹⁴ He brought them out of darkness and the deep (deathly) darkness
And broke their bonds apart. [Ps 68:6; Acts 12:7; 16:26]

¹⁵ Let them give thanks to the LORD for His lovingkindness,
And for His wonderful acts to the children of men!

¹⁶ For He has shattered the gates of bronze
And cut the bars of iron apart.

¹⁷ Fools, because of their rebellious way,
And because of their sins, were afflicted.

¹⁸ They detested all kinds of food,
And they drew near to the gates of death.

KEYS *to a* Victorious Life *God's Word Brings Healing*

Psalm 107:20 is an important scripture to me because I have experienced firsthand that there is power in God's Word to heal us everywhere we hurt. After being abused during my childhood years, I had many wrong mind-sets. I frequently verbalized the defeated life I had and expected to continue having, and I truly had no hope of change. I was bitter, resentful, and filled with hatred toward those who had hurt me.

As God's Word renewed my mind (see Rom. 12:2), I began to think differently and talk differently. Eventually my attitude changed, and I finally began behaving differently. The same outcome will happen for anyone who truly studies and believes God's Word. His Word has power inherent in it to change lives.

Before our lives can change, our thinking must change. Satan attempts to build strongholds in our minds from the time we are very young. A stronghold is an area in which an enemy occupies and hides, and from that place makes his attack. We learn in God's Word that we can tear down strongholds by believing God's Word. Truth always defeats lies! Always remember that there is no pit so deep that God cannot reach down into it and lift us out. He is our Healer, and He delights in making us whole.

¹⁹ Then they cried out to the LORD in their trouble,

And He saved them from their distresses.

²⁰ He sent His word and healed them,

And rescued them from their destruction. [2 Kin 20:4, 5; Matt 8:8]

²¹ Let them give thanks to the LORD for His lovingkindness,

And for His wonderful acts to the children of men! [Heb 13:15]

²² And let them offer the sacrifices of thanksgiving,

And speak of His deeds with shouts of joy!

²³ Those who go down to the sea in ships,

Who do business on great waters;

²⁴ They have seen the works of the LORD,

And His wonders in the deep.

²⁵ For He spoke and raised up a stormy wind,

Which lifted up the waves of the sea.

²⁶ They went up toward the heavens [on the crest of the wave], they went down again to the depths [of the watery trough];

Their courage melted away in their misery.

²⁷ They staggered and trembled like a drunken man,

And were at their wits' end [all their wisdom was useless].

²⁸ Then they cried out to the LORD in their trouble,

And He brought them out of their distresses.

²⁹ He hushed the storm to a gentle whisper,

So that the waves of the sea were still. [Ps 65:7; 89:9; Matt 8:26]

³⁰ Then they were glad because of the calm,

And He guided them to their desired haven (harbor).

³¹ Let them give thanks to the LORD for His lovingkindness,

And for His wonderful acts to the children of men!

³² Let them exalt Him also in the congregation of the people,

And praise Him at the seat of the elders.

³³ He turns rivers into a wilderness,

And springs of water into a thirsty ground; [1 Kin 17:1, 7]

³⁴ A productive land into a [barren] salt waste,

Because of the wickedness of those who dwell in it. [Gen 13:10; 14:3; 19:25]

³⁵ He turns a wilderness into a pool of water

And a dry land into springs of water; [Is 41:18]

³⁶ And there He has the hungry dwell,

So that they may establish an inhabited city,

³⁷ And sow fields and plant vineyards,

And produce an abundant harvest.

³⁸ Also He blesses them so that they multiply greatly,

And He does not let [the number of] their cattle decrease.

³⁹ When they are diminished and bowed down (humbled)

Through oppression, misery, and sorrow,

⁴⁰ He pours contempt on princes

And makes them wander in a pathless wasteland.

⁴¹ Yet He sets the needy securely on high, away from affliction,

And makes their families like a flock.

⁴² The upright see it and rejoice;

But all unrighteousness shuts its mouth.

⁴³ Who is wise? Let him observe *and* heed these things;

And [thoughtfully] consider the lovingkindness of the LORD.

Psalm 108

Praise and Supplication to God for Victory.

A Song. A Psalm of David.

¹ O GOD, my heart is steadfast [with confident faith];

I will sing, I will sing praises, even with my soul.

² Awake, harp and lyre;

I will awaken the dawn!

³ I will praise *and* give thanks to You, O LORD, among the people;

And I will sing praises to You among the nations.

⁴ For Your lovingkindness is great *and* higher than the heavens;

Your truth *reaches* to the skies.
[Ps 57:7–11]
5 Be exalted [in majesty], O God, above
the heavens,
And Your glory above all the earth.
6 That Your beloved [ones] may be
rescued,
Save with Your right hand, and answer
me!

7 God has spoken in His holiness:
"I will rejoice, I will portion out
Shechem [as I divide Canaan among
My people],
And measure out the Valley of Succoth.
8 "Gilead is Mine, Manasseh is Mine;
Ephraim also is the helmet of My head
[My stronghold, My defense];
Judah is My scepter. [Gen 49:10]
9 "Moab is My washbowl;
Over Edom I will throw My shoe [to
show Edom is Mine];
Over Philistia I will shout [in triumph]."

10 Who will bring me into the fortified city
[of Petra]?
Who will lead me to Edom?
11 Have You not rejected us, O God?
And will You not go out, O God, with
our armies?
12 Give us help against the adversary,
For deliverance by man is in vain [a
worthless hope].
13 With God we will do valiantly,
For it is He who will trample down our
enemies. [Ps 60:5–12]

Psalm 109

Vengeance Invoked upon
Adversaries.

To the Chief Musician.
A Psalm of David.

1 O GOD of my praise!
Do not keep silent,
2 For the mouth of the wicked and the
mouth of the deceitful are opened
against me;
They have spoken against me with a
lying tongue.
3 They have also surrounded me with
words of hatred,
And have fought against me without a
cause.

4 In return for my love, they attack me,
But I am in prayer.
5 They have repaid me evil for good,
And hatred for my love.

6 Appoint a wicked man against him,
And let an attacker stand at his right
hand [to kill him].
7 When he enters into dispute, let
wickedness come about.
Let his prayer [for help] result [only] in
sin.
8 Let his days be few;
And let another take his office. [Acts
1:20]
9 Let his children be fatherless
And his wife a widow.
10 Let his children wander and beg;
Let them seek their food *and* be driven
far from their ruined homes. [Gen
4:12]
11 Let the creditor seize all that he has,
And let strangers plunder the product of
his labor.
12 Let there be no one to extend kindness
to him,
Nor let anyone be gracious to his
fatherless children.
13 Let his descendants be cut off,
And in the following generation let their
name be blotted out.

14 Let the wickedness of his fathers be
remembered by the LORD;
And do not let the sin of his mother be
blotted out.
15 Let them be before the LORD
continually,
That He may cut off their memory from
the earth;
16 Because the man did not remember to
show kindness,
But persecuted the suffering and needy
man,
And the brokenhearted, to put them to
death.
17 He also loved cursing, and it came [back]
to him;
He did not delight in blessing, so it was
far from him.
18 He clothed himself with cursing as with
his garment,
And it seeped into his inner self like
water

POWERPOINT

If you have a wounded heart (see Ps. 109:22), you can receive God's healing and move forward with your life. I have found that when I have a relationship problem, or get wounded, or when someone hurts my feelings, these circumstances will take away my strength and affect my faith unless I am quick to forgive. Ask God to help you forgive and heal you everywhere you hurt.

And like [anointing] oil into his bones.
19 Let it be to him as a robe with which he covers himself,

And as a sash with which he is constantly bound.
20 Let this be the reward of my attackers from the LORD,

And of those who speak evil against my life.

21 But You, O GOD, the Lord, show *kindness* to me, for Your name's sake;
Because Your lovingkindness (faithfulness, compassion) is good, O rescue me;
22 For I am suffering and needy,
And my heart is wounded within me.
23 I am vanishing like a shadow when it lengthens *and* fades;
I am shaken off like the locust.
24 My knees are unsteady from fasting;
And my flesh is gaunt and without fatness.
25 I also have become a reproach *and* an object of taunting to others;
When they see me, they shake their heads [in derision]. [Matt 26:39]

26 Help me, O LORD my God;
Save me according to Your lovingkindness—
27 And let them know that this is Your hand;
You, LORD, have done it.
28 Let them curse, but You bless.

When adversaries arise, let them be ashamed,
But let Your servant rejoice.
29 Let my attackers be clothed with dishonor,
And let them cover themselves with their own shame as with a robe.

30 I will give great praise *and* thanks to the LORD with my mouth;
And in the midst of many I will praise Him.
31 For He will stand at the right hand of the needy,
To save him from those who judge his soul.

Psalm 110

The LORD Gives Dominion to the King.

A Psalm of David.

1 THE LORD (Father) says to my Lord (the Messiah, His Son),
"Sit at My right hand
Until I make Your enemies a footstool for Your feet [subjugating them into complete submission]." [Josh 10:24; Matt 26:64; Acts 2:34; 1 Cor 15:25; Col 3:1; Heb 12:2]
2 The LORD will send the scepter of Your strength from Zion, *saying,*
"Rule in the midst of Your enemies." [Rom 11:26, 27]
3 Your people will offer themselves willingly [to participate in Your battle] in the day of Your power;
In the splendor of holiness, from the womb of the dawn,
Your young men are to You as the dew.

4 The LORD has sworn [an oath] and will not change His mind:
"You are a priest forever
According to the order of Melchizedek." [Heb 5:10; 7:11, 15, 21]
5 The LORD is at Your right hand,
He will crush kings in the day of His wrath.
6 He will execute judgment [in overwhelming punishment] among the nations;
He will fill them with corpses,

He will crush the chief men over a broad country. [Ezek 38:21, 22; 39:11, 12]
[7] He will drink from the brook by the wayside;
Therefore He will lift up His head [triumphantly].

Psalm 111

The LORD Praised for His Goodness.

[1] PRAISE THE LORD! (Hallelujah!)
I will give thanks to the LORD with all my heart,
In the company of the upright and in the congregation.
[2] Great are the works of the LORD,
Studied by all those who delight in them.
[3] Splendid and majestic is His work,
And His righteousness endures forever.
[4] He has made His wonderful acts to be remembered;
The LORD is gracious and merciful *and* full of loving compassion.
[5] He has given food to those who fear Him [with awe-inspired reverence];
He will remember His covenant forever. [Deut 10:12; Ps 96:9]
[6] He has declared *and* made known to His people the power of His works,
In giving them the heritage of the nations.
[7] The works of His hands are truth and [absolute] justice;
All His precepts are sure (established, reliable, trustworthy).
[8] They are upheld forever and ever;
They are done in [absolute] truth and uprightness.
[9] He has sent redemption to His people;
He has ordained His covenant forever;
Holy and awesome is His name—
[inspiring reverence and godly fear].

Speak God's Word

I know that the reverent fear of the Lord is the beginning of wisdom. I possess a good understanding and a teachable heart as I do God's will.

| *adapted from* PSALM 111:10 |

[10] The [reverent] fear of the LORD is the beginning (the prerequisite, the absolute essential, the alphabet) of wisdom;
A good understanding *and* a teachable heart are possessed by all those who do *the will of the LORD*;
His praise endures forever. [Job 28:28; Prov 1:7; Matt 22:37, 38; Rev 14:7]

Psalm 112

Prosperity of the One Who Fears the LORD.

[1] PRAISE THE LORD! (Hallelujah!)
Blessed [fortunate, prosperous, and favored by God] is the man who fears the LORD [with awe-inspired reverence and worships Him with obedience],
Who delights greatly in His commandments. [Deut 10:12]
[2] His descendants will be mighty on earth;
The generation of the upright will be blessed.
[3] Wealth and riches are in his house,
And his righteousness endures forever.
[4] Light arises in the darkness for the upright;
He is gracious and compassionate and righteous (upright—in right standing with God).
[5] It is well with the man who is gracious and lends;
He conducts his affairs with justice. [Ps 37:26; Luke 6:35; Col 4:5]
[6] He will never be shaken;
The righteous will be remembered forever. [Prov 10:7]
[7] He will not fear bad news;
His heart is steadfast, trusting [confidently relying on and believing] in the LORD.
[8] His heart is upheld, he will not fear
While he looks [with satisfaction] on his adversaries.
[9] He has given freely to the poor;
His righteousness endures forever;
His horn will be exalted in honor. [2 Cor 9:9]
[10] The wicked will see it and be angered,

KEYS *to a* Victorious Life *Trusting God with Our Minds*

Many times we say that we are trusting God, but our minds are busy worrying. Proverbs 3:5 confirms that we are to trust the Lord not only with our hearts, but also with our minds.

What do you allow your mind to do when you have problems? Do you worry and try to figure things out, or do you leave them in God's capable hands? If you operate with the mind of the Spirit, trusting God instead of worrying, you can have "the peace of God which transcends all understanding" (Phil. 4:7); you can have inexpressible and glorious joy (see 1 Pet. 1:8) right in the middle of terrible trials and tribulations; you "will not fear bad news," because your "heart is steadfast, trusting [confidently relying on and believing] in the LORD" (Ps. 112:7). Trusting God instead of worrying releases joy in us and provides answers to our problems.

He will gnash his teeth and melt away
[in despair and death];
The desire of the wicked will perish *and*
come to nothing.

Psalm 113

The LORD Exalts the Humble.

1 PRAISE THE LORD! (Hallelujah!)
Praise, O servants of the LORD,
Praise the name of the LORD.
2 Blessed be the name of the LORD
From this time forth and forever.
3 From the rising of the sun to its setting
The name of the LORD is to be praised
[with awe-inspired reverence].
4 The LORD is high above all nations,
And His glory above the heavens.

5 Who is like the LORD our God,
Who is enthroned on high,

A Prayer To Renew Your Mind

Thank You, Lord, that You raise the poor out of the dust and lift the needy from the ash heap.

· *adapted from Psalm 113:7*

6 Who humbles Himself to regard
The heavens and the earth? [Ps 138:6; Is
57:15]
7 He raises the poor out of the dust
And lifts the needy from the ash heap,
8 That He may seat them with princes,
With the princes of His people.
9 He makes the barren woman live in the
house
As a joyful mother of children.
Praise the LORD! (Hallelujah!)

Psalm 114

God's Rescue of Israel from Egypt.

1 WHEN ISRAEL came out of Egypt,
The house of Jacob from a people of
strange language,
2 Judah became His sanctuary,
And Israel His dominion. [Ex 29:45, 46;
Deut 27:9]

3 The [Red] Sea looked and fled;
The Jordan turned back. [Ex 14:21; Josh
3:13, 16; Ps 77:16]
4 The mountains leaped like rams,
The [little] hills, like lambs.
5 What ails you, O sea, that you flee?
O Jordan, that you turn back?

⁶O mountains, that you leap like rams,
O [little] hills, like lambs?

⁷Tremble, O earth, at the presence of the Lord,
At the presence of the God of Jacob (Israel),

⁸Who turned the rock into a pool of water,
The flint into a fountain of water. [Ex 17:6; Num 20:11]

Psalm 115

Pagan Idols Contrasted with the Lord.

¹NOT TO us, O Lord, not to us,
But to Your name give glory
Because of Your lovingkindness, because of Your truth *and* faithfulness.

²Why should the nations say,
"Where, now, is their God?"

³But our God is in heaven;
He does whatever He pleases.

⁴The idols [of the nations] are silver and gold,
The work of man's hands.

⁵They have mouths, but they cannot speak;
They have eyes, but they cannot see;

⁶They have ears, but they cannot hear;

They have noses, but they cannot smell;

⁷They have hands, but they cannot feel;
They have feet, but they cannot walk;
Nor can they make a sound with their throats.

⁸Those who make them will become like them,
Everyone who trusts in them. [Ps 135:15–18]

⁹O Israel, trust *and* take refuge in the Lord! [Be confident in Him, cling to Him, rely on His word!]
He is their help and their shield.

¹⁰O house of Aaron, trust in the Lord;
He is their help and their shield.

¹¹You who [reverently] fear the Lord, trust in Lord;
He is their help and their shield.

¹²The Lord has been mindful of us; He will bless,
He will bless the house of Israel;
He will bless the house of Aaron.

¹³He will bless those who fear *and* worship the Lord [with awe-inspired reverence and submissive wonder],
Both the small and the great. [Ps 103:11; Rev 11:18; 19:5]

¹⁴May the Lord give you [great] increase,
You and your children.

¹⁵May you be blessed of the Lord,
Who made heaven and earth.

¹⁶The heavens are the heavens of the Lord,
But the earth He has given to the children of men.

¹⁷The dead do not praise the Lord,
Nor do any who go down into silence;

¹⁸But as for us, we will bless *and* affectionately and gratefully praise the Lord
From this time forth and forever.
Praise the Lord! (Hallelujah!)

POWERPOINT

God gives us understanding on many issues, but we do not have to understand everything in order to walk with the Lord and be obedient to His will. There are times when God leaves huge question marks as tools to stretch our faith because He sees things from a heavenly perspective and does what He pleases (see Ps. 115:3).

Unanswered questions crucify the fleshly life. It is difficult for us to give up reasoning and simply trust God, but once the process is accomplished, the mind enters into a place of rest.

Psalm 116

Thanksgiving for Rescue from Death.

¹I LOVE the Lord, because He hears [and continues to hear]
My voice and my supplications (my pleas, my cries, my specific needs).

²Because He has inclined His ear to me,

KEYS *to a* Victorious Life *Thanksgiving Destroys Discontent*

When the apostle Paul said he had learned to be content, he was saying he still trusted God even if he did not particularly like the situation in which he found himself (see Phil. 4:12). Therefore, his trust kept him in perfect peace. When our minds are fixed on the Lord, we are content and peaceful.

Trusting God and refusing to complain in hard times greatly honors Him. There is no value in saying how much we trust God when all is well if, when the test comes, we can't say and sincerely mean, "I trust You, Lord." The psalmist said, "I believed [and clung to my God] when I said, 'I am greatly afflicted'" (Ps. 116:10). Through gratitude and thanksgiving, you can close the destructive doors of discontentment. Don't wait until everything is perfect before you decide to enjoy your everyday life.

Therefore I will call on Him as long as I live.
3 The cords *and* sorrows of death encompassed me,
And the terrors of Sheol came upon me;
I found distress and sorrow.
4 Then I called on the name of the LORD:
"O LORD, please save my life!"

5 Gracious is the LORD, and [consistently] righteous;
Yes, our God is compassionate.
6 The LORD protects the simple (childlike);
I was brought low [humbled and discouraged], and He saved me.
7 Return to your rest, O my soul,
For the LORD has dealt bountifully with you. [Matt 11:29]
8 For You have rescued my life from death,
My eyes from tears,
And my feet from stumbling *and* falling.
9 I will walk [in submissive wonder] before the LORD
In the land of the living.
10 I believed [and clung to my God] when I said,
"I am greatly afflicted." [2 Cor 4:13]
11 I said in my alarm,
"All men are liars."

12 What will I give to the LORD [in return]
For all His benefits toward me?

[How can I repay Him for His precious blessings?]
13 I will lift up the cup of salvation
And call on the name of the LORD.
14 I will pay my vows to the LORD,
Yes, in the presence of all His people.
15 Precious [and of great consequence] in the sight of the LORD
Is the death of His godly ones [so He watches over them].
16 O LORD, truly I am Your servant;
I am Your servant, the son of Your handmaid;
You have unfastened my chains.
17 I will offer to You the sacrifice of thanksgiving,
And will call on the name of the LORD.
18 I will pay my vows to the LORD,
Yes, in the presence of all His people,
19 In the courts of the LORD's house (temple)—
In the midst of you, O Jerusalem.
Praise the LORD! (Hallelujah!)

Psalm 117

A Psalm of Praise.

1 O PRAISE the LORD, all you nations!
Praise Him, all you people! [Rom 15:11]

A Prayer To Renew Your Mind

Thank You, Lord, that Your lovingkindness prevails over me. I triumph and overcome through You. And Your truth endures forever.

· adapted from Psalm 117:2

²For His lovingkindness prevails over us [and we triumph and overcome through Him],
And the truth of the Lord endures forever.
Praise the Lord! (Hallelujah!)

Psalm 118

Thanksgiving for the Lord's Saving Goodness.

¹O GIVE thanks to the Lord, for He is good;
For His lovingkindness endures forever.
²Oh let Israel say,
"His lovingkindness endures forever."
³Oh let the house of Aaron say,
"His lovingkindness endures forever."
⁴Oh let those who [reverently] fear the Lord, say,
"His lovingkindness endures forever."

⁵Out of my distress I called on the Lord;
The Lord answered me and set me free.
⁶The Lord is on my side; I will not fear.
What can [mere] man do to me? [Heb 13:6]
⁷The Lord is on my side, He is among those who help me;
Therefore I will look [in triumph] on those who hate me.
⁸It is better to take refuge in the Lord Than to trust in man.
⁹It is better to take refuge in the Lord Than to trust in princes.

¹⁰All nations encompassed me;
In the name of the Lord I will surely cut them off.
¹¹They encompassed me, yes, they surrounded me [on every side];
In the name of the Lord I will cut them off.
¹²They swarmed around me like bees;

They flare up *and* are extinguished like a fire of thorns;
In the name of the Lord I will surely cut them off. [Deut 1:44]
¹³You [my enemy] pushed me violently so that I was falling,
But the Lord helped me.
¹⁴The Lord is my strength and song,
And He has become my salvation.

¹⁵The sound of joyful shouting and salvation is in the tents of the righteous:
The right hand of the Lord does valiantly.
¹⁶The right hand of the Lord is exalted;
The right hand of the Lord does valiantly.
¹⁷I will not die, but live,
And declare the works *and* recount the illustrious acts of the Lord.
¹⁸The Lord has disciplined me severely,
But He has not given me over to death. [2 Cor 6:9]

¹⁹Open to me the [temple] gates of righteousness;
I shall enter through them, I shall give thanks to the Lord.
²⁰This is the gate of the Lord;
The righteous will enter through it. [Ps 24:7]
²¹I will give thanks to You, for You have heard *and* answered me;
And You have become my salvation [my Rescuer, my Savior].

²²The stone which the builders rejected Has become the chief corner *stone.*
²³This is from the Lord *and* is His doing;
It is marvelous in our eyes. [Matt 21:42; Acts 4:11; 1 Pet 2:7]
²⁴This [day in which God has saved me] is the day which the Lord has made;
Let us rejoice and be glad in it.
²⁵O Lord, save now, we beseech You;
O Lord, we beseech You, send now prosperity *and* give us success!
²⁶Blessed is the one who comes in the name of the Lord;
We have blessed you from the house of the Lord [you who come into His sanctuary under His guardianship]. [Mark 11:9, 10]

WINNING THE BATTLES *of the* MIND
Rejoice in Today

Winning the battle of the mind involves learning to relax and take things as they come without becoming stressed or fearful. In spite of troubling events taking place around us, we can learn to embrace each day, confessing and believing, "This [day in which God has saved me] is the day which the LORD has made; let us rejoice and be glad in it" (Ps. 118:24).

When the psalmist writes, *"This* is the day which the LORD has made" he is encouraging us to embrace and enjoy the present moment. We often postpone our rejoicing and our being glad until we think certain circumstances are perfect. The fact is, perfection will never happen in this life; we will always be hoping for and praying about something.

If we wait until we think everything in our lives is ideal before we rejoice, we will miss a lot of the joy and blessing that God has for us. We need to learn to enjoy each day and every moment. Even in circumstances that are difficult, when we rejoice and are thankful in "this," whatever "this" situation may be, we will grow in spiritual maturity and be happier, more peaceful people.

People often say, "I will be so happy when…" Almost everyone can fill in the blank after "when." "When I get married," "when I don't have to drive my teenagers everywhere they want to go," "when my bills are paid off," or "when I get a promotion at work." People who are always waiting for *when,* miss so much of *this.*

Those who think they will be glad when God does something specific for them may rejoice when they get what they want; but typically it is not long before they once again cannot be glad until He does something else for them. Then they become anxious about that next thing, and could easily spend their entire lives waiting for another time to be glad, never experiencing the peace that is available to them each day. Psalm 118:24 teaches us that *today* is the day to rejoice and be glad, no matter what is going on or what we hope will happen tomorrow, next week, next month, or next year.

A PRAYER FOR VICTORY

Heavenly Father, help me to be content with who I am and what I have, no matter what my circumstances are right now. I choose to rejoice in this day, and not to miss any of the peace or blessing You have for me today. Amen.

KEYS *to a* Victorious Life *Have an Extraordinary Day*

The psalmist said, "This is the day which the LORD has made; let us rejoice and be glad in it" (Ps. 118:24). I believe he discovered the secret to living ordinary days with extraordinary enthusiasm. He simply decided and declared that since the Lord had made each day, and that it was a gift to him, he would enjoy it and be glad. He made a decision that produced the feelings he wanted rather than waiting to see how he felt.

God's presence makes life exciting if we have a proper understanding of life as a whole. Everything we do is sacred and amazing if we do it as unto the Lord and believe He is with us. Ask yourself right now whether you truly believe that God is with you even in the midst of very ordinary tasks. If your answer is yes, you can have an extraordinary day!

---

27 The LORD is God, and He has given us light [illuminating us with His grace and freedom and joy].
Bind the festival sacrifices with cords to the horns of the altar.
28 You are my God, and I give thanks to You;
[You are] my God, I extol You.
29 O give thanks to the LORD, for He is good;
For His lovingkindness endures forever.

Psalm 119

Meditations and Prayers Relating to the Law of God.

א

Aleph.

1 HOW BLESSED *and* favored by God are those whose way is blameless [those with personal integrity, the upright, the guileless],
Who walk in the law [and who are guided by the precepts and revealed will] of the LORD.
2 Blessed *and* favored by God are those who keep His testimonies,
And who [consistently] seek Him *and* long for Him with all their heart.

3 They do no unrighteousness;
They walk in His ways. [1 John 3:9; 5:18]
4 You have ordained Your precepts,
That we should follow them with [careful] diligence.
5 Oh, that my ways may be established
To observe *and* keep Your statutes [obediently accepting and honoring them]!
6 Then I will not be ashamed
When I look [with respect] to all Your commandments [as my guide].
7 I will give thanks to You with an upright heart,
When I learn [through discipline] Your righteous judgments [for my transgressions].
8 I shall keep Your statutes;
Do not utterly abandon me [when I fail].

Speak God's Word

I consistently seek God and long for Him with all my heart. I do no unrighteousness; I walk in His ways.

| *adapted from* PSALM 119:2–3 |

KEYS *to a* Victorious Life *Choose To Study the Word*

David said, "Blessed and *favored by God are those who keep His testimonies, and who [consistently] seek Him* and *long for Him with all their heart" (Ps. 119:2). In order to know God—what to expect from Him and what He expects from you—you must know His Word. It's not possible for God to say one thing but do another. He cannot lie, and He's always faithful to perform what He has promised.*

I know many people who would like their lives to improve but they won't discipline themselves to study and learn the Word or to speak the Word. Spending time with God by studying the Word is your choice, and only you can make it. When you make that choice to seek Him with your whole heart, it won't take long before your desires will begin to change and God will become more important to you than anything else.

ב
Beth.

9 How can a young man keep his way pure?
　By keeping watch [on himself] according
　　to Your word [conforming his life to
　　Your precepts].
10 With all my heart I have sought You,
　[inquiring of You and longing for You];
　Do not let me wander from
　　Your commandments [neither
　　through ignorance nor by willful
　　disobedience]. [2 Chr 15:15]
11 Your word I have treasured *and* stored
　in my heart,
　That I may not sin against You.
12 Blessed *and* reverently praised are You,
　O LORD;
　Teach me Your statutes.
13 With my lips I have told of
　All the ordinances of Your mouth.
14 I have rejoiced in the way of Your
　testimonies,
　As much as in all riches.
15 I will meditate on Your precepts
　And [thoughtfully] regard Your ways
　　[the path of life established by Your
　　precepts]. [Ps 104:34]
16 I will delight in Your statutes;
　I will not forget Your word.

ג
Gimel.

17 Deal bountifully with Your servant,
　That I may live and keep Your word
　　[treasuring it and being guided by it
　　day by day]. [Ps 119:97–101]
18 Open my eyes [to spiritual truth] so that
　I may behold
　Wonderful things from Your law.
19 I am a stranger on the earth;

POWERPOINT

We cannot tell of God's ordinances
(see Ps. 119:13), or truths, unless we
know them. If we want to be able to
say what God says, we have to know
what He says, and the way to know
that is to study His Word diligently.
In order to know God and what to
expect from Him, we need to know His
Word—because they are one. It is not
possible for God to say one thing
and do another.

WINNING THE BATTLES *of the* MIND
Ask for Understanding

I have heard many people say that reading the Bible is confusing and that they don't understand what God is saying. Sometimes that's because people keep trying to figure it out with their minds. We cannot always rely on our understanding (see Prov. 3:5), and we need to realize we're not smart enough to understand the mind of God. Moses explained to the children of Israel that there are "secret things" known only to God (see Deut. 29:29). He pointed out that when God revealed His will—making things clear—those were the words they should obey.

It really is that simple. Like the psalmist, we can say, "Give me understanding [a teachable heart and the ability to learn], that I may keep Your law; and observe it with all my heart" (Ps. 119:34). We need to ask God to show us what we are to do, and follow Him when He reveals that to us. Before reading or studying God's Word, always ask the Holy Spirit to teach you.

Reasoning can move us in a direction that may not reflect God's will even though it seems logical. This happened to King Saul. It was unlawful for him—even as the king—to offer sacrifices. After Saul and his army waited several days for Samuel, the high priest, to arrive, Saul grew impatient (or perhaps fearful) and offered sacrifices on his own. When Samuel rebuked Saul, the king explained that the imminent threat from the Philistines and the immediate need to ask for the Lord's help "forced" him to act (1 Sam. 13:12). Saul foolishly reasoned that he was wiser than God.

By contrast, the apostle Paul said: "I am telling the truth in Christ, I am not lying, my conscience testifies with me [enlightened and prompted] by the Holy Spirit" (Rom. 9:1). He was doing the right thing—not because he had figured it out or analyzed the situation, but because his actions bore witness in his spirit.

That's the attitude we need. We need to depend on God to show us things in such a way that we know—with an inner certainty—that what has been revealed to our minds is correct. We may be tempted to reason in our minds and search for logical solutions, but discernment and revelation are always better than reasoning.

A PRAYER FOR VICTORY

Dear God, thank You for loving me more than I could ever comprehend. In the name of Jesus Christ, I ask You to help me love and honor You so much that when You speak, I will have only one thought in my mind, and that is to obey. Amen.

Do not hide Your commandments from me. [Gen 47:9; 1 Chr 29:15; Ps 39:12; 2 Cor 5:6; Heb 11:13]

20 My soul is crushed with longing
For Your ordinances at all times.

21 You rebuke the presumptuous *and* arrogant, the cursed *ones,*
Who wander from Your commandments.

22 Take reproach and contempt away from me,
For I observe Your testimonies.

23 Even though princes sit and talk to one another against me,
Your servant meditates on Your statutes.

24 Your testimonies also are my delight
And my counselors.

ד

Daleth.

25 My earthly life clings to the dust;
Revive *and* refresh me according to Your word. [Ps 143:11]

26 I have told of my ways, and You have answered me;
Teach me Your statutes.

27 Make me understand the way of Your precepts,
So that I will meditate (focus my thoughts) on Your wonderful works. [Ps 145:5, 6]

28 My soul dissolves because of grief;
Renew *and* strengthen me according to [the promises of] Your word.

29 Remove from me the way of falsehood *and* unfaithfulness,
And graciously grant me Your law.

30 I have chosen the faithful way;
I have placed Your ordinances *before me.*

31 I cling tightly to Your testimonies;
O LORD, do not put me to shame!

32 I will run the way of Your commandments [with purpose],
For You will give me a heart that is willing.

ה

He.

33 Teach me, O LORD, the way of Your statutes,
And I will [steadfastly] observe it to the end.

34 Give me understanding [a teachable heart and the ability to learn], that I may keep Your law;
And observe it with all my heart. [Prov 2:6; James 1:5]

35 Make me walk in the path of Your commandments,
For I delight in it.

36 Incline my heart to Your testimonies
And not to *dishonest* gain *and* envy. [Ezek 33:31; Mark 7:21, 22; 1 Tim 6:10; Heb 13:5]

37 Turn my eyes away from vanity [all those worldly, meaningless things that distract—let Your priorities be mine],
And restore me [with renewed energy] in Your ways.

38 Establish Your word *and* confirm Your promise to Your servant,
As that which produces [awe-inspired] reverence for You. [Deut 10:12; Ps 96:9]

39 Turn away my reproach which I dread,
For Your ordinances are good.

40 I long for Your precepts;
Renew me through Your righteousness.

ו

Vav.

41 May Your lovingkindness also come to me, O LORD,
Your salvation according to Your promise;

42 So I will have an answer for the one who taunts me,
For I trust [completely] in Your word [and its reliability].

43 And do not take the word of truth utterly out of my mouth,
For I wait for Your ordinances.

44 I will keep Your law continually,
Forever and ever [writing Your precepts on my heart].

45 And I will walk at liberty,
For I seek *and* deeply long for Your precepts.

46 I will also speak of Your testimonies before kings
And shall not be ashamed. [Ps 138:1; Matt 10:18, 19; Acts 26:1, 2]

47 For I shall delight in Your commandments,
Which I love.

A Prayer To
Renew Your Mind

This is my comfort in my affliction, Lord,
that Your word has revived me and
given me life.

· *adapted from Psalm 119:50*

48 And I shall lift up my hands to Your
    commandments,
  Which I love;
  And I will meditate on Your statutes.

ז

Zayin.

49 Remember [always] the word *and*
    promise to Your servant,
  In which You have made me hope.
50 This is my comfort in my affliction,
  That Your word has revived me *and*
    given me life. [Rom 15:4]
51 The arrogant utterly ridicule me,
  Yet I do not turn away from Your law.
52 I have remembered [carefully] Your
    ancient ordinances, O LORD,
  And I have taken comfort.
53 Burning indignation has seized me
    because of the wicked,
  Who reject Your law.
54 Your statutes are my songs
  In the house of my pilgrimage.
55 O LORD, I remember Your name in the
    night,
  And keep Your law.
56 This has become mine [as the gift of
    Your grace],
  That I observe Your precepts [accepting
    them with loving obedience].

ח

Heth.

57 The LORD is my portion;
  I have promised to keep Your words.
58 I sought Your favor with all my heart;
  Be merciful *and* gracious to me
    according to Your promise.
59 I considered my ways
  And turned my feet to [follow and obey]
    Your testimonies.
60 I hurried and did not delay
  To keep Your commandments.
61 The cords of the wicked have encircled
    and ensnared me,

  But I have not forgotten Your law.
62 At midnight I will rise to give thanks to
    You
  Because of Your righteous ordinances.
63 I am a companion of all who [reverently]
    fear You,
  And of those who keep *and* honor Your
    precepts.
64 The earth, O LORD, is full of Your
    lovingkindness *and* goodness;
  Teach me Your statutes.

ט

Teth.

65 You have dealt well with Your servant,
  O LORD, according to Your promise.
66 Teach me good judgment (discernment)
    and knowledge,
  For I have believed *and* trusted *and*
    relied on Your commandments.
67 Before I was afflicted I went astray,
  But now I keep *and* honor Your word
    [with loving obedience].
68 You are good and do good;
  Teach me Your statutes.
69 The arrogant have forged a lie against
    me,
  But I will keep Your precepts with all my
    heart.
70 Their heart is insensitive like fat [their
    minds are dull and brutal],
  But I delight in Your law.
71 It is good for me that I have been
    afflicted,
  That I may learn Your statutes.
72 The law from Your mouth is better to
    me
  Than thousands of gold and silver
    pieces.

י

Yodh.

73 Your hands have made me and
    established me;

A Prayer To
Renew Your Mind

Lord, teach me good judgment,
discernment, and knowledge, for I have
believed and trusted and relied on Your
commandments.

· *adapted from Psalm 119:66*

Give me understanding *and* a teachable heart, that I may learn Your commandments.

74 May those who [reverently] fear You see me and be glad,

Because I wait for Your word.

75 I know, O LORD, that Your judgments are fair,

And that in faithfulness You have disciplined me. [Heb 12:10]

76 O may Your lovingkindness *and* graciousness comfort me,

According to Your word (promise) to Your servant.

77 Let Your compassion come to me that I may live,

For Your law is my delight.

78 Let the arrogant be ashamed *and* humiliated, for they sabotage me with a lie;

But I will meditate on Your precepts.

79 May those who fear You [with submissive wonder] turn to me,

Even those who have known Your testimonies.

80 May my heart be blameless in Your statutes,

So that I will not be ashamed.

‫כ‬

Kaph.

81 My soul languishes *and* grows weak for Your salvation;

I wait for Your word.

82 My eyes fail [with longing, watching] for [the fulfillment of] Your promise,

Saying, "When will You comfort me?"

83 For I have become like a wineskin [blackened and shriveled] in the smoke [in which it hangs],

Yet I do not forget Your statutes.

84 How many are the days of Your servant [which he must endure]?

When will You execute judgment on those who persecute me? [Rev 6:10]

85 The arrogant (godless) have dug pits for me,

Men who do not conform to Your law.

86 All Your commandments are faithful *and* trustworthy.

They have persecuted me with a lie; help me [LORD]!

87 They had almost destroyed me on earth,

But as for me, I did not turn away from Your precepts.

88 According to Your steadfast love refresh me *and* give me life,

So that I may keep *and* obey the testimony of Your mouth.

‫ל‬

Lamedh.

89 Forever, O LORD,

Your word is settled in heaven [standing firm and unchangeable]. [Ps 89:2; Matt 24:34, 35; 1 Pet 1:25]

90 Your faithfulness *continues* from generation to generation;

You have established the earth, and it stands [securely].

91 They continue this day according to Your ordinances,

For all things [all parts of the universe] are Your servants. [Jer 33:25]

92 If Your law had not been my delight,

Then I would have perished in my time of trouble.

93 I will never forget Your precepts,

For by them You have revived me *and* given me life.

94 I am Yours, save me [as Your own];

For I have [diligently] sought Your precepts *and* required them [as my greatest need]. [Ps 42:1]

95 The wicked wait for me to destroy me,

But I will consider Your testimonies.

96 I have seen that all [human] perfection has its limits [no matter how grand and perfect and noble];

Your commandment is exceedingly broad *and* extends without limits [into eternity]. [Rom 3:10–19]

‫מ‬

Mem.

97 Oh, how I love Your law!

It is my meditation all the day. [Ps 1:2]

98 Your commandments make me wiser than my enemies,

For Your words are always with me.

99 I have better understanding *and* deeper insight than all my teachers [because of Your word],

For Your testimonies are my meditation. [2 Tim 3:15]

WINNING THE BATTLES *of the* MIND
Biblical Meditation

Because of terms such as "transcendental meditation" and "New Age," some Christians avoid any reference to meditation. They're afraid of the occult or pagan worship, while not realizing how often the Bible urges us to meditate on God's Word. In fact, Psalm 119 explains biblical meditation in a number of ways, such as, "Oh, how I love Your law! It is my meditation all the day" (Ps. 119:97).

God's Word teaches us three significant lessons about meditation.

First, the Scriptures refer to more than a quick reading or pausing for a few brief, reflecting thoughts. The Bible presents meditation as serious pondering done by serious, committed followers. It is a call to deep, serious concentration.

Second, the biblical contexts show meditation as ongoing and habitual. "It is my meditation all the day." Both Joshua 1:8 and Psalm 1:2 say that the godly person meditates on God's law day and night. The people who spoke of meditating did so seriously and gave their minds fully to it.

Third, meditation is not a religious ritual. In most of the biblical passages where the term occurs, the writer goes on to point out the results. In Joshua 1:8: "for then you will make your way prosperous, and then you will be successful." And Psalm 1:3 says, "And in whatever he does, he prospers [and comes to maturity]."

We don't talk or teach much about meditation today. It's hard work! It demands time and undivided attention. It requires that we cut all the noise out of our lives for a season and give ourselves to deeper study of God's Word.

If you want to win the battle for the mind, meditation is a powerful weapon for you to use. The Word of God is a treasure chest of powerful, life-giving secrets that God wants to reveal to us. These truths are manifested to those who meditate on, ponder, study, think about, practice mentally, and speak the Word of God. Some people repeat a verse again and again until the meaning fills their mind. There is value in repetition!

You'll be amazed at how much power is released into your life from this practice. The more you meditate on God's Word (think about it over and over), the more you will be able to draw readily upon its strength in times of trouble.

As we spend time in God's presence and ponder His Word, we grow, we encourage others, and we win the battle against the enemy of our mind.

A PRAYER FOR VICTORY

Holy Spirit of God, help me to spend time every day meditating on the treasures of Your Word. I thank You for showing me that as I fill my mind with pure and holy thoughts, I will become a stronger and better disciple. Amen.

Speak God's Word

*God's Word is a lamp to my feet
and a light to my path.*

[*adapted from* PSALM 119:105]

100 I understand more than the aged [who
have not observed Your precepts],
Because I have observed *and* kept Your
precepts.
101 I have restrained my feet from every
evil way,
That I may keep Your word. [Prov 1:15]
102 I have not turned aside from Your
ordinances,
For You Yourself have taught me.
103 How sweet are Your words to my
taste,
Sweeter than honey to my mouth! [Ps
19:10; Prov 8:11]
104 From Your precepts I get
understanding;
Therefore I hate every false way.

נ

Nun.

105 Your word is a lamp to my feet
And a light to my path. [Prov 6:23]
106 I have sworn [an oath] and have
confirmed it,
That I will keep Your righteous
ordinances. [Neh 10:29]
107 I am greatly afflicted;
Renew *and* revive me [giving me life],
O LORD, according to Your word.
108 Accept *and* take pleasure in the
freewill offerings of my mouth,
O LORD,
And teach me Your ordinances. [Hos
14:2; Heb 13:15]
109 My life is continually in my hand,
Yet I do not forget Your law.
110 The wicked have laid a snare for me,
Yet I do not wander from Your precepts.
111 I have taken Your testimonies as a
heritage forever,
For they are the joy of my heart. [Deut
33:4]
112 I have inclined my heart to perform
Your statutes
Forever, even to the end.

ס

Samekh.

113 I hate those who are double-minded,
But I love *and* treasure Your law.
114 You are my hiding place and my
shield;
I wait for Your word. [Ps 32:7; 91:1]
115 Leave me, you evildoers,
That I may keep the commandments
of my God [honoring and obeying
them]. [Ps 6:8; 139:19; Matt 7:23]
116 Uphold me according to Your word [of
promise], so that I may live;
And do not let me be ashamed of my
hope [in Your great goodness]. [Ps
25:2; Rom 5:5; 9:33; 10:11]
117 Uphold me that I may be safe,
That I may have regard for Your
statutes continually.
118 You have turned Your back on all those
who wander from Your statutes,
For their deceitfulness is useless.
119 You have removed all the wicked of
the earth like dross [for they have no
value];
Therefore I love Your testimonies.
120 My flesh trembles in [reverent] fear of
You,
And I am afraid *and* in awe of Your
judgments.

ע

Ayin.

121 I have done justice and righteousness;
Do not leave me to those who
oppress me.
122 Be the guarantee for Your servant for
good [as Judah was the guarantee for
Benjamin];
Do not let the arrogant oppress me.
[Gen 43:9]
123 My eyes fail [with longing, watching]
for [the fulfillment of] Your
salvation,
And for [the fulfillment of] Your
righteous word.
124 Deal with Your servant according to
Your [gracious] lovingkindness,
And teach me Your statutes.
125 I am Your servant; give me
understanding [the ability to learn
and a teachable heart]
That I may know Your testimonies.

KEYS *to a* **Victorious Life** *The Treasures of God's Word*

God's Word has tremendous treasures, powerful life-giving secrets that God wants to reveal to us. They are manifested to those who ponder, study, think about, practice mentally, and meditate on the Word.

Psalm 119:130 says that the unfolding of God's Words to us gives us light and that "their unfolding gives understanding to the simple (childlike)." There is no end to what God can show you out of even one verse of Scripture. You can study a scripture one time and get one thing, and in studying that same verse another time you'll see something else you did not even notice before.

The Lord keeps revealing His secrets to those who are diligent about studying the Word. Don't be the person who always settles for living off someone else's revelation. Study the Word for yourself, and allow the Holy Spirit to bless your life with truth.

---

126 It is time for the LORD to act;
They have broken Your law.
127 Therefore I love Your commandments more than gold,
Yes, more than refined gold.
128 Therefore I esteem as right all Your precepts concerning everything;
I hate every false way.

ב

Pe.

129 Your testimonies are wonderful;
Therefore my soul keeps them.
130 The unfolding of Your [glorious] words give light;
Their unfolding gives understanding to the simple (childlike).
131 I opened my mouth and panted [with anticipation],
Because I longed for Your commandments.
132 Turn to me and be gracious to me *and* show me favor,
As is Your way to those who love Your name.
133 Establish my footsteps in [the way of] Your word;

Do not let any human weakness have power over me [causing me to be separated from You].
134 Redeem me from the oppression of man;
That I may keep Your precepts. [Luke 1:74]
135 Make Your face shine [with pleasure] upon Your servant,
And teach me Your statutes. [Ps 4:6]
136 My eyes weep streams of water
Because people do not keep Your law.

צ

Tsadhe.

137 Righteous are You, O LORD,
And upright are Your judgments.
138 You have commanded Your testimonies in righteousness
And in great faithfulness.
139 My zeal has [completely] consumed me,
Because my enemies have forgotten Your words.
140 Your word is very pure (refined);
Therefore Your servant loves it.
141 I am small and despised,
But I do not forget Your precepts.

142 Your righteousness is an everlasting righteousness,
And Your law is truth. [Ps 19:9; John 17:17]

143 Trouble and anguish have found me,
Yet Your commandments are my delight *and* my joy.

144 Your righteous testimonies are everlasting;
Give me understanding [the ability to learn and a teachable heart] that I may live.

ק
Qoph.

145 I cried with all my heart; answer me, O Lord!
I will observe Your statutes.

146 I cried to You; save me
And I will keep Your testimonies.

147 I rise before dawn and cry [in prayer] for help;
I wait for Your word.

148 My eyes anticipate the night watches *and* I awake before the call of the watchman,
That I may meditate on Your word.

149 Hear my voice according to Your [steadfast] lovingkindness;
O Lord, renew *and* refresh me according to Your ordinances.

150 Those who follow after wickedness approach;
They are far from Your law.

151 You are near, O Lord,
And all Your commandments are truth.

152 Of old I have known from Your testimonies
That You have founded them forever. [Luke 21:33]

ר
Resh.

153 Look upon my agony and rescue me,
For I do not forget Your law.

154 Plead my cause and redeem me;
Revive me *and* give me life according to [the promise of] Your word.

155 Salvation is far from the wicked,
For they do not seek Your statutes.

156 Great are Your tender mercies *and* steadfast love, O Lord;
Revive me *and* give me life according to Your ordinances.

157 Many are my persecutors and my adversaries,
Yet I do not turn away from Your testimonies.

158 I see the treacherous and loathe them,
Because they do not respect Your law.

159 Consider how I love Your precepts;

KEYS *to a* Victorious Life *Devote Your Thoughts to God's Word*

Reading or hearing the Word is good, but when we also devote our thoughts to it, we begin to understand it more deeply. The Word of God is filled with power, and it has the ability to change us. Just as good, nutritious food must be chewed well and swallowed for us to benefit from it, so the Word of God must be taken in and digested to become a part of us.

The psalmist said, "I rise before dawn and cry [in prayer] for help; I wait for Your word . . . . that I may meditate on Your word" (Ps. 119:147–148). Let me encourage you to make a habit of choosing a Bible verse and meditating on it all throughout the day. That way it will become rooted in your heart and become more meaningful to you. Soon, you'll realize that it's changing your life.

Revive me *and* give me life, O Lord,
according to Your lovingkindness.
160 The sum of Your word is truth [the full
meaning of all Your precepts],
And every one of Your righteous
ordinances endures forever.

שׁ

Shin.

161 Princes persecute me without cause,
But my heart stands in [reverent] awe
of Your words [so I can expect You to
help me]. [1 Sam 24:11, 14; 26:18]
162 I rejoice at Your word,
As one who finds great treasure.
163 I hate and detest falsehood,
But I love Your law.
164 Seven times a day I praise You,
Because of Your righteous ordinances.
165 Those who love Your law have great
peace;
Nothing makes them stumble. [Prov
3:2; Is 32:17]
166 I hope *and* wait [with complete
confidence] for Your salvation,
O Lord,
And I do Your commandments. [Gen
49:18]
167 My soul keeps Your testimonies
[hearing and accepting and obeying
them];
I love them greatly.
168 I keep Your precepts and Your
testimonies,
For all my ways are [fully known]
before You.

ת

Tav.

169 Let my [mournful] cry come before
You, O Lord;
Give me understanding [the ability
to learn and a teachable heart]
according to Your word [of promise].
170 Let my supplication come before You;
Deliver me according to Your word.
171 Let my lips speak praise [with
thanksgiving],
For You teach me Your statutes.
172 Let my tongue sing [praise for the
fulfillment] of Your word,
For all Your commandments are
righteous.

173 Let Your hand be ready to help me,
For I have chosen Your precepts.
174 I long for Your salvation, O Lord,
And Your law is my delight.
175 Let my soul live that it may praise You,
And let Your ordinances help me.
176 I have gone astray like a lost sheep;
Seek Your servant, for I do not forget
Your commandments. [Is 53:6; Luke
15:4; 1 Pet 2:25]

Psalm 120

Prayer for Breaking Away from
the Treacherous.

A Song of Ascents.

1 IN MY trouble I cried to the Lord,
And He answered me.
2 Rescue my soul, O Lord, from lying
lips,
And from a deceitful tongue.
3 What shall be given to you, and what
more shall be done to you,
You deceitful tongue?—
4 Sharp arrows of the warrior,
With the burning coals of the broom
tree.

5 Woe to me, for I sojourn in Meshech,
and I live among the tents of Kedar
[among hostile people]! [Gen 10:2;
25:13; Jer 49:28, 29]

POWERPOINT

While seeking advice or counsel
from wise people is certainly not
wrong, we should be mature enough
in our faith that we don't run to
somebody else every time we need to
know what to do in a certain situation.
Discipline yourself to go to God first,
and let Him choose whether He wants
to speak to you Himself or use the
wisdom and advice of others to clarify
things to you. Our only true help comes
from the Lord (see Ps. 121:2).

6 Too long my soul has had its dwelling
   With those who hate peace.
7 I am for peace, but when I speak,
   They are for war.

Psalm 121

The Lord the Keeper of Israel.

A Song of Ascents.

1 I WILL lift up my eyes to the hills [of
   Jerusalem]—
   From where shall my help come? [Jer
   3:23]
2 My help comes from the Lord,
   Who made heaven and earth.
3 He will not allow your foot to slip;
   He who keeps you will not slumber.
      [1 Sam 2:9; Ps 127:1; Prov 3:23, 26; Is
      27:3]
4 Behold, He who keeps Israel
   Will neither slumber [briefly] nor sleep
   [soundly].

5 The Lord is your keeper;
   The Lord is your shade on your right
   hand. [Is 25:4]
6 The sun will not strike you by day,
   Nor the moon by night. [Ps 91:5; Is 49:10;
   Rev 7:16]

7 The Lord will protect you from all evil;
   He will keep your life.
8 The Lord will guard your going out and
   your coming in [everything that you
   do]
   From this time forth and forever. [Deut
   28:6; Prov 2:8; 3:6]

Psalm 122

Prayer for the Peace of Jerusalem.

A Song of Ascents. Of David.

1 I WAS glad when they said to me,
   "Let us go to the house of the Lord." [Is
   2:3; Zech 8:21]
2 Our feet are standing
   Within your gates, O Jerusalem,
3 Jerusalem, that is built
   As a city that is firmly joined together;
4 To which the [twelve] tribes go up, even
   the tribes of the Lord,
   [As was decreed as] an ordinance for
   Israel,
   To give thanks to the name of the
   Lord.
5 For there the thrones of judgment were
   set,
   The thrones of the house of David.

KEYS *to a*
Victorious
   Life *Confess God's Promises*
                        Instead of Past Pain

One of the ways God has taught me to deal with the past is to confess His promises instead of talking about how I feel. We all grapple with certain painful issues from our past. Perhaps you were teased mercilessly as a child and still feel insecure or sensitive because of that old pain. Maybe someone you loved left you without explanation. Maybe someone you trusted betrayed you. Whatever the source of your pain, always remember that God loves you, and you do not have to continue living in the past.

You don't have to spend your life mourning over something you can't do anything about. God wants to heal what was damaged and restore what was lost through every hurt, injustice, and mistake in your life. David said, "Our help is in the name of the Lord, Who made heaven and earth" (Ps. 124:8). God will help you. In fact, He's waiting to help you, so ask for His help today.

KEYS *to a* **Victorious Life** *Expect Good Things To Happen Today*

Live with an attitude of expectancy. The psalmist said, "Those who trust in and rely on the LORD [with confident expectation] are like Mount Zion, which cannot be moved but remains forever" (Ps. 125:1). He was confident in his expectation.

To live expectantly is not the same as living with a sense of entitlement, which is an attitude that says we deserve everything. We don't deserve anything from God, but because of His great love and His mercy toward us, He desires that we live in holy expectancy, believing we will so we can receive His best.

Even if you have had a problem or a need for a long time, that can change if you will do your part. Your part is to believe God's Word, obey Him, sow good seeds, have a vision of breakthrough, and think and say right things in agreement with God's Word—and be persistent. As you continue doing this, you will develop a healthy mind-set that enables you to prosper in all areas.

---

⁶Pray for the peace of Jerusalem:
"May they prosper who love you [holy city].
⁷"May peace be within your walls
And prosperity within your palaces."
⁸For the sake of my brothers and my friends,
I will now say, "May peace be within you."
⁹For the sake of the house of the LORD our God [which is Jerusalem],
I will seek your (the city's) good.

Psalm 123

Prayer for the LORD's Help.

A Song of Ascents.

¹UNTO YOU I lift up my eyes,
O You who are enthroned in the heavens!
²Behold, as the eyes of servants look to the hand of their master,
And as the eyes of a maid to the hand of her mistress,
So our eyes look to the LORD our God,
Until He is gracious *and* favorable toward us.

³Be gracious to us, O LORD, be gracious *and* favorable toward us,
For we are greatly filled with contempt.
⁴Our soul is greatly filled
With the scoffing of those who are at ease,
And with the contempt of the proud [who disregard God's law].

Psalm 124

Praise for Rescue from Enemies.

A Song of Ascents. Of David.

¹"IF IT had not been the LORD who was on our side,"
Let Israel now say,
²"If it had not been the LORD who was on our side
When men rose up against us,
³Then they would have [quickly] swallowed us alive,
When their wrath was kindled against us;
⁴Then the waters would have engulfed us,
The torrent would have swept over our soul;
⁵Then the raging waters would have swept over our soul."

6 Blessed be the LORD,
 Who has not given us as prey to be torn
  by their teeth.
7 We have escaped like a bird from the
  snare of the fowlers;
 The trap is broken and we have escaped.
8 Our help is in the name of the LORD,
 Who made heaven and earth.

Psalm 125

The LORD Surrounds His People.

A Song of Ascents.

1 THOSE WHO trust in *and* rely on the
  LORD [with confident expectation]
 Are like Mount Zion, which cannot be
  moved but remains forever.

2 As the mountains surround Jerusalem,
 So the LORD surrounds His people
  From this time forth and forever.
3 For the scepter of wickedness shall not
  rest on the land of the righteous,
 So that the righteous will not reach out
  their hands to do wrong.

4 Do good, O LORD, to those who are good
 And to those who are upright in their
  hearts.
5 But as for those who turn aside to their
  crooked ways [in unresponsiveness to
  God],
 The LORD will lead them away with
  those who do evil.
 Peace be upon Israel.

KEYS *to a* **Victorious Life** *Let God Build Your Reputation*

Our society places a great deal of emphasis and value on building a good life, including a career and a good reputation. When we try to build our lives and our reputations by ourselves, we are leaning on the arm of flesh (ourselves and other people). We work hard to develop skills, find a career, earn money, build relationships, make a good name for ourselves, and do everything we think will cause us to be successful as the world views success. But Psalm 127:1–2 indicates that all this effort is in vain. The Lord is the One who builds our lives and our reputations, according to the good plans He has for us.

We can be confident that God is working in us, changing us, and helping us grow through our faith in Him, so we can fulfill His good plans for our lives. In Philippians 1:6, Paul writes to assure us of this: "He who has begun a good work in you will [continue to] perfect and complete it until the day of Christ Jesus [the time of His return]." You and I may have confidence that God will complete the good work He has begun in us!

What Paul is saying is simply this: God is the One Who started this good work in you and He is the One Who will finish it! This means we should allow God to do His work without trying to interfere. We should always do the part He gives us to do, but we should never try to do anything without leaning entirely on Him. We need to be patient and rest in Him as He accomplishes what needs to be done instead of getting involved in things when they are not happening as quickly as we would like or in the way we would like. There are certain responsibilities we need to fulfill in our lives, but there are certain things only God can do. Take the pressure off yourself by leaning on the arm of the Lord instead of the arm of the flesh!

Psalm 126

Thanksgiving for Return from Captivity.

A Song of Ascents.

[1] WHEN THE LORD brought back the captives to Zion (Jerusalem),
We were like those who dream [it seemed so unreal]. [Ps 53:6; Acts 12:9]

[2] Then our mouth was filled with laughter
And our tongue with joyful shouting;
Then they said among the nations,
"The LORD has done great things for them."

[3] The LORD has done great things for us;
We are glad!

[4] Restore our captivity, O LORD,
As the stream-beds in the South (the Negev) [are restored by torrents of rain].

[5] They who sow in tears shall reap with joyful singing.

[6] He who goes back and forth weeping, carrying his bag of seed [for planting],
Will indeed come again with a shout of joy, bringing his sheaves with him.

> **!** **REMEMBER**, God always leads you in triumph in Christ!

Psalm 127

Prosperity Comes from the LORD.

A Song of Ascents. Of Solomon.

[1] UNLESS THE LORD builds the house,
They labor in vain who build it;
Unless the LORD guards the city,
The watchman keeps awake in vain. [Ps 121:1, 3, 5]

[2] It is vain for you to rise early,
To retire late,
To eat the bread of anxious labors—
For He gives [blessings] to His beloved
even in his sleep.

[3] Behold, children are a heritage *and* gift from the LORD,
The fruit of the womb a reward. [Deut 28:4]

[4] Like arrows in the hand of a warrior,
So are the children of one's youth.

[5] How blessed [happy and fortunate] is the man whose quiver is filled with them;
They will not be ashamed
When they speak with their enemies [in gatherings] at the [city] gate.

KEYS *to a* Victorious Life *Worry Is a Waste of Time*

Worrying is an absolute waste of time. Every time we get upset, it wastes a lot of emotional energy, tires us out, can harm our health, steals our joy, and still it doesn't change one thing. The Bible says we can't even add an hour to the length of our lives by worrying (see Matt. 6:27). Yet we often worry, worry, worry, which gets us nowhere. Solomon said, "It is vain for you to rise early, to retire late, to eat the bread of anxious labors" (Ps. 127:2). We need to stop trying to fix things only God can fix.

Jesus essentially tells us to calm down (see John 14:27) and cheer up (see John 16:33). I believe these two actions combined serve as a one-two knockout punch to the devil. When you realize you can't fix everything, you calm down; and when you know God can, you cheer up!

Psalm 128

Blessedness of the Fear of the LORD.

A Song of Ascents.

¹ BLESSED [HAPPY and sheltered by God's favor] is everyone who fears the LORD [and worships Him with obedience],

Who walks in His ways *and* lives according to His commandments. [Ps 1:1, 2]

² For you shall eat the fruit of [the labor of] your hands,

You will be happy *and* blessed and it will be well with you.

³ Your wife shall be like a fruitful vine

Within the innermost part of your house;

Your children will be like olive plants

Around your table.

⁴ Behold, for so shall the man be blessed *and* divinely favored

Who fears the LORD [and worships Him with obedience].

⁵ May the LORD bless you from Zion [His holy mountain],

And may you see the prosperity of Jerusalem all the days of your life;

⁶ Indeed, may you see your [family perpetuated in your] children's children.

Peace be upon Israel!

Psalm 129

Prayer for the Overthrow of Zion's Enemies.

A Song of Ascents.

¹ "MANY TIMES they have persecuted me (Israel) from my youth,"

Let Israel now say,

² "Many times they have persecuted me from my youth,

Yet they have not prevailed against me.

³ "The [enemies, like] plowers plowed on my back;

They made their furrows [of suffering] long [in Israel]."

⁴ The LORD is righteous;

He has cut in two the [thick] cords of the wicked [which enslaved the people of Israel].

⁵ May all who hate Zion

Be put to shame and turned backward [in defeat].

KEYS *to a* Victorious Life *Enjoy the Wait*

Patience is extremely important for people who want to glorify God and enjoy their lives (see James 1:4). If people are impatient, the situations they encounter in life will certainly cause them to react emotionally in a wrong way. When pressured by circumstances, we need to tell ourselves, "Wait [patiently] for the LORD, my soul [expectantly] waits" (Ps. 130:5).

The next time you have to wait on something or someone, rather than reacting with impatience, try talking to yourself a little. You might think, Getting upset will not make this go any faster, so I might as well find a way to enjoy the wait. *Then perhaps say out loud, "I am developing patience as I wait, so I am thankful for this situation." When you do this, you are acting on the Word of God rather than reacting with impatience to the unpleasant circumstance.*

KEYS *to a* Victorious Life *Seeking Contentment*

If I am discontent, I easily become upset. But if I choose to be content no matter what is going on, my emotions remain balanced. Our thoughts have a lot to do with our moods. Some thoughts improve our moods and increase our level of contentment, while others send our moods spiraling downward, making us unhappy and discontent. We can think ourselves happy, and we can think ourselves sad! How we talk to ourselves also affects our emotions, so if we talk to ourselves properly, we can stay content and emotionally stable.

Having put his hope in the Lord, David said, "I have calmed and quieted my soul; . . . like a weaned child within me [composed and freed from discontent]" (Ps. 131:2). Trusting God at all times is the pathway to contentment. Even if we don't have all that we want, we can trust God that He will provide what is right for us in His perfect timing.

---

⁶Let them be like the grass on the housetops,

Which withers before it grows up,

⁷With which the reaper does not fill his hand,

Nor the binder of sheaves his arms,

⁸Nor do those who pass by say,

"The blessing of the LORD be upon you;

We bless you in the name of the LORD."

Psalm 130

Hope in the LORD's Forgiving Love.

A Song of Ascents.

¹OUT OF the depths [of distress] I have cried to You, O LORD.

²Lord, hear my voice!

Let Your ears be attentive

To the voice of my supplications.

³If You, LORD, should keep an account of our sins *and* treat us accordingly,

O Lord, who could stand [before you in judgment and claim innocence]? [Ps 143:2; Rom 3:20; Gal 2:16]

⁴But there is forgiveness with You,

That You may be feared *and* worshiped [with submissive wonder]. [Deut 10:12]

⁵I wait [patiently] for the LORD, my soul [expectantly] waits,

And in His word do I hope.

⁶My soul waits for the Lord

More than the watchmen for the morning;

More than the watchmen for the morning.

⁷O Israel, hope in the LORD;

For with the LORD there is lovingkindness,

And with Him is abundant redemption.

⁸And He will redeem Israel

From all his sins.

Psalm 131

Childlike Trust in the LORD.

A Song of Ascents. Of David.

¹LORD, MY heart is not proud, nor my eyes haughty;

Nor do I involve myself in great matters,

Or in things too difficult for me.

²Surely I have calmed and quieted my soul;

Like a weaned child [resting] with his mother,

My soul is like a weaned child within
me [composed and freed from
discontent].
3 O Israel, hope in the LORD
From this time forth and forever.

Psalm 132

Prayer for the LORD's Blessing
Upon the Sanctuary.

A Song of Ascents.

1 O LORD, remember on David's behalf
All his hardship *and* affliction;
2 How he swore to the LORD
And vowed to the Mighty One of Jacob:
3 "I absolutely will not enter my house,
Nor get into my bed—
4 I certainly will not permit my eyes to
sleep
Nor my eyelids to slumber,
5 Until I find a place for the LORD,
A dwelling place for the Mighty One of
Jacob (Israel)." [Acts 7:46]

6 Behold, we heard of it at Ephrathah;
We found it in the field of Jaar. [1 Sam
6:21]
7 Let us go into His tabernacle;
Let us worship at His footstool.
8 Arise, O LORD, to Your resting place,
You and the ark [the symbol] of Your
strength.
9 Let Your priests be clothed with
righteousness (right living),
And let Your godly ones shout for joy.

10 For the sake of Your servant David,
Do not turn away the face of Your
anointed.
11 The LORD swore to David
A truth from which He will not turn
back:
"One of your descendants I will set upon
your throne. [Ps 89:3, 4; Luke 1:69;
Acts 2:30, 31]
12 "If your children will keep My covenant
And My testimony which I will teach
them,
Their children also shall sit upon your
throne forever."

13 For the LORD has chosen Zion;
He has desired it for His dwelling
place:

14 "This is My resting place forever" [says
the LORD];
"Here will I dwell, for I have desired it.
15 "I will abundantly bless her
provisions;
I will satisfy her poor with bread.
16 "Her priests also I will clothe with
salvation,
And her godly ones will shout aloud for
joy.
17 "There I will make the horn (strength) of
David grow;
I have prepared a lamp for My anointed
[fulfilling the promises]. [1 Kin 11:36;
15:4; 2 Chr 21:7; Luke 1:69]
18 "His enemies I will clothe with shame,
But upon himself shall his crown
shine."

Psalm 133

The Excellency of Brotherly Unity.

A Song of Ascents.
Of David.

1 BEHOLD, HOW good and how pleasant
it is
For brothers to dwell together in unity!
2 It is like the precious oil [of
consecration] poured on the head,
Coming down on the beard,
Even the beard of Aaron,
Coming down upon the edge of his
[priestly] robes [consecrating the
whole body]. [Ex 30:25, 30]
3 It is like the dew of [Mount] Hermon
Coming down on the hills of Zion;
For there the LORD has commanded the
blessing: life forevermore.

Psalm 134

Greetings of Night Watchers.

A Song of Ascents.

1 BEHOLD, BLESS *and* praise the LORD,
all servants of the LORD (priests,
Levites),
Who stand *and* serve by night in the
house of the LORD. [1 Chr 9:33]
2 Lift up your hands to the sanctuary
And bless the LORD.
3 May the LORD bless you from Zion,
He who made heaven and earth.

POWERPOINT

Psalm 135:3 is one of many Bible verses that says "the LORD is good." No matter what has happened in our lives, God is good, and we need to believe that. God is good and He does not show partiality. In other words, He is good all the time; goodness is part of His nature. His goodness radiates from Him. Not everything in life is good, but God is always good, and He will turn negative situations into positive ones as we trust Him (see Gen. 50:20).

Psalm 135

Praise the LORD's Wonderful Works. Vanity of Idols.

¹ PRAISE THE LORD! (Hallelujah!)
Praise the name of the LORD;
Praise Him, O servants of the LORD (priests, Levites),
² You who stand in the house of the LORD,
In the courts of the house of our God,
³ Praise the LORD, for the LORD is good;
Sing praises to His name, for it is gracious *and* lovely.
⁴ For the LORD has chosen [the descendants of] Jacob for Himself,
Israel for His own special treasure *and* possession. [Deut 7:6]

⁵ For I know that the LORD is great
And that our Lord is above all gods.
⁶ Whatever the LORD pleases, He does,
In the heavens and on the earth, in the seas and all deeps—
⁷ Who causes the clouds to rise from the ends of the earth;
Who makes lightning for the rain,
Who brings the wind from His storehouses;

⁸ Who struck the firstborn of Egypt,
Both of man and animal; [Ex 12:12, 29; Ps 78:51; 136:10]

⁹ Who sent signs and wonders into your midst, O Egypt,
Upon Pharaoh and all his servants.
¹⁰ Who struck many nations
And killed mighty kings,
¹¹ Sihon, king of the Amorites,
Og, king of Bashan,
And all the kingdoms of Canaan;
¹² And He gave their land as a heritage,
A heritage to Israel His people.
¹³ Your name, O LORD, endures forever,
Your fame *and* remembrance, O LORD,
[endures] throughout all generations.
¹⁴ For the LORD will judge His people
And He will have compassion on His servants [revealing His mercy]. [Heb 10:30]
¹⁵ The idols of the nations are silver and gold,
The work of men's hands.
¹⁶ They have mouths, but they do not speak;
They have eyes, but they do not see;
¹⁷ They have ears, but they do not hear,
Nor is there any breath in their mouths.
¹⁸ Those who make idols are like them [absolutely worthless—spiritually blind, deaf, and powerless];
So is everyone who trusts in *and* relies on them. [Ps 115:4–8]

¹⁹ O house of Israel, bless *and* praise the LORD [with gratitude];
O house of Aaron, bless the LORD;
²⁰ O house of Levi, bless the LORD;

POWERPOINT

Psalm 136 contains twenty-six verses and each of them ends with, "for His lovingkindness endures forever." You and I can never do so much wrong that there isn't any more mercy left for us. Where sin abounds, grace (mercy) abounds much more (Rom. 5:20). God is much more eager to pardon than to punish.

KEYS *to a* Victorious Life *Active Awareness of God's Love*

When I began my ministry, as I was preparing for my first meeting, I asked the Lord what He wanted me to teach, and what came to my heart was, Tell My people I love them. *My response was, "They know that from Sunday school. I want to teach them something really powerful." The Lord reminded me that if people were actively aware of how much He loved them, as the psalmist was in Psalm 136, they would act differently.*

As I began to study the subject of receiving God's love, I realized I was in desperate need of the message myself. I had a subconscious, vague sort of understanding that God loved me, but I needed a deeper revelation of this life-changing truth. The love of God is meant to be a powerful force in our lives, one that will take us through even the most difficult trials without our ever doubting God's love.

You who fear the LORD [and worship Him with obedience], bless the LORD [with grateful praise]! [Deut 6:5; Ps 31:23]
²¹ Blessed be the LORD from Zion, Who dwells [with us] at Jerusalem. Praise the LORD! (Hallelujah!)

Psalm 136

Thanks for the LORD's Goodness to Israel.

¹ GIVE THANKS to the LORD, for He is good;
For His lovingkindness (graciousness, mercy, compassion) endures forever.
² Give thanks to the God of gods,
For His lovingkindness endures forever.
³ Give thanks to the Lord of lords,
For His lovingkindness endures forever.
⁴ To Him who alone does great wonders,
For His lovingkindness endures forever;
⁵ To Him who made the heavens with skill,
For His lovingkindness endures forever;
⁶ To Him who stretched out the earth upon the waters,
For His lovingkindness endures forever;
⁷ To Him who made the great lights,

For His lovingkindness endures forever;
⁸ The sun to rule over the day,
For His lovingkindness endures forever;
⁹ The moon and stars to rule by night,
For His lovingkindness endures forever;
¹⁰ To Him who struck the firstborn of Egypt,
For His lovingkindness endures forever; [Ex 12:29]
¹¹ And brought Israel out from among them,
For His lovingkindness endures forever; [Ex 12:51; 13:3, 17]
¹² With a strong hand and with an outstretched arm,
For His lovingkindness endures forever;
¹³ To Him who divided the Red Sea into parts,
For His lovingkindness endures forever; [Ex 14:21, 22]
¹⁴ And made Israel pass through the midst of it,
For His lovingkindness endures forever;
¹⁵ But tossed Pharaoh and his army into the Red Sea,
For His lovingkindness endures forever;
¹⁶ To Him who led His people through the wilderness,
For His lovingkindness endures forever;

¹⁷ To Him who struck down great kings,
For His lovingkindness endures forever;
¹⁸ And killed mighty kings,
For His lovingkindness endures forever;
[Deut 29:7]
¹⁹ Sihon, king of the Amorites,
For His lovingkindness endures forever;
[Num 21:21–24]
²⁰ And Og, king of Bashan,
For His lovingkindness endures forever;
[Num 21:33–35]
²¹ And gave their land as a heritage,
For His lovingkindness endures forever;
²² Even a heritage to Israel His servant,
For His lovingkindness endures forever;
[Josh 12:1]

23 Who [faithfully] remembered us in our
lowly condition,
For His lovingkindness endures forever;
²⁴ And has rescued us from our enemies,
For His lovingkindness endures forever;
²⁵ Who gives food to all flesh,
For His lovingkindness endures forever;
²⁶ Give thanks to the God of heaven,
For His lovingkindness (graciousness,
mercy, compassion) endures forever.

Psalm 137

An Experience of the Captivity.

¹ BY THE rivers of Babylon,
There we [captives] sat down and
wept,
When we remembered Zion [the city
God imprinted on our hearts].
² On the willow trees in the midst of
Babylon
We hung our harps.
³ For there they who took us captive
demanded of us a song with words,
And our tormentors [who made a
mockery of us demanded] amusement,
saying,
"Sing us one of the songs of Zion."

4 How can we sing the LORD's song
In a strange *and* foreign land?
⁵ If I forget you, O Jerusalem,
Let my right hand forget [her skill with
the harp].
⁶ Let my tongue cling to the roof of my
mouth
If I do not remember you,

If I do not prefer Jerusalem
Above my chief joy. [Ezek 3:26]

⁷ Remember, O LORD, against the sons of
Edom,
The day of [the fall of] Jerusalem,
Who said "Down, down [with her]
To her very foundation."
⁸ O daughter of Babylon, you devastator,
How blessed will be the one
Who repays you [with destruction] as you
have repaid us. [Is 13:1–22; Jer 25:12, 13]
⁹ How blessed will be the one who seizes
and dashes your little ones
Against the rock.

Psalm 138

Thanksgiving for the LORD's Favor.

A Psalm of David.

¹ I WILL give You thanks with all my heart;
I sing praises to You before the [pagan]
gods.
² I will bow down [in worship] toward
Your holy temple
And give thanks to Your name for Your
lovingkindness and Your truth;
For You have magnified Your word
together with Your name.
³ On the day I called, You answered me;
And You made me bold *and* confident
with [renewed] strength in my life.

4 All the kings of the land will give thanks
and praise You, O LORD,
When they have heard of the promises
of Your mouth [which were fulfilled].
⁵ Yes, they will sing of the ways of the
LORD [joyfully celebrating His
wonderful acts],
For great is the glory *and* majesty of the
LORD.
⁶ Though the LORD is exalted,
He regards the lowly [and invites them
into His fellowship];

A Prayer To
Renew Your Mind

*Lord, when I call to You, You answer me.
You make me bold and confident with
renewed strength in my life.*

· *adapted form Psalm 138:3*

But the proud *and* haughty He knows
  from a distance. [Prov 3:34; James 4:6;
  1 Pet 5:5]

7 Though I walk in the midst of trouble,
  You will revive me;
You will stretch out Your hand against
  the wrath of my enemies,
And Your right hand will save me. [Ps
  23:3, 4]
8 The LORD will accomplish that which
  concerns me;
Your [unwavering] lovingkindness,
  O LORD, endures forever—
Do not abandon the works of Your own
  hands. [Ps 57:2; Phil 1:6]

Psalm 139

God's Omnipresence and Omniscience.

To the Chief Musician.
A Psalm of David.

1 O LORD, you have searched me
  [thoroughly] and have known me.
2 You know when I sit down and when I
  rise up [my entire life, everything I do];

You understand my thought from afar.
  [Matt 9:4; John 2:24, 25]
3 You scrutinize my path and my lying
  down,
And You are intimately acquainted with
  all my ways.
4 Even before there is a word on my
  tongue [still unspoken],
Behold, O LORD, You know it all. [Heb
  4:13]
5 You have enclosed me behind and
  before,
And [You have] placed Your hand
  upon me.
6 Such [infinite] knowledge is too
  wonderful for me;
It is too high [above me], I cannot
  reach it.

7 Where can I go from Your Spirit?
  Or where can I flee from Your presence?
8 If I ascend to heaven, You are there;
  If I make my bed in Sheol (the nether
  world, the place of the dead), behold,
  You are there. [Rom 11:33]
9 If I take the wings of the dawn,
  If I dwell in the remotest part of the sea,

KEYS *to a* Victorious Life *A Healthy Relationship with Yourself*

Take comfort in knowing that God knew all about you even before you were born, and He still chose to be in relationship with you (see Ps. 139:13–16; Jer. 1:5). How you think God views you and how you feel about yourself on the inside determines the quality of life you will have. Learn to see yourself as God sees you!

It's important to ask yourself what kind of relationship you have with you. Do you enjoy spending time alone? Are you able to forgive yourself (receive God's forgiveness) when you make mistakes? Are you patient with yourself while God is changing you? Are you able to be yourself and freely be the unique individual God created you to be?

When you ask these questions and answer them honestly, you can begin to understand what kind of relationship you have with yourself. If it is not what it should be, you can learn from God's Word how to love yourself in a balanced way. If you can relax about who you are, you can usually relax about life in general.

WINNING THE BATTLES *of the* MIND

Appreciate Uniqueness

When it comes to having good relationships, it is vital that we learn to accept the differences in people. God creates each of us differently on purpose. Those who are different from you are unique and special, and not people who got in all the wrong lines when God was passing out personality traits. I used to think, *Where was I when God handed out the "nice genes"?* I was right where I was supposed to be, receiving what God wanted me to have, and so were you and so was everyone else. Let's remember that God created each of us in our mother's womb carefully and intricately (see Ps. 139:13–16). We are not a mistake just because we are not like someone else.

Thinking that everyone should be like we are, as well as thinking that we should be like everyone else, is one of our biggest problems in relationships. This kind of wrong thinking causes wrong attitudes that are damaging to healthy and satisfying marriages, friendships, and work relationships. The truth is that God has created us all differently on purpose, and although I don't always understand why He created some people the way He did, I do know I am called by Him to love and accept them and not to think something is wrong with them because they don't seem to be a perfect match for me.

How dull and uninteresting life would be if everyone looked and behaved exactly alike and had the same temperament. What if every tree and flower were the same, and every bird, dog, cat, et cetera? Boring! We can learn to appreciate the variety of people God has placed in the world, and we can learn how to think about the differences between ourselves in a way that honors God and improves our relationships.

How many people do we shut out of our lives, exclude, and criticize, making them feel inferior just because they are not like we are? Probably more than we care to count. We each connect with some people more than others, but even if we don't want to be a person's best friend, we can appreciate their uniqueness as God's creation and make every effort to make them feel loved and significant.

A PRAYER FOR VICTORY

Wise and wonderful God, I am sorry for the many people I've shut out of my life in one way or another because they were different from me. Help me to love and accept others and to enjoy them as Your amazing creations.
In Jesus' name. Amen.

POWERPOINT

Most people struggle greatly with jealousy, envy, and comparison. This is a common trait found in people who are insecure. Learning that I was an individual (see Ps. 139:14)—that God has a unique, personal plan for my life—has been one of the most valuable and precious freedoms the Lord has granted me. I am assured that I need not compare myself with anyone, and neither do you.

10 Even there Your hand will lead me,
And Your right hand will take hold of me.
11 If I say, "Surely the darkness will cover me,
And the night will be the only light around me,"
12 Even the darkness is not dark to You *and* conceals nothing from You,
But the night shines as bright as the day;
Darkness and light are alike *to You.* [Dan 2:22]

13 For You formed my innermost parts;
You knit me [together] in my mother's womb.
14 I will give thanks *and* praise to You, for I am fearfully and wonderfully made;
Wonderful are Your works,
And my soul knows it very well.
15 My frame was not hidden from You,
When I was being formed in secret,
And intricately *and* skillfully formed [as if embroidered with many colors] in the depths of the earth.
16 Your eyes have seen my unformed substance;
And in Your book were all written
The days that were appointed *for me,*
When as yet there was not one of them [even taking shape].

17 How precious also are Your thoughts to me, O God!
How vast is the sum of them! [Ps 40:5]

18 If I could count them, they would outnumber the sand.
When I awake, I am still with You.

19 O that You would kill the wicked, O God;
Go away from me, therefore, men of bloodshed. [Is 11:4]
20 For they speak against You wickedly,
Your enemies take *Your name* in vain. [Jude 15]
21 Do I not hate those who hate You, O Lord?
And do I not loathe those who rise up against You?
22 I hate them with perfect *and* utmost hatred;
They have become my enemies.

23 Search me [thoroughly], O God, and know my heart;
Test me and know my anxious thoughts;
24 And see if there is any wicked *or* hurtful way in me,
And lead me in the everlasting way.

Psalm 140

Prayer for Protection against the Wicked.

To the Chief Musician. A Psalm of David.

1 RESCUE ME, O Lord, from evil men;
Protect me from violent men.
2 They devise evil things in their hearts;
They continually [gather together and] stir up wars.
3 They sharpen their tongues like a serpent's;
Poison of a viper is under their lips. [Rom 3:13]   *Selah.*

4 Keep me, O Lord, from the hands of the wicked;
Protect me from violent men
Who intend to trip up my steps.
5 The proud have hidden a trap for me, and cords;
They have spread a net by the wayside;
They have set traps for me.   *Selah.*

6 I said to the Lord, "You are my God;
Listen to the voice of my supplications, O Lord.
7 "O God the Lord, the strength of my salvation,

POWERPOINT

Scripture lets us know how very important it is that we think properly. Thoughts are powerful, and they have creative ability. If our thoughts are going to affect what we become, thinking right thoughts should certainly be a priority for us. For our head to be protected in the day of battle (see Ps. 140:7), it is an absolute necessity to get your thinking in line with God's Word. You cannot have a positive life and a negative mind.

You have covered my head in the day of battle.

8 "Do not grant, O LORD, the desires of the wicked;
Do not further their evil device, that they not be exalted.   *Selah.*

9 "Those who surround me raise their heads;
May the mischief of their own lips come upon them.

10 "Let burning coals fall upon them;
Let them be thrown into the fire,
Into deep [water] pits from which they cannot rise.

11 "Do not let a slanderer be established in the earth;
Let evil quickly hunt the violent man [to overthrow him and stop his evil acts]."

12 I know [with confidence] that the LORD will maintain the cause of the afflicted,
And [will secure] justice for the poor.

13 Surely the righteous will give thanks to Your name;
The upright will dwell in Your presence.

Psalm 141

An Evening Prayer for Sanctification and Protection.

A Psalm of David.

1 LORD, I call upon You; hurry to me.
Listen to my voice when I call to You.

2 Let my prayer be counted as incense before You;
The lifting up of my hands as the evening offering. [1 Tim 2:8; Rev 8:3, 4]

3 Set a guard, O LORD, over my mouth;
Keep watch over the door of my lips [to keep me from speaking thoughtlessly].

KEYS *to a* Victorious Life *Think About What You Say*

I strongly recommend confessing the Word of God out loud. Even though what you confess may be the opposite of how you initially feel, keep confessing it; God's Word has inherent power to change your feelings. God's Word also brings comfort to us and quiets our distraught emotions.

David said, "Set a guard, O LORD, over my mouth; keep watch over the door of my lips [to keep me from speaking thoughtlessly]" (Ps. 141:3). There is a time to speak and a time to keep silent. Sometimes the best thing we can do is to say nothing. When we do speak, it is wise to be purposeful in what we say and to think about our words beforehand. If we truly believe our words are filled with life or death (see Prov. 18:21), why wouldn't we more carefully choose what we say?

⁴Do not incline my heart to [consent to or
   tolerate] any evil thing,
   Or to practice deeds of wickedness
   With men who plan *and* do evil;
   And let me not eat of their delicacies (be
   tempted by their gain).

⁵Let the righteous [thoughtfully] strike
   (correct) me—it is a kindness [done to
   encourage my spiritual maturity].
   It is [the choicest anointing] oil on the
   head;
   Let my head not refuse [to accept and
   acknowledge and learn from] it;
   For still my prayer is against their
   wicked deeds. [Prov 9:8; 19:25; 25:12;
   Gal 6:1]
⁶Their [wicked, godless] judges are thrown
   down the sides of the rocky cliff,
   And they [who followed them] will hear
   my words, for they are pleasant (just).
⁷As when the one plows and breaks open
   the ground [and the soil scatters
   behind him],
   Our bones have been scattered at the
   mouth of Sheol [by the injustices of
   the wicked]. [2 Cor 1:9]

⁸For my eyes are toward You, O God, the
   Lord;
   In You I take refuge; do not pour out my
   life *nor* leave me defenseless.
⁹Keep me from the jaws of the trap which
   they have set for me,
   And from the snares of those who do evil.
¹⁰Let the wicked fall into their own nets,
   While I pass by *and* safely escape [from
   danger].

Psalm 142

Prayer for Help in Trouble.

A skillful song, *or* a didactic *or*
reflective poem, of David; when he was
in the cave. A Prayer.

¹I CRY aloud with my voice to the Lord;
   I make supplication with my voice to the
   Lord.
²I pour out my complaint before Him;
   I declare my trouble before Him.
³When my spirit was overwhelmed
   and weak within me [wrapped in
   darkness],

POWERPOINT

David, the author of Psalm 142, was
a man through whom deep emotions
ran. His response to his feelings of
depression and being wrapped in
darkness was not to meditate on the
problem. Instead, he literally came
against the problem by choosing to
cry out to the Lord, his refuge and
portion in the land of the living. In
other words, he thought on Someone
good, his Deliverer, and it helped him
to overcome depression.

   You knew my path.
   In the way where I walk
   They have hidden a trap for me.
⁴Look to the right [the point of attack]
   and see;
   For there is no one who has regard for
   me [to act in my favor].
   Escape has failed me *and* I have nowhere
   to run;
   No one cares about my life.

⁵I cried out to You, O Lord;
   I said, "You are my refuge,
   My portion in the land of the living.
⁶"Give attention to my cry,
   For I am brought very low;
   Rescue me from my persecutors,
   For they are stronger than I.
⁷"Bring my soul out of prison (adversity),
   So that I may give thanks *and* praise
   Your name;
   The righteous will surround me [in
   triumph],
   For You will look after me."

Psalm 143

Prayer for Help and Guidance.

A Psalm of David.

¹HEAR MY prayer, O Lord,
   Listen to my supplications!
   Answer me in Your faithfulness, and in
   Your righteousness.

KEYS *to a* Victorious Life *Choose To Think About God*

The psalmist David talked frequently about meditating on or thinking about all the wonderful works of the Lord—the mighty acts of God. He thought on the name of the Lord, the mercy of God, the love of God, and many other such things.

When he felt depressed, he wrote in Psalm 143:4–5 that his response was not to meditate on the problem. Instead, he actively came against the problem by choosing to remember the good times of past days—pondering the doings of God and the works of His hands. In other words, David focused his thoughts on something good, and it helped him overcome depression.

Never forget this: Your mind plays an important role in your victory. Think thoughts that will add power to your life, not ones that drain your strength and energy.

---

² And do not enter into judgment with Your servant,
For in Your sight no man living is righteous *or* justified. [Ps 130:3; Rom 3:20–26; Gal 2:16]
³ For the enemy has persecuted me,
He has crushed my life down to the ground;
He has made me dwell in dark places, like those who have been long dead.
⁴ Therefore my spirit is overwhelmed *and* weak within me [wrapped in darkness];
My heart grows numb within me.

⁵ I remember the days of old;
I meditate on all that You have done;
I ponder the work of Your hands.
⁶ I reach out my hands to You;
My throat *thirsts* for You, as a parched land [thirsts for water].   *Selah.*

⁷ Answer me quickly, O Lord, my spirit fails;
Do not hide Your face from me,
Or I will become like those who go down into the pit (grave).
⁸ Let me hear Your lovingkindness in the morning,
For I trust in You.

Teach me the way in which I should walk,
For I lift up my soul to You.
⁹ Rescue me, O Lord, from my enemies;
I take refuge in You.

¹⁰ Teach me to do Your will [so that I may please You],
For You are my God;
Let Your good Spirit lead me on level ground.
¹¹ Save my life, O Lord, for Your name's sake;
In Your righteousness bring my life out of trouble.
¹² In your lovingkindness, silence *and* destroy my enemies
And destroy all those who afflict my life,
For I am Your servant.

Psalm 144

Prayer for Rescue and Prosperity.

A Psalm of David.

¹ BLESSED BE the Lord, my Rock *and* my great strength,
Who trains my hands for war
And my fingers for battle;

POWERPOINT

David praises the Lord with strong, compelling words in Psalm 144—Rock, fortress, high tower, and more. The Lord subdued David's enemies under him, but David also had to do his part. We are partners with God. He has a part, and we have a part. We cannot do His part, and He will not do ours. If we do our part, He will train us to conquer in battle.

2 My [steadfast] lovingkindness and my fortress,
My high tower and my rescuer,
My shield and He in whom I take refuge,
Who subdues my people under me.
3 LORD, what is man that You take notice of him?
Or the son of man that You think of him? [Job 7:17; Ps 8:4; Heb 2:6]
4 Man is like a mere breath;
His days are like a shadow that passes away.

5 Bow Your heavens, O LORD, and come down;
Touch the mountains, and they will smoke.
6 Flash lightning and scatter my enemies;
Send out Your arrows and confuse *and* embarrass *and* frustrate them.
7 Stretch out Your hand from above;
Set me free and rescue me from great waters,
Out of the hands of [hostile] foreigners [who surround us]
8 Whose mouths speak deceit [without restraint],
And whose right hand is a right hand of falsehood.

9 I will sing a new song to You, O God;
Upon a harp of ten strings I will sing praises to You,
10 Who gives salvation to kings,
Who sets David His servant free from the evil sword.
11 Set me free and rescue me from the hand of [hostile] foreigners,
Whose mouth speaks deceit [without restraint],
And whose right hand is a right hand of falsehood.

12 Let our sons in their youth be like plants full grown,
And our daughters like corner pillars fashioned for a palace;
13 Let our barns be full, supplying every kind of produce,
And our flocks bring forth thousands and ten thousands in our fields;
14 Let our cattle bear
Without mishap and without loss,
And let there be no outcry in our streets!
15 How blessed *and* favored are the people in such circumstance;
How blessed [fortunate, prosperous, and favored] are the people whose God is the LORD!

Psalm 145

The LORD Extolled for His Goodness.

A Psalm of praise. Of David.

1 I WILL exalt You, my God, O King,
And [with gratitude and submissive wonder] I will bless Your name forever and ever.
2 Every day I will bless You *and* lovingly praise You;
Yes, [with awe-inspired reverence] I will praise Your name forever and ever.
3 Great is the LORD, and highly to be praised,
And His greatness is [so vast and profound as to be] unsearchable [incomprehensible to man]. [Job 5:9; 9:10; Rom 11:33]
4 One generation shall praise Your works to another,
And shall declare Your mighty *and* remarkable acts.
5 On the glorious splendor of Your majesty
And on Your wonderful works, I will meditate.

6 People will speak of the power of Your
   awesome acts,
And [with gratitude and submissive
   wonder] I will tell of Your greatness.
7 They will overflow [like a fountain]
   when they speak of Your great *and*
   abundant goodness
And will sing joyfully of Your
   righteousness.

8 The LORD is gracious and full of
   compassion,
Slow to anger and abounding in
   lovingkindness.
9 The LORD is good to all,
And His tender mercies are over all His
   works [the entirety of things
   created].
10 All Your works shall give thanks to You
   and praise You, O LORD,
And Your godly ones will bless You.
11 They shall speak of the glory of Your
   kingdom
And talk of Your power,
12 To make known to the sons of men Your
   mighty acts
And the glorious majesty of Your
   kingdom.
13 Your kingdom is an everlasting
   kingdom,

And Your dominion *endures* throughout
   all generations. [Dan 7:14, 27]
14 The LORD upholds all those [of His own]
   who fall
And raises up all those who are bowed
   down.
15 The eyes of all look to You [in hopeful
   expectation],
And You give them their food in due
   time.
16 You open Your hand
And satisfy the desire of every living
   thing.
17 The LORD is [unwaveringly] righteous in
   all His ways
And gracious *and* kind in all His
   works.

KEYS to a Victorious Life *Speak Words that Edify and Encourage*

*Words are wonderful when used with good intentions. They can encourage, edify,
and give confidence. When we understand the power of words and realize we can
choose what we think and speak, our lives can be transformed. Our words are not
forced on us—they formulate in our thoughts and then we speak them. We can
learn to choose our thoughts, to resist the wrong ones, and to think on the good,
healthy, right ones.*

*When you get up in the morning, if there is something you need to attend to that
you're not looking forward to, you can say, "I dread this day," or you can say, "I
will exalt You, my God, O King . . . . Every day I will bless You* and *lovingly praise
You" (Ps. 145:1–2). God will give you the strength today to do whatever you need
to do and to do it with joy.*

KEYS *to a* **Victorious Life** *God Liberally Meets Your Needs*

Paul tells us that God will "liberally supply (fill until full) your every need according to His riches in glory in Christ Jesus" (Phil. 4:19). He doesn't promise that God will give us everything we want, but he does assure us that God will meet our every need.

Many times we think of needs in terms of the basic necessities of life. These represent our physical needs, but I believe God created us to need more than the essentials. We don't simply need money, nourishment, roofs over our heads, and clothes to wear. We also need wisdom, strength, health, friends, and loved ones; and we need the gifts and talents and abilities to help us do what we are supposed to do in life. We need many things, and God is willing to open His hand "and satisfy the desire of every living thing" (Ps. 145:16).

18 The LORD is near to all who call on Him,
To all who call on Him in truth (without guile).
19 He will fulfill the desire of those who fear *and* worship Him [with awe-inspired reverence and obedience];
He also will hear their cry and will save them.
20 The LORD keeps all who love Him,
But all the wicked He will destroy.
21 My mouth will speak the praise of the LORD,
And all flesh will bless *and* gratefully praise His holy name forever and ever.

Psalm 146

The LORD an Abundant Helper.

1 PRAISE THE LORD! (Hallelujah!)
Praise the LORD, O my soul!
2 While I live I will praise the LORD;
I will sing praises to my God as long as I live.
3 Do not trust in princes,
In mortal man, in whom there is no salvation (help).
4 When his spirit leaves him, he returns to the earth;
In that very day his thoughts *and* plans perish. [1 Cor 2:6]

5 How blessed *and* graciously favored is he whose help is the God of Jacob (Israel),
Whose hope is in the LORD his God,
[Gen 32:30]
6 Who made heaven and earth,
The sea, and all that is in them,
Who keeps truth *and* is faithful forever,
[Gen 1:3]

POWERPOINT

Disappointments hurt! So rather than be hurt again and again, many people simply refuse to hope or to believe that anything good will ever happen to them. This type of behavior sets up a negative lifestyle. When thoughts are negative, everything else becomes negative, too. No matter what comes against us, God wants each of us to be "blessed *and* graciously favored" (Ps. 146:5) as we look to Him as our help and set our hope in Him. Positive minds are always full of faith and hope.

KEYS *to a* Victorious Life *Think About Where Your Thoughts Come From*

Not every thought in your head is from you, from your circumstances, or from God. Some of the thoughts you think are from Satan's placing wrong thoughts in your mind because he wants to control your life. Did you know you don't have to continue thinking about everything that comes into your mind? You can cast wrong thoughts down and replace them with right thoughts (see 2 Cor. 10:5).

When you wake up feeling depressed and think, This is not going to be a good day, *you don't have to remain depressed. Instead, you can believe,* Great is our Lord and abundant in strength. He lifts up the humble. This will be a fantastic day! *(see Ps. 147:5–6).*

Negative thoughts and attitudes can be avoided simply by saying, "That's not a God thought. I cast it down in Jesus' name, and I am going to think about something beneficial to me today."

---

7 Who executes justice for the
  oppressed,
   Who gives food to the hungry.
   The LORD sets free the prisoners.

8 The LORD opens *the eyes of* the
   blind;
   The LORD lifts up those who are bowed
   down;
   The LORD loves the righteous [the
   upright in heart]. [Luke 13:13; John
   9:7, 32]

9 The LORD protects the strangers;
   He supports the fatherless and the widow;
   But He makes crooked the way of the
   wicked.

10 The LORD shall reign forever,
   Your God, O Zion, to all generations.
   Praise the LORD! (Hallelujah!) [Ps 10:16;
   Rev 11:15]

A Prayer To Renew Your Mind

Thank You, God, that You heal the brokenhearted and bind up my wounds, healing my pain and comforting my sorrow.

· *adapted from Psalm 147:3*

Psalm 147

Praise for Jerusalem's Restoration and Prosperity.

1 PRAISE THE LORD!
   For it is good to sing praises to our
   [gracious and majestic] God;
   Praise is becoming *and* appropriate.

2 The LORD is building up Jerusalem;
   He is gathering [together] the exiles of
   Israel.

3 He heals the brokenhearted
   And binds up their wounds [healing
   their pain and comforting their
   sorrow]. [Ps 34:18; Is 57:15; 61:1; Luke
   4:18]

4 He counts the number of the stars;
   He calls them all by their names.

5 Great is our [majestic and mighty] Lord
   and abundant in strength;
   His understanding is inexhaustible
   [infinite, boundless].

6 The LORD lifts up the humble;
   He casts the wicked down to the ground.

7 Sing to the LORD with thanksgiving;
   Sing praises to our God with the lyre,

8 Who covers the heavens with clouds,
   Who provides rain for the earth,

WINNING THE BATTLES *of the* MIND
A New Perspective on the Past

Our perspectives on life involve our thought processes and they also affect our moods. If I am in a bad mood, I may need a perspective adjustment. Perhaps I am thinking too much about what I don't have and not enough about what I do have. Or I may be looking at what people don't do for me, instead of what they have done for me. Our perspective on anything, especially events and people we don't like, will have a long-range effect. How we view events that took place as far back as childhood may still be affecting us negatively today.

When I learned to think of the abuse in my childhood as something that was unfortunate, but something that God could use for good, the pain began to lessen and I began to heal emotionally. As long as I deeply resented my father for sexually abusing me, and I resented my mother for not protecting me, I had a wound in my soul that could not heal. When I decided to try to understand the way my father was raised, and my mother's fear and weakness of character, I actually started feeling more sorry for them than I did for myself.

If you are dealing with a broken heart or a wounded soul, try asking God to help you make a connection between your perspective and your current feelings. If you are willing to change the way you view the situation, you will begin to make progress toward wholeness instead of remaining broken. Life breaks each of us in one way or another. It is up to us whether we will remain broken and bitter or let God use it to make us better and more powerful.

We have God's promise: "He heals the brokenhearted and binds up their wounds [healing their pain and comforting their sorrow]" (Ps. 147:3). Although opening up old wounds for the purpose of having them cleansed is painful, it is more painful to remain wounded and broken all our lives. We cannot do anything about our past, but we can do a great deal about our future. I encourage you to not remain stuck in a painful place when God is offering you healing. It's never too late for a new beginning.

A PRAYER FOR VICTORY

Lord God of heaven, I commit to You my heart and soul and mind for the healing of what is broken in my life. Help me to see what I need to know about my past, and cleanse my wounds that I may be healed.
It's in Jesus' name, I pray. Amen.

Who makes grass grow on the mountains.
9 He gives to the beast its food,
And to the young ravens that for which they cry.
10 He does not delight in the strength (military power) of the horse,
Nor does He take pleasure in the legs (strength) of a man.
11 The LORD favors those who fear *and* worship Him [with awe-inspired reverence and obedience],
Those who wait for His mercy *and* lovingkindness. [Ps 145:20]

12 Praise the LORD, O Jerusalem!
Praise your God, O Zion!
13 For He has strengthened the bars of your gates,
He has blessed your children within you.
14 He makes peace in your borders;
He satisfies you with the finest of the wheat.
15 He sends His command to the earth;
His word runs very swiftly.
16 He gives [to the earth] snow like [a blanket of] wool;
He scatters the frost like ashes.
17 He casts out His ice like fragments;
Who can stand before His cold?
18 He sends out His word and melts the ice;
He causes His wind to blow and the waters to flow.
19 He declares His word to Jacob,
His statutes and His ordinances to Israel. [Mal 4:4]
20 He has not dealt this way with any [other] nation;
They have not known [understood, appreciated, heeded, or cherished] His ordinances.
Praise the LORD! (Hallelujah!) [Ps 79:6; Jer 10:25]

Psalm 148

The Whole Creation Invoked to Praise the LORD.

1 PRAISE THE LORD!
Praise the LORD from the heavens;
Praise Him in the heights!
2 Praise Him, all His angels;
Praise Him, all His hosts (armies)!

3 Praise Him, sun and moon:
Praise Him, all stars of light!
4 Praise Him, highest heavens,
And the waters above the heavens!
5 Let them praise the name of the LORD,
For He commanded and they were created.
6 He has also established them forever and ever;
He has made a decree which shall not pass away.

7 Praise the LORD from the earth,
Sea monsters and all deeps;
8 Lightning and hail, snow and fog;
Stormy wind, fulfilling His orders;
9 Mountains and all hills;
Fruitful trees and all cedars;
10 Beasts and all cattle;
Creeping things and winged birds;
11 Kings of the earth and all people;
Princes and all judges of the earth;
12 Both young men and virgins;
Old men and children.

13 Let them praise the name of the LORD,
For His name alone is exalted *and* supreme;
His glory *and* majesty are above earth and heaven.
14 He has lifted up a horn for His people [giving them strength, prosperity, dignity, and preeminence],
Praise for all His godly ones;
For the people of Israel, a people near to Him.
Praise the LORD! (Hallelujah!) [Ps 75:10; Eph 2:17]

Psalm 149

Israel Invoked to Praise the LORD.

1 PRAISE THE LORD!
Sing to the LORD a new song,
And praise Him in the congregation of His godly ones (believers).
2 Let Israel rejoice in their Maker;
Let Zion's children rejoice in their King. [Zech 9:9; Matt 21:5]
3 Let them praise His name with dancing;
Let them sing praises to Him with the tambourine and lyre.
4 For the LORD takes pleasure in His people;

KEYS *to a* Victorious Life *High Praises*

In David's Psalm 149, he gives us a picture of the position God's people should take—with "the high praises of God . . . in their throats, and a two-edged sword" of the Word of God in their hands (v. 6). In the remainder of the psalm, he goes on to infer that the saints of God take this position in order to defeat their enemies.

Praise defeats the devil more quickly than any other battle plan. Praise is a garment we put on that will protect us from defeat and negativity in our minds. This garment should be genuine heart praise and not just lip service or a method being tried to see if it works. Praise always involves the Word of God. We praise God according to His Word and His goodness.

Worship is a battle position! As we worship God for Who He is and for His attributes, for His ability and might, we will witness His power and attributes released on our behalf.

I am sure your heart frequently fills up with love and worship for God. Bow your heart and give thanks to Him. Praise and worship confuse the enemy. Take your position, and you will see the enemy's defeat.

God never loses a battle. He has a definite battle plan, and when we follow it, we will win with Him.

He will beautify the humble with
salvation.
⁵ Let the godly ones exult in glory;
Let them sing for joy on their beds.
⁶ Let the high praises of God be in their
throats,
And a two-edged sword in their hands,
[Heb 4:12; Rev 1:16]
⁷ To execute vengeance on the nations
And punishment on the peoples,
⁸ To bind their kings with chains
And their nobles with fetters of iron,
⁹ To execute on them the judgment
written.
This is the honor for all His godly ones.
Praise the Lᴏʀᴅ! (Hallelujah!)

Speak God's Word
*With every breath of my life,
I will praise the Lord!*
| *adapted from* PSALM 150:6 |

Psalm 150

A Psalm of Praise.

¹ PRAISE THE Lᴏʀᴅ!
Praise God in His sanctuary;
Praise Him in His mighty heavens.
² Praise Him for His mighty acts;
Praise Him according to [the abundance
of] His greatness. [Deut 3:24;
Ps 145:5, 6]

³ Praise Him with trumpet sound;
Praise Him with harp and lyre.
⁴ Praise Him with tambourine and
dancing;
Praise Him with stringed instruments
and flute.
⁵ Praise Him with resounding cymbals;
Praise Him with loud cymbals.
⁶ Let everything that has breath *and* every
breath of life praise the Lᴏʀᴅ!
Praise the Lᴏʀᴅ! (Hallelujah!)

THE
PROVERBS

Proverbs

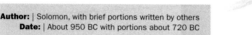

Author: | Solomon, with brief portions written by others
Date: | About 950 BC with portions about 720 BC

Proverbs is the Bible's greatest book of wisdom. Wisdom should be one of our primary goals for our thinking. The wiser we are, the better we can recognize and overcome the enemy's attempts to influence our thoughts and use them against us. Throughout Proverbs, we see the words *knowledge*, *understanding*, and *learning*, which are all aspects of godly wisdom. It offers wisdom on relationships, decision-making, time management, how to handle finances, and many other aspects of life.

Proverbs also includes many verses pertaining to thoughts and words. From start to finish, it teaches us how to think and how to speak and emphasizes the importance of thoughts and words. If you want to see change in any area of your life, it will start with changing the way you think and the way you speak.

WINNING THOUGHTS FROM PROVERBS:

Words are not merely words. They are containers for power (see Proverbs 18:21).

As human beings, we think about and plan many things, but it is the Lord's purpose that will stand strong (see Proverbs 19:21).

Whatever you think, that's what you become (see Proverbs 23:7).

VERSES FOR VICTORY FROM PROVERBS:

The wise will hear and increase their learning, and the person of understanding will acquire wise counsel and the skill [to steer his course wisely and lead others to the truth]. | Proverbs 1:5

Trust in and rely confidently on the LORD with all your heart and do not rely on your own insight or understanding. In all your ways know and acknowledge and recognize Him, and He will make your paths straight and smooth [removing obstacles that block your way]. | Proverbs 3:5–6

He who guards his mouth and his tongue guards himself from troubles. | Proverbs 21:23

PROVERBS

1 THE PROVERBS (truths obscurely expressed, maxims) of Solomon son of David, king of Israel:

2 To know [skillful and godly] wisdom and instruction;
To discern *and* comprehend the words of understanding *and* insight,

3 To receive instruction in wise behavior *and* the discipline of wise thoughtfulness,
Righteousness, justice, and integrity;

4 That prudence (good judgment, astute common sense) may be given to the naive *or* inexperienced [who are easily misled],
And knowledge and discretion (intelligent discernment) to the youth,

5 The wise will hear and increase their learning,
And the person of understanding will acquire wise counsel *and* the skill [to steer his course wisely and lead others to the truth], [Prov 9:9]

6 To understand a proverb and a figure [of speech] *or* an enigma with its interpretation,
And the words of the wise and their riddles [that require reflection].

7 The [reverent] fear of the Lord [that is, worshiping Him and regarding Him as truly awesome] is the beginning *and* the preeminent part of knowledge [its starting point and its essence];

But arrogant fools despise [skillful and godly] wisdom and instruction *and* self-discipline. [Ps 111:10]

8 My son, hear the instruction of your father,
And do not reject the teaching of your mother.

9 For they are a garland of grace on your head,
And chains *and* ornaments [of gold] around your neck.

10 My son, if sinners entice you,
Do not consent. [Ps 1:1; Eph 5:11]

11 If they say, "Come with us;
Let us lie in wait to *shed* blood,
Let us ambush the innocent without cause;

12 Let us swallow them alive like Sheol (the place of the dead),
Even whole, as those who go down to the pit [of death];

13 We will find *and* take all kinds of precious possessions,
We will fill our houses with spoil;

14 Throw in your lot with us [they insist];
We will all have one money bag [in common],"

15 My son, do not walk on the road with them;
Keep your foot [far] away from their path,

16 For their feet run to evil,
And they hurry to shed blood.

17 Indeed, it is useless to spread the *baited* net
In the sight of any bird;

18 But [when these people set a trap for others] they lie in wait for their own blood;
They set an ambush for their own lives [and rush to their destruction].

19 So are the ways of everyone who is greedy for gain;
Greed takes away the lives of its possessors. [Prov 15:27; 1 Tim 6:10]

20 Wisdom shouts in the street,

A Prayer To Renew Your Mind

Lord, I pray that You will help me grow in wisdom. As I become wiser, I will hear and increase in learning, and I will acquire wise counsel and the skill to steer my course wisely through life and lead others to the truth.

· adapted from Proverbs 1:5–6

KEYS *to a* **Victorious Life** *Live Fearlessly*

Solomon said, "Whoever listens to me (Wisdom) will live securely and *in confident trust and will be at ease, without fear* or *dread of evil" (Prov. 1:33). That is a powerful promise for us today.*

Similarly, the apostle Paul stated that we should not, even for one moment, be frightened or intimidated by anything our opponents try to do to us (see Phil. 1:28), that our fearlessness is a sign to our enemies of their impending destruction and evidence of our deliverance and salvation through God. In other words, when we have trials, the spiritual world is watching. God is watching and Satan is watching; therefore, how we respond and what we say and do are very important. If you can hold your tongue and remain emotionally stable during times of difficulty, it is a sign of spiritual maturity and you are honoring God and letting the enemy know he is not going to control you.

She raises her voice in the markets;
²¹ She calls out at the head of the noisy streets [where large crowds gather];
At the entrance of the city gates she speaks her words:
²² "How long, O naive ones [you who are easily misled], will you love being simple-minded *and* undiscerning?
How long will scoffers [who ridicule and deride] delight in scoffing,
How long will fools [who obstinately mock truth] hate knowledge?
²³ "If you will turn *and* pay attention to my rebuke,
Behold, I [Wisdom] will pour out my spirit on you;
I will make my words known to you. [Is 11:2; Eph 1:17–20]
²⁴ "Because I called and you refused [to answer],
I stretched out my hand and no one has paid attention [to my offer]; [Is 65:11, 12; 66:4; Jer 7:13, 14; Zech 7:11–13]
²⁵ And you treated all my counsel as nothing
And would not accept my reprimand,
²⁶ I also will laugh at your disaster;
I will mock when your dread *and* panic come,

²⁷ When your dread *and* panic come like a storm,
And your disaster comes like a whirlwind,
When anxiety and distress come upon you [as retribution].
²⁸ "Then they will call upon me (Wisdom), but I will not answer;
They will seek me eagerly but they will not find me, [Job 27:9; 35:12, 13; Is 1:15, 16; Jer 11:11; Mic 3:4; James 4:3]
²⁹ Because they hated knowledge
And did not choose the fear of the LORD [that is, obeying Him with reverence and awe-filled respect], [Prov 8:13]
³⁰ They would not accept my counsel,
And they spurned all my rebuke.
³¹ "Therefore they shall eat of the fruit of their own [wicked] way
And be satiated with [the penalty of] their own devices.
³² "For the turning away of the naive will kill them,
And the careless ease of [self-righteous] fools will destroy them. [Is 32:6]
³³ "But whoever listens to me (Wisdom) will live securely *and* in confident trust
And will be at ease, without fear *or* dread of evil."

2 MY SON, if you will receive my words
And treasure my commandments within you,

2 So that your ear is attentive to [skillful and godly] wisdom,
And apply your heart to understanding [seeking it conscientiously and striving for it eagerly];

3 Yes, if you cry out for insight,
And lift up your voice for understanding;

4 If you seek skillful *and* godly wisdom as you would silver
And search for her as you would hidden treasures;

5 Then you will understand the [reverent] fear of the LORD [that is, worshiping Him and regarding Him as truly awesome]
And discover the knowledge of God. [Prov 1:7]

6 For the LORD gives [skillful and godly] wisdom;
From His mouth come knowledge and understanding.

7 He stores away sound wisdom for the righteous [those who are in right standing with Him];
He is a shield to those who walk in integrity [those of honorable character and moral courage],

8 He guards the paths of justice;
And He preserves the way of His saints (believers). [1 Sam 2:9; Ps 66:8, 9]

9 Then you will understand righteousness and justice [in every circumstance]
And integrity and every good path.

10 For [skillful and godly] wisdom will enter your heart
And knowledge will be pleasant to your soul.

11 Discretion will watch over you,
Understanding *and* discernment will guard you,

12 To keep you from the way of evil *and* the evil man,
From the man who speaks perverse things;

13 From those who leave the paths of uprightness
To walk in the ways of darkness;

14 Who find joy in doing evil
And delight in the perversity of evil,

15 Whose paths are crooked,
And who are devious in their ways;

16 To keep you from the immoral woman;
From the seductress with her flattering words, [Prov 2:11]

17 Who leaves the companion (husband) of her youth,
And forgets the covenant of her God.

18 For her house leads down to death
And her paths lead to the dead;

19 None who go to her return again,
Nor do they regain the paths of life—

20 So you will walk in the way of good men [that is, those of personal integrity, moral courage and honorable character],
And keep to the paths of the righteous.

21 For the upright [those who are in right standing with God] will live in the land
And those [of integrity] who are blameless [in God's sight] will remain in it;

22 But the wicked will be cut off from the land
And the treacherous shall be [forcibly] uprooted *and* removed from it.

3 MY SON, do not forget my teaching,
But let your heart keep my commandments;

2 For length of days and years of life [worth living]
And tranquility *and* prosperity [the wholeness of life's blessings] they will add to you.

3 Do not let mercy *and* kindness and truth leave you [instead let these qualities define you];
Bind them [securely] around your neck,

Speak God's Word

I will trust in and rely confidently on the Lord with all my heart and not rely on my own insight or understanding. In all my ways I will know and acknowledge and recognize Him, and He will make my paths straight and smooth, removing obstacles in my way.

| *adapted from* PROVERBS 3:5–6 |

Write them on the tablet of your heart. [Col 3:9–12]

⁴So find favor and high esteem
In the sight of God and man. [Luke 2:52]

⁵Trust in *and* rely confidently on the LORD with all your heart
And do not rely on your own insight *or* understanding.

⁶In all your ways know *and* acknowledge *and* recognize Him,
And He will make your paths straight *and* smooth [removing obstacles that block your way].

⁷Do not be wise in your own eyes;

Fear the LORD [with reverent awe and obedience] and turn [entirely] away from evil. [Prov 8:13]

⁸It will be health to your body [your marrow, your nerves, your sinews, your muscles—all your inner parts]
And refreshment (physical well-being) to your bones.

⁹Honor the LORD with your wealth
And with the first fruits of all your crops (income); [Deut 26:2; Mal 3:10; Luke 14:13, 14]

¹⁰Then your barns will be abundantly filled
And your vats will overflow with new wine. [Deut 28:8]

¹¹My son, do not reject *or* take lightly the discipline of the LORD [learn from your mistakes and the testing that comes from His correction through discipline];
Nor despise His rebuke, [Ps 94:12; Heb 12:5, 6; Rev 3:19]

¹²For those whom the LORD loves He corrects,
Even as a father *corrects* the son in whom he delights.

KEYS *to a* Victorious Life *Trust God with Your Mind*

God wants us to trust Him not only with our whole heart, but also with our mind (our thoughts). I found in my own life that I would often say I trusted God, yet I mentally tried to come up with reasons for and answers to my problems. I spent a lot of time in confusion saying, "Lord, I just don't understand! I don't know what to do." God wasn't asking me to understand or to take action apart from His instructions. He wanted me to trust!

Surveys taken in my conferences reveal that most people say they are confused, but God is not the author of confusion (see 1 Cor. 14:33). We can eliminate confusion in our lives if we cease trying to figure everything out and trust God to let us know what He wants us to know at the right time.

Acknowledge God in all that you do and He promises to direct your path (see Prov. 3:6). You may not always understand the direction He is leading you, but you can be assured that you will arrive at the right place at the right time.

13 Happy [blessed, considered fortunate,
to be admired] is the man who finds
[skillful and godly] wisdom,
And the man who gains understanding
and insight [learning from God's word
and life's experiences],

14 For wisdom's profit is better than the
profit of silver,
And her gain is better than fine gold.

15 She is more precious than rubies;
And nothing you can wish for compares
with her [in value]. [Job 28:12–18]

16 Long life is in her right hand;
In her left hand are riches and honor.
[Prov 8:12–21; 1 Tim 4:8]

17 Her ways are highways of pleasantness
and favor,
And all her paths are peace.

18 She is a tree of life to those who take
hold of her,
And happy [blessed, considered
fortunate, to be admired] is everyone
who holds her tightly.

19 The LORD by His wisdom has founded
the earth;
By His understanding He has
established the heavens. [Col 1:16]

20 By His knowledge the deeps were broken
up
And the clouds drip with dew.

21 My son, let them not escape from your
sight,
But keep sound wisdom and
discretion,

22 And they will be life to your soul (your
inner self)
And a gracious adornment to your neck
(your outer self).

23 Then you will walk on your way [of life]
securely
And your foot will not stumble. [Ps
91:11, 12; Prov 10:9]

24 When you lie down, you will not be
afraid;
When you lie down, your sleep will be
sweet.

25 Do not be afraid of sudden fear
Nor of the storm of the wicked when it
comes [since you will be blameless];

26 For the LORD will be your confidence,
firm *and* strong,
And will keep your foot from being
caught [in a trap].

27 Do not withhold good from those to
whom it is due [its rightful recipients],
When it is in your power to do it. [Rom
13:7; Gal 6:10]

28 Do not say to your neighbor, "Go, and
come back,
And tomorrow I will give it,"
When you have it with you. [Lev 19:13;
Deut 24:15]

29 Do not devise evil against your neighbor,
Who lives securely beside you.

30 Do not quarrel with a man without cause,
If he has done you no harm. [Rom 12:18]

31 Do not envy a man of violence
And do not choose any of his ways. [Ps
37:1; 73:3; Prov 24:1]

32 For the devious are repulsive to the LORD;
But His private counsel is with the
upright [those with spiritual integrity
and moral courage]. [Ps 25:14]

33 The curse of the LORD is on the house of
the wicked,
But He blesses the home of the just *and*
righteous. [Ps 37:22; Zech 5:4; Mal 2:2]

34 Though He scoffs at the scoffers *and*
scorns the scorners,
Yet He gives His grace [His undeserved
favor] to the humble [those who give up
self-importance]. [James 4:6; 1 Pet 5:5]

35 The wise will inherit honor *and* glory,
But dishonor *and* shame is conferred on
fools. [Is 32:6]

4 HEAR, O children, the instruction
of a father,
And pay attention [and be willing
to learn] so that you may gain
understanding *and* intelligent
discernment.

2 For I give you good doctrine;
Do not turn away from my instruction.

3 When I was a son with my father (David),
Tender and the only son in the sight of
my mother (Bathsheba),

4 He taught me and said to me,
"Let your heart hold fast my words;
Keep my commandments and live.
[1 Chr 28:9; Eph 6:4]

5 "Get [skillful and godly] wisdom!
Acquire understanding [actively
seek spiritual discernment, mature
comprehension, and logical
interpretation]!

Do not forget nor turn away from the
words of my mouth.

6 "Do not turn away from her (Wisdom)
and she will guard *and* protect you;
Love her, and she will watch over you.

7 "The beginning of wisdom is: Get
[skillful and godly] wisdom [it is
preeminent]!
And with all your acquiring, get
understanding [actively seek spiritual
discernment, mature comprehension,
and logical interpretation]. [James 1:5]

8 "Prize wisdom [and exalt her], and she
will exalt you;
She will honor you if you embrace her.

9 "She will place on your head a garland of
grace;
She will present you with a crown of
beauty *and* glory."

10 Hear, my son, and accept my sayings,
And the years of your life will be many.

11 I have instructed you in the way of
[skillful and godly] wisdom;
I have led you in upright paths.

12 When you walk, your steps will not be
impeded [for your path will be clear
and open];
And when you run, you will not
stumble.

13 Take hold of instruction; [actively seek
it, grip it firmly and] do not let go.
Guard her, for she is your life.

14 Do not enter the path of the wicked,
And do not go the way of evil men.

15 Avoid it, do not travel on it;
Turn away from it and pass on.

16 For the wicked cannot sleep unless they
do evil;
And they are deprived of sleep unless
they make someone stumble *and* fall.

17 For they eat the bread of wickedness
And drink the wine of violence.

18 But the path of the just (righteous) is like
the light of dawn,
That shines brighter and brighter until
[it reaches its full strength and glory
in] the perfect day. [2 Sam 23:4; Matt
5:14; Phil 2:15]

19 The way of the wicked is like [deep]
darkness;
They do not know over what they
stumble. [John 12:35]

A Prayer To Renew Your Mind

*Lord, open my ears to Your sayings. I
will not let them escape from my sight.
I will keep them in the center of my
heart. For they are life to all who find
them, and healing and health to all
my flesh.*   · *adapted from Proverbs 4:20–22*

20 My son, pay attention to my words *and*
be willing to learn;
Open your ears to my sayings.

21 Do not let them escape from your sight;
Keep them in the center of your heart.

22 For they are life to those who find them,
And healing *and* health to all their flesh.

23 Watch over your heart with all
diligence,
For from it *flow* the springs of life.

24 Put away from you a deceitful (lying,
misleading) mouth,
And put devious lips far from you.

25 Let your eyes look directly ahead
[toward the path of moral courage]
And let your gaze be fixed straight
in front of you [toward the path of
integrity].

26 Consider well *and* watch carefully the
path of your feet,
And all your ways will be steadfast *and*
sure.

27 Do not turn away to the right nor to the
left [where evil may lurk];
Turn your foot from [the path of] evil.

5 MY SON, be attentive to my wisdom
[godly wisdom learned by costly
experience],
Incline your ear to my understanding;
[1 Kin 4:29]

2 That you may exercise discrimination
and discretion (good judgment),
And your lips may reserve knowledge
and answer wisely [to temptation].

3 For the lips of an immoral woman drip
honey [like a honeycomb]
And her speech is smoother than oil;
[Ezek 20:30; Col 2:8–10; 2 Pet 2:14–17]

4 But in the end she is bitter like [the
extract of] wormwood,
Sharp as a two-edged sword.

KEYS *to a* Victorious Life *Post a Guard Around Your Heart*

To watch over our hearts with all diligence (see Prov. 4:23) means to be alert or watchful to Satan's subtle tactics at all times. We can learn about how to do this from Philippians 4:6–7: "Do not be anxious or worried about anything, but in everything [every circumstance and situation] by prayer and petition with thanksgiving, continue to make your [specific] requests known to God. And the peace of God [that peace which reassures the heart, that peace] which transcends all understanding, [that peace which] stands guard over your hearts and your minds in Christ Jesus [is yours]."

When we guard something, we watch over it with special care and stand ready to protect it at all times. To me, Proverbs 4:23 means that I am to be alert, to be conscious and aware of my thoughts and attitudes, and to not let the enemy or anything else poison my heart with lies and deceits. Many wrong and vicious thought patterns and attitudes are built up in us little by little. We must remember that Satan is very patient, and he is relentless, so we must be even more relentless than he is. Guard your heart with all diligence!

Sometimes when riding along in the car, looking out the window, I catch myself thinking some thoughts that are really unproductive, unkind, and suspicious of others. Thankfully, because of what I have learned from God's Word, I know to immediately cast down these thoughts and choose to think on something good. This is how we guard our hearts. We need to also be careful not to spend too much time with people who are given to gossiping, complaining, and being negative. We can become like what we surround ourselves with if we don't guard our hearts carefully!

---

5 Her feet go down to death;
  Her steps take hold of Sheol (the nether world, the place of the dead),
6 So that she does not think [seriously] about the path of life;
  Her ways are aimless *and* unstable; you cannot know where her path leads.

7 Now then, my sons, listen to me
  And do not depart from (forget) the words of my mouth.
8 Let your way [in life] be far from her,
  And do not go near the door of her house [avoid even being near the places of temptation], [Prov 4:15; Rom 16:17; 1 Thess 5:19–22]

9 Or you will give your honor to others,
  And your years to the cruel one,
10 And strangers will be filled with your strength
  And your hard-earned wealth will go to the house of a foreigner [who does not know God];
11 And you will groan when your *life is* ending,
  When your flesh and your body are consumed;
12 And you say, "How I hated instruction *and* discipline,
  And my heart despised correction *and* reproof!

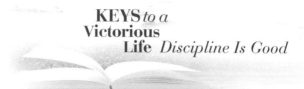

KEYS *to a* Victorious Life *Discipline Is Good*

Some people, such as the person described in Proverbs 5:12–13, cringe at the mention of the word discipline. Their mental attitudes toward discipline are unhealthy and self-defeating and lead to a defeated life. We need to realize that discipline is our friend, not our enemy. It helps us be what we say we want to be, do what we say we want to do, and have what we say we want to have.

Discipline doesn't prevent you from having fun and doing what you want to do in life; instead it helps you obtain what you truly want, which includes peace, joy, and right relationships. Learn to love discipline (it will keep you out of trouble!), and embrace it as your companion in life.

---

13 "I have not listened to the voice of my teachers,
Nor have I inclined my ear to those who instructed me.
14 "I was almost in total ruin
In the midst of the assembly and congregation."

15 Drink water from your own cistern [of a pure marriage relationship]
And fresh running water from your own well.
16 Should your springs (children) be dispersed,
As streams of water in the streets?
17 [Confine yourself to your own wife.] Let *your children* be yours alone,
And not *the children* of strangers with you.
18 Let your fountain (wife) be blessed [with the rewards of fidelity],
And rejoice in the wife of your youth. [Song 4:12, 15]

19 *Let her be as* a loving hind and graceful doe,
Let her breasts refresh *and* satisfy you at all times;
Always be exhilarated *and* delight in her love.
20 Why should you, my son, be exhilarated with an immoral woman
And embrace the bosom of an outsider (pagan)?
21 For the ways of man are directly before the eyes of the LORD,
And He carefully watches all of his paths [all of his comings and goings]. [2 Chr 16:9; Job 31:4; 34:21; Prov 15:3; Jer 16:17; Hos 7:2; Heb 4:13]
22 The iniquities done by a wicked man will trap him,
And he will be held with the cords of his sin.
23 He will die for lack of instruction (discipline),
And in the greatness of his foolishness he will go astray *and* be lost.

A Prayer To Renew Your Mind

Thank You, Lord, that my ways are before Your eyes, and You carefully watch all my comings and goings.

· *adapted from Proverbs 5:21*

6 MY SON, if you have become surety (guaranteed a debt or obligation) for your neighbor,
If you have given your pledge for [the debt of] a stranger *or* another [outside your family],

² If you have been snared with the words
   of your lips,
   If you have been trapped by the speech
   of your mouth,
³ Do this now, my son, and release
   yourself [from the obligation];
   Since you have come into the hand of
   your neighbor,
   Go humble yourself, and plead with your
   neighbor [to pay his debt and release
   you].
⁴ Give no [unnecessary] sleep to your eyes,
   Nor slumber to your eyelids;
⁵ Tear yourself away like a gazelle from
   the hand of *the hunter*
   And like a bird from the hand of the
   fowler.

6 Go to the ant, O lazy one;
   Observe her ways and be wise, [Job 12:7]
⁷ Which, having no chief,
   Overseer or ruler,
⁸ She prepares her food in the summer
   And brings in her provisions [of food for
   the winter] in the harvest.
⁹ How long will you lie down, O lazy
   one?
   When will you arise from your sleep
   [and learn self-discipline]?
   [Prov 24:33, 34]
¹⁰ "Yet a little sleep, a little slumber,
   A little folding of the hands to lie down
   and rest"—

POWERPOINT

We can learn a lot when we read about
the ant, which works and provides
for itself with no supervision. People
who must always have someone else
pushing them to do things rarely do
something great. Those who only do
what is right when someone is looking
won't get very far either. We should be
motivated from within and live our lives
before God, knowing that He sees all
and trusting that our reward will
come from Him.

¹¹ So your poverty will come like an
   approaching prowler who walks
   [slowly, but surely]
   And your need [will come] like an armed
   man [making you helpless]. [Prov 10:4;
   13:4; 20:4]

12 A worthless person, a wicked man,
   Is one who walks with a perverse
   (corrupt, vulgar) mouth.
¹³ Who winks with his eyes [in mockery],
   who shuffles his feet [to signal],
   Who points with his fingers [to give
   subversive instruction];
¹⁴ Who perversely in his heart plots
   trouble *and* evil continually;
   Who spreads discord *and* strife.
¹⁵ Therefore [the crushing weight of] his
   disaster will come suddenly *upon him;*
   Instantly he will be broken, and there
   will be no healing *or* remedy [because
   he has no heart for God].

16 These six things the LORD hates;
   Indeed, seven are repulsive to Him:
¹⁷ A proud look [the attitude that makes
   one overestimate oneself and discount
   others], a lying tongue,
   And hands that shed innocent blood, [Ps
   120:2, 3]
¹⁸ A heart that creates wicked plans,
   Feet that run swiftly to evil,
¹⁹ A false witness who breathes out lies
   [even half-truths],
   And one who spreads discord (rumors)
   among brothers.

20 My son, be guided by your father's [God-
   given] commandment (instruction)
   And do not reject the teaching of your
   mother; [Eph 6:1–3]
²¹ Bind them continually upon your heart
   (in your thoughts),
   And tie them around your neck. [Prov
   3:3; 7:3]
²² When you walk about, they (the godly
   teachings of your parents) will guide
   you;
   When you sleep, they will keep watch
   over you;
   And when you awake, they will talk to
   you.
²³ For the commandment is a lamp, and
   the teaching [of the law] is light,

And reproofs (rebukes) for discipline are
the way of life, [Ps 19:8; 119:105]
24 To keep you from the evil woman,
From [the flattery of] the smooth tongue
of an immoral woman.
25 Do not desire (lust after) her beauty in
your heart,
Nor let her capture you with her
eyelashes.
26 For on account of a prostitute one is
reduced to a piece of bread [to be
eaten up],
And the immoral woman hunts [with a
hook] the precious life [of a man].
27 Can a man take fire to his chest
And his clothes not be burned?
28 Or can a man walk on hot coals
And his feet not be scorched?
29 So is the one who goes in to his
neighbor's wife;
Whoever touches her will not be found
innocent *or* go unpunished.
30 People do not despise a thief if he steals
To satisfy himself when he is hungry;
31 But when he is found, he must repay
seven times [what he stole];
He must give all the property of his
house [if necessary to meet his fine].
32 But whoever commits adultery with
a woman lacks common sense
and sound judgment *and* an
understanding [of moral principles];
He who would destroy his soul does it.
33 Wounds and disgrace he will find,
And his reproach (blame) will not be
blotted out.
34 For jealousy enrages the [wronged]
husband;
He will not spare [the guilty one] on the
day of vengeance.
35 He will not accept any ransom [offered
to buy him off from demanding full
punishment];
Nor will he be satisfied though you offer
him many gifts (bribes).

7 MY SON, keep my words
And treasure my commandments
within you [so they are readily
available to guide you].
2 Keep my commandments and live,
And keep my teaching *and* law as the
apple of your eye.

3 Bind them [securely] on your fingers;
Write them on the tablet of your heart.
4 Say to [skillful and godly] wisdom, "You
are my sister,"
And regard understanding *and*
intelligent insight as your intimate
friends;
5 That they may keep you from the
immoral woman,
From the foreigner [who does not
observe God's laws and] who flatters
with her [smooth] words.

6 For at the window of my house
I looked out through my lattice.
7 And among the naive [the inexperienced
and gullible],
I saw among the youths
A young man lacking [good] sense,
8 Passing through the street near her
corner;
And he took the path to her house
9 In the twilight, in the evening;
In the black and dark night.
10 And there a woman met him,
Dressed as a prostitute and sly *and*
cunning of heart.
11 She was boisterous and rebellious;
She would not stay at home.
12 At times *she was* in the streets, at times
in the market places,
Lurking *and* setting her ambush at every
corner.
13 So she caught him and kissed him
And with a brazen *and* impudent face
she said to him:
14 "I have peace offerings with me;
Today I have paid my vows.
15 "So I came out to meet you [that you
might share with me the feast of my
offering],
Diligently I sought your face and I have
found you.
16 "I have spread my couch with coverings
and cushions of tapestry,
With colored fine linen of Egypt.
17 "I have perfumed my bed
With myrrh, aloes, and cinnamon.
18 "Come, let us drink our fill of love until
morning;
Let us console *and* delight ourselves
with love.
19 "For my husband is not at home.

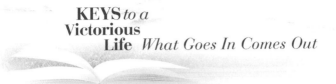

KEYS *to a* Victorious Life *What Goes In Comes Out*

When we think thoughts and speak words, especially frequently, they are written on the tablet of our heart, embedded in our hard drive, so to speak. Just as a computer can only put out the information programmed into it, so our heart can only put out what is written on it: "For the mouth speaks out of that which fills the heart" (Matt. 12:34). If you don't like the results you are getting from your computer, you don't hesitate to install a new program or perhaps even get a new computer. You can take similar steps with your life.

Start rewriting what has been programmed into your heart by choosing more carefully what you think and speak. "Keep my commandments and live, and keep my teaching and law as the apple of your eye. Bind them [securely] on your fingers; write them on the tablet of your heart" (Prov. 7:2–3).

He has gone on a long journey;
20 He has taken a bag of money with him,
   And he will come home on the
      appointed day."
21 With her many persuasions she caused
      him to yield;
   With her flattering lips she seduced him.
22 Suddenly he went after her, as an ox
      goes to the slaughter [not knowing the
      outcome],
   Or as one in stocks going to the
      correction [to be given] to a fool,
23 Until an arrow pierced his liver [with a
      mortal wound];
   Like a bird fluttering straight into the
      net,
   He did not know that it *would cost* him
      his life.

24 Now therefore, my sons, listen to me,
   And pay attention to the words of my
      mouth.
25 Do not let your heart turn aside to her
      ways,
   Do not stray into her [evil, immoral]
      paths.
26 For she has cast down many [mortally]
      wounded;
   Indeed, all who were killed by her were
      strong. [Neh 13:26]

27 Her house is the way to Sheol,
   Descending to the chambers of death.
      [1 Cor 6:9]

8 DOES NOT wisdom call,
   And understanding lift up her voice?
2 On the top of the heights beside the
      way,
   Where the paths meet, wisdom takes
      her stand;
3 Beside the gates, at the entrance to the
      city,
   At the entrance of the doors, she cries
      out:
4 "To you, O men, I call,
   And my voice is directed to the sons of
      men.
5 "O you naive *or* inexperienced [who are
      easily misled], understand prudence
      and seek astute common sense;
   And, O you [closed-minded, self-
      confident] fools, understand wisdom
      [seek the insight and self-discipline
      that leads to godly living]. [Is 32:6]
6 "Listen, for I will speak excellent *and*
      noble things;
   And the opening of my lips *will reveal*
      right things.
7 "For my mouth will utter truth,

KEYS *to a* Victorious Life *An Excellent Life*

In Proverbs 8:6, Solomon made a decision about how he would talk, and we would be wise to follow his example. Just as we can direct our thoughts, we can also direct our words with God's help. We should choose to "speak excellent and noble things."

Our words affect us and the people around us. They also affect what God is able to do for us. We cannot have a negative mouth and a positive life. In 1 Peter 3:10, the apostle Peter teaches us that if we want to enjoy life and see good days— even in the midst of trials—we must keep our tongue free from evil.

What kind of life do you want? Do you want an excellent life? If so, then be excellent in your choice of words. Change your words, and you will change your life!

And wickedness is repulsive *and* loathsome to my lips.

8 "All the words of my mouth are in righteousness (upright, in right standing with God);

There is nothing contrary to truth or perverted (crooked) in them.

9 "They are all straightforward to him who understands [with an open and willing mind],

And right to those who find knowledge *and* live by it.

10 "Take my instruction rather than [seeking] silver,

And take knowledge rather than choicest gold,

11 "For wisdom is better than rubies; And all desirable things cannot compare with her. [Job 28:15; Ps 19:10; 119:127]

12 "I, [godly] wisdom, reside with prudence [good judgment, moral courage and astute common sense],

And I find knowledge and discretion. [James 1:5]

13 "The [reverent] fear *and* worshipful awe of the LORD *includes* the hatred of evil; Pride and arrogance and the evil way, And the perverted mouth, I hate.

14 "Counsel is mine and sound wisdom;

I am understanding, power *and* strength are mine.

15 "By me kings reign And rulers decide *and* decree justice. [Dan 2:21; Rom 13:1]

16 "By me princes rule, and nobles, All who judge *and* govern rightly.

17 "I love those who love me; And those who seek me early *and* diligently will find me. [1 Sam 2:30; Ps 91:14; John 14:21; James 1:5]

18 "Riches and honor are with me, Enduring wealth and righteousness (right standing with God). [Prov 3:16; Matt 6:33]

19 "My fruit is better than gold, even pure gold,

And my yield is better than choicest silver.

20 "I, [Wisdom, continuously] walk in the way of righteousness,

In the midst of the paths of justice,

21 That I may cause those who love me to inherit wealth *and* true riches,

And that I may fill their treasuries.

22 "The LORD created *and* possessed me at the beginning of His way,

Before His works of old [were accomplished].

²³"From everlasting I was established *and* ordained,

From the beginning, before the earth existed, [I, godly wisdom, existed]. [John 1:1; 1 Cor 1:24]

²⁴"When there were no ocean depths I was born,

When there were no fountains *and* springs overflowing with water.

²⁵"Before the mountains were settled, Before the hills, I was born; [Job 15:7, 8]

²⁶While He had not yet made the earth and the fields,

Or the first of the dust of the earth.

²⁷"When He established the heavens, I [Wisdom] was there;

When He drew a circle upon the face of the deep,

²⁸When He made firm the skies above, When the fountains and springs of the deep became fixed *and* strong,

²⁹When He set for the sea its boundary So that the waters would not transgress [the boundaries set by] His command,

When He marked out the foundations of the earth— [Job 38:10, 11; Ps 104:6–9; Jer 5:22]

³⁰Then I was beside Him, as a master craftsman;

And I was daily His delight;

Rejoicing before Him always, [Matt 3:17; John 1:2, 18]

³¹Rejoicing in the world, His inhabited earth,

And having my delight in the sons of men. [Ps 16:3]

³²"Now therefore, O sons, listen to me, For blessed [happy, prosperous, to be admired] are they who keep my ways. [Ps 119:1, 2; 128:1, 2; Luke 11:28]

³³"Heed (pay attention to) instruction and be wise,

And do not ignore *or* neglect it.

³⁴"Blessed [happy, prosperous, to be admired] is the man who listens to me, Watching daily at my gates, Waiting at my doorposts.

³⁵"For whoever finds me (Wisdom) finds life

And obtains favor *and* grace from the Lord.

³⁶"But he who fails to find me *or* sins against me injures himself;

All those who hate me love *and* court death."

POWERPOINT

The Bible mentions seven things the Lord hates, and a lying tongue is one of them (see Prov. 6:16–19). In Proverbs 8:7–8, Solomon says he will speak truth. Satan is known as the deceiver; he is a liar and the father of lies (see John 8:44), and one way he wages war in our minds is to whisper lies to us. God, on the other hand is truth, and we can assume that since He hates a lying tongue, He loves words that are truthful. Jesus said that He is the Way, the Truth, and the Life (see John 14:6). Satan lies to all of us, and the only way we can recognize and resist his lies is to know God's Word, which is truth. The more we know the truth, the more we can speak truthfully.

9 WISDOM HAS built her [spacious and sufficient] house;

She has hewn out *and* set up her seven pillars.

²She has prepared her food, she has mixed her wine;

She has also set her table. [Matt 22:2–4]

³She has sent out her maidens, she calls From the highest places of the city:

⁴"Whoever is naive *or* inexperienced, let him turn in here!"

As for him who lacks understanding, she says,

⁵"Come, eat my food

And drink the wine I have mixed [and accept my gifts]. [Is 55:1; John 6:27]

⁶"Leave [behind] your foolishness [and the foolish] and live,

And walk in the way of insight *and* understanding."

A Prayer To Renew Your Mind

Help me to always remember, Lord, that the reverent fear of You is the beginning of wisdom and that regarding You as truly awesome is the beginning and preeminent part of wisdom, its starting place and its essence.

· *adapted from Proverbs 9:10*

7 He who corrects *and* instructs a scoffer gets dishonor for himself,
And he who rebukes a wicked man gets insults for himself.

8 Do not correct a scoffer [who foolishly ridicules and takes no responsibility for his error] or he will hate you;
Correct a wise man [who learns from his error], and he will love you. [Ps 141:5]

9 Give *instruction* to a wise man and he will become even wiser;
Teach a righteous man and he will increase his learning.

10 The [reverent] fear of the LORD [that is, worshiping Him and regarding Him as truly awesome] is the beginning *and* the preeminent part of wisdom [its starting point and its essence],
And the knowledge of the Holy One is understanding *and* spiritual insight.

11 For by me (wisdom from God) your days will be multiplied,
And years of life shall be increased.

12 If you are wise, you are wise for yourself [for your own benefit];
If you scoff [thoughtlessly ridicule and disdain], you alone will pay the penalty.

13 The foolish woman is restless *and* noisy;
She is naive *and* easily misled *and* thoughtless, and knows nothing at all [of eternal value].

14 She sits at the doorway of her house,
On a seat by the high *and* conspicuous places of the city,

15 Calling to those who pass by,
Who are making their paths straight:

16 "Whoever is naive *or* inexperienced, let him turn in here!"

And to him who lacks understanding (common sense), she says,

17 "Stolen waters (pleasures) are sweet [because they are forbidden];
And bread *eaten* in secret is pleasant." [Prov 20:17]

18 But he does not know that the spirits of the dead are there,
And that her guests are [already] in the depths of Sheol (the nether world, the place of the dead).

10

THE PROVERBS of Solomon:

A wise son makes a father glad,
But a foolish [stubborn] son [who refuses to learn] is a grief to his mother.

2 Treasures of wickedness *and* ill-gotten gains do not profit,
But righteousness *and* moral integrity in daily life rescues from death.

3 The LORD will not allow the righteous to hunger [God will meet all his needs],
But He will reject *and* cast away the craving of the wicked. [Ps 34:9, 10; 37:25]

4 Poor is he who works with a negligent *and* idle hand,
But the hand of the diligent makes *him* rich.

5 He who gathers during summer *and* takes advantage of his opportunities is a son who acts wisely,
But he who sleeps during harvest *and* ignores the moment of opportunity is a son who acts shamefully.

6 Blessings are on the head of the righteous [the upright, those in right standing with God],
But the mouth of the wicked conceals violence.

7 The *memory of the righteous [person] is a [source of] blessing,
But the name of the wicked will [be forgotten and] rot [like a corpse]. [Ps 112:6; 9:5]

8 The wise in heart [are willing to learn so they] will accept *and* obey commands (instruction),
But the babbling fool [who is arrogant and thinks himself wise] will come to ruin.

10:7 Lit *mention.*

KEYS *to a* Victorious Life *Remember To Speak Positively*

Jesus often experienced adverse circumstances, and while He talked about the situations He was facing, He never did so in a negative way. In the book of John, He told His disciples He was going away, but they should be happy for Him because it was the will of God. He went on to say He wouldn't be talking much more with them (see John 14:28–31).

Proverbs 10:11 says, "The mouth of the righteous is a fountain of life and *his words of wisdom are a source of blessing," which Jesus demonstrated perfectly. He knew when to speak, when not to speak, and how to speak. He obviously knew the power and impact of words. I believe His choosing to say fewer words and making sure that the ones He did say were the right ones helped Him to complete God's perfect plan for Him.*

9 He who walks in integrity *and* with moral character walks securely,
But he who takes a crooked way will be discovered *and* punished.

10 He who [maliciously] winks the eye [of evil intent] causes trouble;
And the babbling fool [who is arrogant and thinks himself wise] will come to ruin.

11 The mouth of the righteous is a fountain of life *and* his words of wisdom are a source of blessing,
But the mouth of the wicked conceals violence *and* evil.

12 Hatred stirs up strife,
But love covers *and* overwhelms all transgressions [forgiving and overlooking another's faults].

13 On the lips of the discerning, [skillful and godly] wisdom is found,
But discipline *and* the rod are for the back of the one who is without common sense *and* understanding.

14 Wise men store up *and* treasure knowledge [in mind and heart],
But with the mouth of the foolish, ruin is at hand.

15 The rich man's wealth is his fortress;
The ruin of the poor is their poverty.
[Ps 52:7; 1 Tim 6:17]

16 The wages of the righteous [the upright, those in right standing with God] is [a worthwhile, meaningful] life,
The income of the wicked, punishment.
[Rom 6:21–23; 1 Tim 6:10]

17 He who learns from instruction *and* correction is on the [right] path of life [and for others his example is a path toward wisdom and blessing],
But he who ignores *and* refuses correction goes off course [and for others his example is a path toward sin and ruin].

18 He who hides hatred has lying lips,
And he who spreads slander is a fool.
[Prov 26:24–26]

19 When there are many words, transgression *and* offense are unavoidable,
But he who controls his lips *and* keeps thoughtful silence is wise.

20 The tongue of the righteous is like precious silver (greatly valued);
The heart of the wicked is worth little.

21 The lips of the righteous feed *and* guide many,
But fools [who reject God and His wisdom] die for lack of understanding.

WINNING THE BATTLES *of the* MIND
Avoiding "Loose Mouth Disease"

According to Proverbs 10:19 people who talk too much can easily get themselves into trouble. Without meaning to cause problems, they talk about something they were to keep confidential, sharing information with someone who wasn't to find out about it, hurting someone's feelings, spreading gossip or rumors, or making casual comments that others might easily misinterpret. I refer to this kind of undisciplined speech as "loose mouth disease." People who have it merely love to talk and take every opportunity available to say something.

One aspect of loose mouth disease that almost all of us are susceptible to is making comments that other people perceive as promises. I once hurt a friend deeply in this very way. I said something that she took as a long-term commitment, and at the time I thought it would be the case. But God later led me in a different direction, and she was wounded. I felt terrible that I didn't speak more wisely. Since then I have learned to say to people, "We will do such and such unless God leads us in a different direction." That was what I meant when speaking with my friend, but I didn't actually say it. I was not careful enough with my words.

When you make a commitment to someone, speak carefully and make your intention clear. Try not to leave room for the other person to misinterpret your intent, and qualify your commitment if necessary with a comment such as, "We can do that as long as it's good for both of us," or "We can do that if I do not have to work overtime that weekend," or, as I mentioned earlier, "We can do that unless God leads us in a different direction." If we believe what God's Word says about the words of our mouths, we must also take seriously the issue of keeping our word.

If you have ever told someone you would do something and not done it, even if you had a good reason, you know you will feel awkward and uncomfortable the next time you see that person. This kind of trouble can be avoided by practicing wisdom and thinking before you speak. Proverbs 21:23 says, "He who guards his mouth and his tongue guards himself from troubles."

A PRAYER FOR VICTORY

Dear Lord, please help me understand how serious my words are and to be more careful about them, especially when making promises or commitments. I want to be a person of integrity where my words are concerned, and I believe You will help me do it. In Jesus' name. Amen.

22 The blessing of the LORD brings [true] riches,

And He adds no sorrow to it [for it comes as a blessing from God].

23 Engaging in evil is like sport to the fool [who refuses wisdom and chases sin],

But to a man of understanding [skillful and godly] wisdom *brings joy.*

24 What the wicked fears will come upon him,

But the desire of the righteous [for the blessings of God] will be granted.

25 When the whirlwind passes, the wicked is no more,

But the righteous has an everlasting foundation. [Ps 125:1; Matt 7:24–27]

26 Like vinegar to the teeth and smoke to the eyes,

So is the lazy one to those who send him *to work.*

27 The [reverent] fear of the LORD [worshiping, obeying, serving, and trusting Him with awe-filled respect] prolongs one's life,

But the years of the wicked will be shortened.

28 The hope of the righteous [those of honorable character and integrity] is joy,

But the expectation of the wicked [those who oppose God and ignore His wisdom] comes to nothing.

29 The way of the LORD is a stronghold to the upright,

But it is ruin to those who do evil.

30 The [consistently] righteous will never be shaken,

But the wicked will not inhabit the earth. [Ps 37:22; 125:1]

31 The mouth of the righteous flows with [skillful and godly] wisdom,

But the perverted tongue will be cut out.

32 The lips of the righteous know (speak) what is acceptable,

But the mouth of the wicked knows (speaks) what is perverted (twisted).

11 A FALSE balance *and* dishonest business practices are extremely offensive to the LORD,

But an accurate scale is His delight. [Lev 19:35, 36; Prov 16:11]

2 When pride comes [boiling up with an arrogant attitude of self-importance], then come dishonor *and* shame,

But with the humble [the teachable who have been chiseled by trial and who have learned to walk humbly with God] there is wisdom *and* soundness of mind.

3 The integrity *and* moral courage of the upright will guide them,

But the crookedness of the treacherous will destroy them.

4 Riches will not provide security in the day of wrath *and* judgment,

But righteousness rescues from death. [Prov 10:2; Zeph 1:18]

5 The righteousness of the blameless will smooth their way *and* keep it straight,

But the wicked will fall by his own wickedness.

6 The righteousness of the upright will rescue them,

But the treacherous will be caught by their own greed.

7 When the wicked man dies, his expectation will perish;

And the hope of [godless] strong men perishes.

8 The righteous is rescued from trouble,

And the wicked takes his place.

9 With his mouth the godless man destroys his neighbor,

But through knowledge *and* discernment the righteous will be rescued.

10 When it goes well for the righteous, the city rejoices,

And when the wicked perish, there are shouts of joy.

11 By the blessing [of the influence] of the upright the city is exalted,

But by the mouth of the wicked it is torn down.

12 He who despises his neighbor lacks sense,

But a man of understanding keeps silent.

13 He who goes about as a gossip reveals secrets,

But he who is trustworthy *and* faithful keeps a matter hidden.

14 Where there is no [wise, intelligent] guidance, the people fall [and go off course like a ship without a helm],

WINNING THE BATTLES *of the* MIND
Seek the Right Kind of Advice

When you are facing a dilemma, it is important to run to the throne (to God), not to the phone to ask a friend for advice. It's always best to go to God first and seek His wisdom and to not start asking other people what they think. There are situations in life when you can benefit from a trustworthy person's good advice and times when God chooses to speak to you through other people, so I want to offer a couple of guidelines for seeking advice.

First, anytime we talk to someone else about our problems, we should do so with a purpose in mind. When we speak of our troubles just to be talking about them or trying to gain nothing more than sympathy, we often say things that don't really need to be said.

Second, know that bad advice is worse than no advice at all. So the first guideline for talking to people about your problems is to speak with someone you respect and are willing to listen to. Talk with someone who is known to be wise, who knows God's Word thoroughly, and who will keep your secrets. God's Word clearly teaches us that we are to not follow the advice of the ungodly (see Ps. 1:1). Seek advice from true friends who will not simply agree with you, but will disagree if they see that you may be wrong about something.

Third, talk with someone whom you can trust not to discuss with anyone else what you have discussed with them. Only people with mature character will keep secrets, so if you need to talk about something confidential, seek someone who is disciplined with their mouth and has been proven trustworthy.

You can protect yourself and hopefully gain the good advice you need by following God's wisdom in these areas. I can tell you from firsthand experience that I have sacrificed my joy and peace on numerous occasions simply because I talked to the wrong people. Proverbs 11:14 says there is victory in the abundance of counselors, but it also says they must be "wise and godly" counselors. When you need advice, look for wise, godly people who can give you good advice—and you'll be on your way to victory.

A PRAYER FOR VICTORY

Help me, Lord, to look to You for advice first anytime I have a problem. If I need to seek advice from another human being, lead me to the right people, people who are wise and trustworthy and will help me find the wisdom you want me to have. In Jesus' name. Amen.

But in the abundance of [wise and godly] counselors there is victory.

15 He who puts up security *and* guarantees a debt for an outsider will surely suffer [for his foolishness],

But he who hates (declines) being a guarantor is secure [from its penalties].

16 A gracious *and* good woman attains honor,

And ruthless men attain riches [but not respect].

17 The merciful *and* generous man benefits his soul [for his behavior returns to bless him],

But the cruel *and* callous man does himself harm.

18 The wicked man earns deceptive wages,

But he who sows righteousness *and* lives his life with integrity will have a true reward [that is both permanent and satisfying]. [Hos 10:12; Gal 6:8, 9; James 3:18]

19 He who is steadfast in righteousness *attains* life,

But he who pursues evil *attains* his own death.

20 The perverse in heart are repulsive *and* shamefully vile to the LORD,

But those who are blameless *and* above reproach in their walk are His delight!

21 Assuredly, the evil man will not go unpunished,

But the descendants of the righteous will be freed.

22 As a ring of gold in a swine's snout,

So is a beautiful woman who is without discretion [her lack of character mocks her beauty].

23 The desire of the righteous brings only good,

But the expectation of the wicked brings wrath.

24 There is the one who [generously] scatters [abroad], and yet increases all the more;

And there is the one who withholds what is justly due, *but it results* only in want *and* poverty.

25 The generous man [is a source of blessing and] shall be prosperous *and* enriched,

And he who waters will himself be watered [reaping the generosity he has sown]. [2 Cor 9:6–10]

26 The people curse him who holds back grain [when the public needs it],

But a blessing [from God and man] is upon the head of him who sells it.

27 He who diligently seeks good seeks favor *and* grace,

But he who seeks evil, evil will come to him.

28 He who leans on *and* trusts in *and* is confident in his riches will fall,

But the righteous [who trust in God's provision] will flourish like a *green* leaf.

29 He who troubles (mismanages) his own house will inherit the wind (nothing),

And the foolish will be a servant to the wise-hearted.

30 The fruit of the [consistently] righteous is a tree of life,

And he who is wise captures *and* wins souls [for God—he gathers them for eternity]. [Matt 4:19; 1 Cor 9:19; James 5:20]

31 If the righteous will be rewarded on the earth [with godly blessings],

How much more [will] the wicked and the sinner [be repaid with punishment]!

12 WHOEVER LOVES instruction *and* discipline loves knowledge, But he who hates reproof *and* correction is stupid.

2 A good man will obtain favor from the LORD,

But He will condemn a man who devises evil.

3 A man will not be established by wickedness,

But the root of the [consistently] righteous will not be moved.

4 A virtuous *and* excellent wife [worthy of honor] is the crown of her husband,

But she who shames him [with her foolishness] is like rottenness in his bones. [Prov 31:23; 1 Cor 11:7]

5 The thoughts *and* purposes of the [consistently] righteous are just (honest, reliable),

But the counsels *and* schemes of the wicked are deceitful.

KEYS *to a* **Victorious** **Life** *The Power of Words*

The Bible says that we need to control our tongue if we want to enjoy life (see 1 Pet. 3:10) and that "the tongue of the wise brings healing" (Prov. 12:18). I find that reading and meditating on what God's Word says about the power of words is helpful to me. Here are some of my favorites: "The one who guards his mouth [thinking before he speaks] protects his life" (Prov. 13:3). "Let the words of my mouth and the meditation of my heart be acceptable and pleasing in Your sight, O LORD, my [firm, immovable] rock and my Redeemer" (Ps. 19:14).

Look up these additional Scriptures and meditate on them as you seek to live a powerful life: Proverbs 8:8; 11:9; 15:4; 18:21; James 1:26. God's Word has power in it that will strengthen and enable you to speak words of life that will benefit you.

---

6 The [malevolent] words of the wicked lie in wait for [innocent] blood [to slander], But the mouth of the upright will rescue *and* protect them.

7 The wicked are overthrown [by their evil] and are no more, But the house of the [consistently] righteous will stand [securely].

8 A man will be commended according to his insight *and* sound judgment, But the one who is of a perverse mind will be despised.

9 Better is he who is lightly esteemed and has a servant, Than he who [boastfully] honors himself [pretending to be what he is not] and lacks bread.

10 A righteous man has kind regard for the life of his animal, But even the compassion of the wicked is cruel. [Deut 25:4]

11 He who tills his land will have plenty of bread, But he who follows worthless *things* lacks common sense *and* good judgment.

12 The wicked desire the plunder of evil men, But the root of the righteous yields *richer* fruit.

13 An evil man is [dangerously] ensnared by the transgression of his lips, But the righteous will escape from trouble.

14 A man will be satisfied with good from the fruit of his words, And the deeds of a man's hands will return to him [as a harvest].

15 The way of the [arrogant] fool [who rejects God's wisdom] is right in his own eyes, But a wise *and* prudent man is he who listens to counsel. [Prov 3:7; 9:9; 21:2]

16 The [arrogant] fool's anger is quickly known [because he lacks self-control and common sense], But a prudent man ignores an insult.

17 He who speaks truth [when he testifies] tells what is right, But a false witness utters deceit [in court].

18 There is one who speaks rashly like the thrusts of a sword, But the tongue of the wise brings healing.

19 Truthful lips will be established forever, But a lying tongue is [credited] only for a moment.

20 Deceit is in the heart of those who devise evil, But counselors of peace have joy.

POWERPOINT

I have certainly experienced the fact that anxiety weighs us down and keeps us from being lighthearted and glad (see Prov. 12:25)—and perhaps you have, too. Anxiety on a regular basis becomes a real burden and keeps us from enjoying life and moving forward in God's plans for us. People who allow their lives to consist of being anxious over one little thing after another do not experience much peace and joy. The good news is that we do have a choice. We can choose to be upset or we can choose to be at peace. Thankfully, we don't have to live by our feelings; we can learn to live beyond them.

21 No harm befalls the righteous,
But the wicked are filled with trouble. [Job 5:19; Ps 91:3; Prov 12:13; Is 46:4; Jer 1:8; Dan 6:27; 2 Tim 4:18]

22 Lying lips are extremely disgusting to the LORD,
But those who deal faithfully are His delight. [Prov 6:17; 11:20; Rev 22:15]

23 A shrewd man is reluctant to display his knowledge [until the proper time],
But the heart of [over-confident] fools proclaims foolishness. [Is 32:6]

24 The hand of the diligent will rule,
But the negligent *and* lazy will be put to forced labor.

25 Anxiety in a man's heart weighs it down,
But a good (encouraging) word makes it glad. [Ps 50:4; Prov 15:13]

26 The righteous man is a guide to his neighbor,
But the way of the wicked leads them astray.

27 The lazy man does not catch *and* roast his prey,
But the precious possession of a [wise] man is diligence [because he recognizes opportunities and seizes them].

28 In the way of righteousness is life,
And in its pathway there is no death [but immortality—eternal life]. [John 3:36; 4:36; 8:51; 11:26; 1 Cor 15:54; Gal 6:8]

13 A WISE son heeds *and* accepts [and is the result of] his father's discipline *and* instruction,
But a scoffer does not listen to reprimand *and* does not learn from his errors.

2 From the fruit of his mouth a [wise] man enjoys good,
But the desire of the treacherous is for violence.

3 The one who guards his mouth [thinking before he speaks] protects his life;
The one who opens his lips wide [and chatters without thinking] comes to ruin.

4 The soul (appetite) of the lazy person craves and gets nothing [for lethargy overcomes ambition],
But the soul (appetite) of the diligent [who works willingly] is rich *and* abundantly supplied. [Prov 10:4]

5 A righteous man hates lies,
But a wicked man is loathsome, and he acts shamefully.

6 Righteousness (being in right standing with God) guards the one whose way is blameless,
But wickedness undermines *and* overthrows the sinner.

7 There is one who pretends to be rich, yet has nothing at all;
Another pretends to be poor, yet has great wealth. [Prov 12:9; Luke 12:20, 21]

8 The ransom for a man's life is his wealth,
But the poor man does not even have to listen to a rebuke *or* threats [from the envious].

9 The light of the righteous [within him—grows brighter and] rejoices,
But the lamp of the wicked [is a temporary light and] goes out.

10 Through pride *and* presumption come nothing but strife,
But [skillful and godly] wisdom is with those who welcome [well-advised] counsel.

11 Wealth *obtained* by fraud dwindles,

KEYS to a Victorious Life *What Are You Talking About?*

The Bible says, "From the fruit of his mouth a [wise] man enjoys good" (Prov. 13:2). We talk a lot, and sometimes we pay little attention to what we are saying, let alone think seriously about the impact of our words. If we are honest with ourselves, we may find that some of our moods—good and bad—are directly linked to our conversations.

Anytime you become aware of your mood, whether you are feeling a bit gloomy or feeling cheerful and blessed, you should ask yourself: "What have I been talking about?" Soon you will begin to see how your words connect to your moods and attitudes.

Why not decide each day before you even get out of bed to ask God to help you talk only about those things that will benefit you and everyone who hears you? Since we have the power to make our days better, we would be foolish indeed if we didn't use it.

But he who gathers gradually by [honest] labor will increase [his riches].

12 Hope deferred makes the heart sick, But when desire is fulfilled, it is a tree of life.

13 Whoever despises the word *and* counsel [of God] brings destruction upon himself, But he who [reverently] fears *and* respects the commandment [of God] will be rewarded.

14 The teaching of the wise is a fountain *and* source of life, So that one may avoid the snares of death.

15 Good understanding wins favor [from others], But the way of the unfaithful is hard [like barren, dry soil].

16 Every prudent *and* self-disciplined man acts with knowledge, But a [closed-minded] fool [who refuses to learn] displays his foolishness [for all to see].

17 A wicked messenger falls into hardship, But a faithful ambassador brings healing.

18 Poverty and shame will come to him who refuses instruction *and* discipline, But he who accepts *and* learns from reproof *or* censure is honored.

19 Desire realized is sweet to the soul; But it is detestable to fools to turn away from evil [which they have planned].

20 He who walks [as a companion] with wise men will be wise, But the companions of [conceited, dull-witted] fools [are fools themselves and] will experience harm. [Is 32:6]

21 Adversity pursues sinners, But the [consistently] upright will be rewarded with prosperity.

22 A good man leaves an inheritance to his children's children, And the wealth of the sinner is stored up for [the hands of] the righteous.

23 Abundant food is in the fallow (uncultivated) ground of the poor, But [without protection] it is swept away by injustice.

24 He who withholds the rod [of discipline] hates his son,

But he who loves him disciplines *and* trains him diligently *and* appropriately [with wisdom and love]. [Prov 19:18; 22:15; 23:13; 29:15, 17; Eph 6:4]

25 The [consistently] righteous has enough to satisfy his appetite,

But the stomach of the wicked is in need [of bread].

14 THE WISE woman builds her house [on a foundation of godly precepts, and her household thrives],

But the foolish one [who lacks spiritual insight] tears it down with her own hands [by ignoring godly principles].

2 He who walks in uprightness [reverently] fears the LORD [and obeys and worships Him with profound respect],

But he who is devious in his ways despises Him.

3 In the mouth of the [arrogant] fool [who rejects God] is a rod for his back,

But the lips of the wise [when they speak with godly wisdom] will protect them.

4 Where there are no oxen, the manger is clean,

But much revenue [because of good crops] comes by the strength of the ox.

5 A faithful *and* trustworthy witness will not lie,

But a false witness speaks lies.

6 A scoffer seeks wisdom and finds none [for his ears are closed to wisdom],

But knowledge is easy for one who understands [because he is willing to learn].

7 Leave the presence of a [shortsighted] fool,

For you will not find knowledge *or* hear godly wisdom from his lips.

8 The wisdom of the sensible is to understand his way,

But the foolishness of [shortsighted] fools is deceit.

9 Fools mock sin [but sin mocks the fools],

KEYS *to a* Victorious Life *Learn To Be Prudent*

A word we don't hear very much about is prudence. The King James Version of Proverbs 14:8 says, "The wisdom of the prudent is to understand his way." To have prudence or to be prudent means being wise stewards of the gifts God has given us to use. Those gifts include time, energy, strength, and health as well as thoughts, words, and material possessions. They include our bodies as well as our minds and spirits.

Prudence is a word that many people are not familiar with, but we should be knowledgeable of it and avidly seek it. In our world today we see a great deal of waste. Jesus doesn't want us to be wasteful. He wants us to be good managers of everything He gives to us. God's giving us increase and promotion is dependent on how well we learn to manage what we already have.

Ask God to reveal when you are being wasteful and make changes accordingly. Sometimes I find myself thinking something that is a total waste of time, or I might be drawn into a conversation that is a waste of time. Thankfully, I can make prudent changes and improve the quality of my life, and so can you.

But among the upright there is good will *and* the favor *and* blessing of God. [Prov 10:23]

10 The heart knows its own bitterness, And no stranger shares its joy.

11 The house of the wicked will be overthrown, But the tent of the upright will thrive.

12 There is a way *which seems* right to a man *and* appears straight before him, But its end is the way of death.

13 Even in laughter the heart may be in pain, And the end of joy may be grief.

14 The backslider in heart will have his fill with his own [rotten] ways, But a good man will *be satisfied* with his ways [the godly thought and action which his heart pursues and in which he delights].

15 The naive *or* inexperienced person [is easily misled and] believes every word he hears, But the prudent man [is discreet and astute and] considers well where he is going.

16 A wise man suspects danger and cautiously avoids evil, But the fool is arrogant and careless.

17 A quick-tempered man acts foolishly *and* without self-control, And a man of wicked schemes is hated.

18 The naive [are unsophisticated and easy to exploit and] inherit foolishness, But the sensible [are thoughtful and far-sighted and] are crowned with knowledge.

19 The evil will bow down before the good, And the wicked [will bow down] at the gates of the righteous.

20 The poor man is hated even by his neighbor, But those who love the rich are many.

21 He who despises his neighbor sins [against God and his fellow man], But happy [blessed and favored by God] is he who is gracious *and* merciful to the poor.

22 Do they not go astray who devise evil *and* wander from the way of righteousness? But kindness and truth will be to those who devise good.

23 In all labor there is profit,

A Prayer To Renew Your Mind

Lord, in the reverent fear of You I have strong confidence, and I will always have a place of refuge.

· adapted from Proverbs 14:26

But mere talk leads only to poverty.

24 The crown of the wise is their wealth [of wisdom], But the foolishness of [closed-minded] fools is [nothing but] folly.

25 A truthful witness saves lives, But he who speaks lies is treacherous.

26 In the [reverent] fear of the LORD there is strong confidence, And His children will [always] have a place of refuge.

27 The [reverent] fear of the LORD [that leads to obedience and worship] is a fountain of life, So that one may avoid the snares of death. [John 4:10, 14]

28 In a multitude of people is a king's glory, But in a lack of people is a [pretentious] prince's ruin.

29 He who is slow to anger has great understanding [and profits from his self-control], But he who is quick-tempered exposes *and* exalts his foolishness [for all to see]. [Prov 16:32; James 1:19]

30 A calm *and* peaceful *and* tranquil heart is life *and* health to the body, But passion *and* envy are like rottenness to the bones.

31 He who oppresses the poor taunts *and* insults his Maker, But he who is kind *and* merciful *and* gracious to the needy honors Him. [Prov 17:5; Matt 25:40, 45]

32 The wicked is overthrown through his wrongdoing, But the righteous has hope *and* confidence *and* a refuge [with God] even in death.

33 Wisdom rests [silently] in the heart of one who has understanding, But what is in the heart of [shortsighted] fools is made known. [Is 32:6]

KEYS *to a* Victorious Life *Your Words Are a Tree of Life*

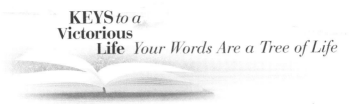

The principle truth in Proverbs 15:4 is the same as the one in Proverbs 18:21, which says we minister either life or death with our mouth: "Death and life are in the power of the tongue."

These two verses explain why God's Word reminds us often to pay attention to the words we speak. In Ephesians 4:29, Paul writes: "Do not let unwholesome [foul, profane, worthless, vulgar] words ever come out of your mouth, but only such speech as is good for building up others, according to the need and the occasion, so that it will be a blessing to those who hear [you speak]."

Notice that the word spirit *in Proverbs 15:4 is spelled with a lowercase "s." This tells us the verse is not talking about the Holy Spirit, but refers to the human spirit. In other words, our words have the power to give life to or to break down the spirit or heart of other people, as well as our own.*

As believers, we are not to speak things that would discourage people or make them want to give up on life, nor are we to pollute ourselves or others with negative words or comments. We are not to use our mouths to hurt people. We should speak words that heal, restore, and uplift. Try giving each person you come in contact with a sincere compliment! People light up when we point out something good about them.

---

34 Righteousness [moral and spiritual integrity and virtuous character] exalts a nation,
But sin is a disgrace to any people.
35 The king's favor *and* good will are toward a servant who acts wisely *and* discreetly,
But his anger *and* wrath are toward him who acts shamefully. [Matt 24:45, 47]

15 A SOFT *and* gentle *and* thoughtful answer turns away wrath,
But harsh *and* painful *and* careless words stir up anger. [Prov 25:15]
2 The tongue of the wise speaks knowledge that is pleasing *and* acceptable,
But the [babbling] mouth of fools spouts folly.
3 The eyes of the LORD are in every place,

Watching the evil and the good [in all their endeavors]. [Job 34:21; Prov 5:21; Jer 16:17; 32:19; Heb 4:13]
4 A soothing tongue [speaking words that build up and encourage] is a tree of life,
But a perverse tongue [speaking words that overwhelm and depress] crushes the spirit.
5 A [flippant, arrogant] fool rejects his father's instruction *and* correction,

Speak God's Word

I speak soft and gentle and thoughtful answers that turn away wrath, not harsh and painful and careless words that stir up anger.

| *adapted from* PROVERBS 15:1 |

But he who [is willing to learn and]
  regards *and* keeps in mind a
  reprimand acquires good sense.
⁶ Great *and* priceless treasure is in the
  house of the [consistently] righteous
  one [who seeks godly instruction and
  grows in wisdom],
But trouble is in the income of the wicked
  one [who rejects the laws of God].
⁷ The lips of the wise spread knowledge
  [sifting it as chaff from the grain];
But the hearts of [shortsighted] fools are
  not so.
⁸ The sacrifice of the wicked is hateful *and*
  exceedingly offensive to the LORD,
But the prayer of the upright is His
  delight! [Is 1:11; Jer 6:20; Amos 5:22]
⁹ The way [of life] of the wicked is hateful
  and exceedingly offensive to the LORD,
But He loves one who pursues
  righteousness [personal integrity,
  moral courage and honorable
  character].
¹⁰ There is severe discipline for him who
  turns from the way [of righteousness];
And he who hates correction will die.
¹¹ Sheol (the nether world, the place of the
  dead) and Abaddon (the abyss, the
  place of eternal punishment) *lie open*
  before the LORD—
How much more the hearts *and* inner
  motives of the children of men. [Job
  26:6; Ps 139:8; Rev 9:2; 20:1, 2]
¹² A scoffer [unlike a wise man] resents one
  who rebukes him *and* tries to teach
  him;
Nor will he go to the wise [for counsel
  and instruction].
¹³ A heart full of joy *and* goodness makes a
  cheerful face,
But when a heart is full of sadness the
  spirit is crushed. [Prov 17:22]
¹⁴ The mind of the intelligent *and*
  discerning seeks knowledge *and*
  eagerly inquires after it,

Speak God's Word

*I have a glad heart that has a continual
feast regardless of the circumstances.*

| adapted from PROVERBS 15:15 |

Speak God's Word

*I will not be hot-tempered and stir up
strife, but I will be slow to anger and
patiently calm disputes.*

| adapted from PROVERBS 15:18 |

But the mouth of the [stubborn] fool
  feeds on foolishness. [Is 32:6]
¹⁵ All the days of the afflicted are
  bad,
But a glad heart has a continual feast
  [regardless of the circumstances].
¹⁶ Better is a little with the [reverent,
  worshipful] fear of the LORD
Than great treasure and trouble with it.
  [Ps 37:16; Prov 16:8; 1 Tim 6:6]
¹⁷ Better is a dinner of vegetables *and*
  herbs where love is present
Than a fattened ox served with hatred.
  [Prov 17:1]
¹⁸ A hot-tempered man stirs up strife,
But he who is slow to anger *and* patient
  calms disputes.
¹⁹ The way of the lazy is like a hedge
  of thorns [it pricks, lacerates, and
  entangles him],
But the way [of life] of the upright is
  smooth *and* open like a highway.
²⁰ A wise son makes a father glad,
But a foolish man despises his mother.
²¹ Foolishness is joy to him who is without
  heart *and* lacks [intelligent, common]
  sense,
But a man of understanding walks
  uprightly [making his course straight].
  [Eph 5:15]
²² Without consultation *and* wise advice,
  plans are frustrated,
But with many counselors they are
  established and succeed.
²³ A man has joy in giving an appropriate
  answer,
And how good *and* delightful is a word
  spoken at the right moment—how
  good it is!
²⁴ The [chosen] path of life leads upward
  for the wise,
That he may keep away from Sheol (the
  nether world, the place of the dead)
  below. [Phil 3:20; Col 3:1, 2]

WINNING THE BATTLES *of the* MIND
Expect Good Things To Happen

Shortly after I began to study the Bible seriously, I often sensed an oppressive atmosphere around me. Everything seemed gloomy—as if something bad was going to happen. It wasn't anything I could explain, just a vague, dreaded sense of something evil or wrong about to happen. When I asked the Lord, "What is this feeling?" He said, "Evil forebodings." I had to meditate on that. I had never heard the phrase before.

I learned that the sense of dread I felt was not based on true circumstances or situations. The problems I was facing were not as critical as the devil was making them appear. My acceptance of his lies, even though they were vague, was opening the door for evil forebodings. I eventually realized that I had encountered so many negative things in my life that I had gotten to the point of expecting more of them. My feelings were based on my past experiences when they should have been based on God's promises.

As I continued to meditate on evil forebodings, God gave me a clear revelation. *I was miserable because my thoughts were miserable*—my thoughts were poisoning my outlook. My thoughts robbed me of the ability to enjoy my life. Instead of being positive because of all the amazing things I was learning from God's Word, I found myself trapped in the gloom and doom that had surrounded me since my abusive childhood.

I had not been taught to let go of what was behind. I couldn't rejoice in the good things going on in my life. I focused on the past and what might lie ahead, which was usually gloom and chaos because that was what I expected. Satan had built a stronghold in my mind, and I was trapped until I learned I could tear down that negative, evil stronghold by applying God's Word to my life and circumstances.

Little by little, my thinking changed, and today I no longer live in evil forebodings. I purposefully expect good things to happen in my life. I realize now that I can choose my thoughts. I don't have to accept Satan's lies.

Like everyone else, negative things do happen to me from time to time, but I don't become negative because of them. I discovered that "a glad heart has a continual feast [regardless of the circumstances]" (Prov. 15:15). I always make an effort to remain positive, and that helps me enjoy my life even in the midst of the storms.

A PRAYER FOR VICTORY

Dear Lord, at times evil forebodings have robbed me of my joy and contentment. When these feelings come, please remind me that You are in control. Help me to rest in You and rejoice in Your Power. Amen.

POWERPOINT

Words are wonderful when used in a proper way. They can encourage, edify, and give confidence to the hearer. A right word spoken at the right time is so good for people (see Prov. 15:23) and can actually be life changing. The words that come out of our mouths go into other people's ears, but they go into our own ears as well. When we hear them, they drop down into our soul, where they give us either joy or sadness, peace or turmoil, depending on what kind of words they are. We can literally increase our own joy and the joy of others by speaking the right words. Confessing good things will make you happier and will make the people around you happier too.

²⁵ The Lord will tear down the house of the proud *and* arrogant (self-righteous),

But He will establish *and* protect the boundaries [of the land] of the [godly] widow.

²⁶ Evil plans *and* thoughts of the wicked are exceedingly vile *and* offensive to the Lord,

But pure words are pleasant words to Him.

²⁷ He who profits unlawfully brings suffering to his own house,

But he who hates bribes [and does not receive nor pay them] will live. [Is 5:8; Jer 17:11]

²⁸ The heart of the righteous thinks carefully about how to answer [in a wise and appropriate and timely way],

But the [babbling] mouth of the wicked pours out malevolent things. [1 Pet 3:15]

²⁹ The Lord is far from the wicked [and distances Himself from them],

But He hears the prayer of the [consistently] righteous [that is, those with spiritual integrity and moral courage].

³⁰ The light of the eyes rejoices the hearts of others,

And good news puts fat on the bones.

³¹ The ear that listens to *and* learns from the life-giving rebuke (reprimand, censure)

Will remain among the wise.

³² He who neglects *and* ignores instruction *and* discipline despises himself,

But he who learns from rebuke acquires understanding [and grows in wisdom].

³³ The [reverent] fear of the Lord [that is, worshiping Him and regarding Him as truly awesome] is the instruction for wisdom [its starting point and its essence];

And before honor comes humility.

16 THE PLANS *and* reflections of the heart belong to man,
But the [wise] answer of the tongue is from the Lord.

² All the ways of a man are clean *and* innocent in his own eyes [and he may see nothing wrong with his actions],

But the Lord weighs *and* examines the motives *and* intents [of the heart and knows the truth]. [1 Sam 16:7; Heb 4:12]

³ Commit your works to the Lord [submit and trust them to Him],

And your plans will succeed [if you respond to His will and guidance].

⁴ The Lord has made everything for its own purpose,

Even the wicked [according to their role] for the day of evil.

⁵ Everyone who is proud *and* arrogant in heart is disgusting *and* exceedingly offensive to the Lord;

Be assured he will not go unpunished. [Prov 8:13; 11:20, 21]

⁶ By mercy *and* lovingkindness and truth [not superficial ritual] wickedness is cleansed from the heart,

And by the fear of the Lord one avoids evil.

⁷ When a man's ways please the Lord, He makes even his enemies to be at peace with him.

⁸ Better is a little with righteousness Than great income [gained] with injustice. [Ps 37:16; Prov 15:16]

WINNING THE BATTLES *of the* MIND
Pleasant, Healing Words

Solomon wrote, "The heart of the wise instructs his mouth [in wisdom] and adds persuasiveness to his lips. Pleasant words are like a honeycomb, sweet *and* delightful to the soul and healing to the body" (Prov. 16:23–24). This proverb means that the thoughts we dwell on will eventually come out in our words. If our words agree with God's Word, we will see miraculous things happen in our lives.

We should be wise in how we think about and speak to others. One of the smartest friends I had in school shared how her father told her she was stupid so many times that eventually her own thoughts said to her, *You aren't intelligent enough to understand this because you are stupid.* We shouldn't determine our worth and value based on what other people have said about us, but on what God says about us!

Many of us struggle at times with insecurity and self-doubt, but for some people it's worse than for others. By speaking encouraging words to others, we are helping them win their own personal battle over the enemy.

I remember times when I've wanted to say a kind word to someone, but then I would think, *Oh, she already knows that.* I have since learned that we cannot edify and encourage anyone too much.

What if each of us decided, *I am God's servant to bring soothing, kind, healing words to wounded and hurting hearts*? Not only would we put the devil to flight, but our friends' joy would soar, and ours, too, because we had been used as God's instruments of healing. It often takes very little effort to do a great deal of good. Often it's only a word of encouragement, a hug, or even just a smile that can brighten someone's day.

A PRAYER FOR VICTORY

Holy Spirit of God, please remind me of the words that dwell inside me. Remind me to hold on to the good, the kind, and the uplifting thoughts, and empower me to cast down those that can hurt and tear down others—and myself. I ask this through Jesus Christ. Amen.

⁹ A man's mind plans his way [as he journeys through life],

But the LORD directs his steps *and* establishes them. [Ps 37:23; Prov 20:24; Jer 10:23]

¹⁰ A divine decision [given by God] is on the lips of the king [as His representative];

His mouth should not be unfaithful *or* unjust in judgment. [Deut 17:18–20; 2 Sam 14:17–20; 1 Kin 3:9–12; Is 11:2]

¹¹ A just balance and [honest] scales are the LORD's;

All the weights of the bag are His concern [established by His eternal principles].

¹² It is repulsive [to God and man] for kings to behave wickedly,

For a throne is established on righteousness (right standing with God).

¹³ Righteous lips are the delight of kings, And he who speaks right is loved.

¹⁴ The wrath of a king is like a messenger of death,

But a wise man will appease it.

¹⁵ In the light of the king's face is life, And his favor is like a cloud bringing the spring rain.

¹⁶ How much better it is to get wisdom than gold!

And to get understanding is to be chosen above silver. [Prov 8:10, 19]

¹⁷ The highway of the upright turns away *and* departs from evil;

He who guards his way protects his life (soul).

¹⁸ Pride goes before destruction, And a haughty spirit before a fall.

¹⁹ It is better to be humble in spirit with the lowly

Than to divide the spoil with the proud (haughty, arrogant).

²⁰ He who pays attention to the word [of God] will find good,

And blessed (happy, prosperous, to be admired) is he who trusts [confidently] in the LORD.

²¹ The wise in heart will be called understanding,

And sweet speech increases persuasiveness *and* learning [in both speaker and listener].

²² Understanding (spiritual insight) is a [refreshing and boundless] wellspring of life to those who have it,

But to give instruction *and* correction to fools is foolishness.

²³ The heart of the wise instructs his mouth [in wisdom]

And adds persuasiveness to his lips.

²⁴ Pleasant words are like a honeycomb, Sweet *and* delightful to the soul and healing to the body.

²⁵ There is a way which seems right to a man *and* appears straight before him, But its end is the way of death.

²⁶ The appetite of a worker works for him, For his hunger urges him on.

²⁷ A worthless man devises *and* digs up evil, And the words on his lips are like a scorching fire.

²⁸ A perverse man spreads strife, And one who gossips separates intimate friends. [Prov 17:9]

²⁹ A violent *and* exceedingly covetous man entices his neighbor [to sin],

And leads him in a way that is not good.

³⁰ He who [slyly] winks his eyes does so to plot perverse things;

And he who compresses his lips [as if in a secret signal] brings evil to pass.

³¹ The silver-haired head is a crown of splendor *and* glory;

It is found in the way of righteousness. [Prov 20:29]

³² He who is slow to anger is better *and* more honorable than the mighty [soldier],

And he who rules *and* controls his own spirit, than he who captures a city.

³³ The lot is cast into the lap, But its every decision is from the LORD.

17 BETTER IS a dry morsel [of food served] with quietness *and* peace

Than a house full of feasting [served] with strife *and* contention.

² A wise servant will rule over the [unworthy] son who acts shamefully *and* brings disgrace [to the family] And [the worthy servant] will share in the inheritance among the brothers.

³ The refining pot is for silver and the furnace for gold,

But the LORD tests hearts. [Ps 26:2; Prov 27:21; Jer 17:10; Mal 3:3]

4 An evildoer listens closely to wicked lips;

And a liar pays attention to a destructive *and* malicious tongue.

5 Whoever mocks the poor taunts his Maker,

And he who rejoices at [another's] disaster will not go unpunished. [Job 31:29; Prov 14:31; Obad 12]

6 Grandchildren are the crown of aged men,

And the glory of children is their fathers [who live godly lives]. [Ps 127:3; 128:3]

7 Excellent speech does not benefit a fool [who is spiritually blind],

Much less do lying lips *benefit* a prince.

8 A bribe is like a bright, precious stone in the eyes of its owner;

Wherever he turns, he prospers.

9 He who covers *and* forgives an offense seeks love,

But he who repeats *or* gossips about a matter separates intimate friends.

10 A reprimand goes deeper into one who has understanding *and* a teachable spirit

Than a hundred lashes into a fool. [Is 32:6]

11 A rebellious man seeks only evil;

Therefore a cruel messenger will be sent against him.

12 Let a man meet a [ferocious] bear robbed of her cubs

Rather than the [angry, narcissistic] fool in his folly. [Hos 13:8]

13 Whoever returns evil for good,

KEYS *to a*
Victorious
Life *Live with Joy and Delight*

God is life, and every good thing He has created is part of that life. We get so caught up in doing and accomplishing, in working and trying to climb the ladder of success, that if we are not careful, we will come to the end of our life and only then realize that we never really lived. God wants us to enjoy life and live it to the full, until it overflows.

We have choices in life. We can grumble our way through our troubles, or we can maintain positive thoughts and attitudes and also have a happy heart. Either way, we have to go through some troubles, so why not take the joy of the Lord as our strength and have our mind filled with energy and vitality and healing. The pressure of any problem is immediately lessened if we choose to believe that God will work something good from it.

In John 15, Jesus talks about abiding in Him. In verse 11, He says, "I have told you these things so that My joy and *delight may be in you, and that your joy may be made full* and *complete* and *overflowing." Jesus wants us to trust Him and have a happy heart (see Prov. 17:22).*

Don't spend your life waiting for things to change before you can be happy. Cultivate and nurture a happy heart now and experience God's "joy and delight" in you all the way to the end of your life.

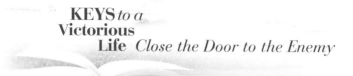

KEYS *to a* Victorious Life *Close the Door to the Enemy*

One of the best commitments we can make is to speak good, positive words. Sometimes, when we truly can't think of anything good to say, it is wise to say nothing at all (see Prov. 17:28). Making a commitment to speak only good things does not mean we will no longer be tempted to speak negative words. In fact, the enemy may tempt us even more than before because he knows the power of words. The very thought that we would commit to improve our words is frightening to him.

We need to remember that the enemy can only influence and control our words to the extent that we allow him to do so. If we ask God for grace, and discipline ourselves to stop speaking negatively, we close a door of opportunity to the enemy. He will always tempt us to do and say what is wrong, but we can resist him and gain victory.

Evil will not depart from his house. [Ps 109:4, 5; Jer 18:20]

14 The beginning of strife is like letting out water [as from a small break in a dam; first it trickles and then it gushes];

Therefore abandon the quarrel before it breaks out *and* tempers explode.

15 He who justifies the wicked, and he who condemns the righteous

Are both repulsive to the LORD. [Ex 23:7; Prov 24:24; Is 5:23]

16 Why is there money in the hand of a fool to buy wisdom,

When he has no common sense *or* even a heart for it?

17 A friend loves at all times,

And a brother is born for adversity.

18 A man lacking common sense gives a pledge

And becomes guarantor [for the debt of another] in the presence of his neighbor.

19 He who loves transgression loves strife *and* is quarrelsome;

He who [proudly] raises his gate seeks destruction [because of his arrogant pride].

20 He who has a crooked mind finds no good, And he who is perverted in his language falls into evil. [James 3:8]

21 He who becomes the parent of a fool [who is spiritually blind] does so to his sorrow,

And the father of a fool [who is spiritually blind] has no joy.

22 A happy heart is good medicine *and* a joyful mind causes healing,

But a broken spirit dries up the bones. [Prov 12:25; 15:13, 15]

23 A wicked man receives a bribe from the [hidden] pocket

To pervert the ways of justice.

24 [Skillful and godly] wisdom is in the presence of a person of understanding [and he recognizes it],

But the eyes of a [thickheaded] fool are on the ends of the earth.

25 A foolish son is a grief *and* anguish to his father

And bitterness to her who gave birth to him.

26 It is also not good to fine the righteous,

Nor to strike the noble for their uprightness.

27 He who has knowledge restrains *and* is careful with his words,

And a man of understanding *and* wisdom has a cool spirit (self-control, an even temper). [James 1:19]

28 Even a [callous, arrogant] fool, when
   he keeps silent, is considered
   wise;
  When he closes his lips he is regarded as
   sensible (prudent, discreet) *and* a man
   of understanding.

18 HE WHO [willfully] separates
   himself [from God and man]
   seeks his own desire,
  He quarrels against all sound wisdom.
2 A [closed-minded] fool does not delight
   in understanding,
  But only in revealing his personal
   opinions [unwittingly displaying his
   self-indulgence and his stupidity].
3 When the wicked man comes [to the
   depth of evil], contempt [of all that is
   pure and good] also comes,
  And with inner baseness (dishonor)
   comes outer shame (scorn).
4 The words of a man's mouth are like
   deep waters [copious and difficult to
   fathom];

  The fountain of [mature, godly] wisdom
   is like a bubbling stream [sparkling,
   fresh, pure, and life-giving].
5 To show respect to the wicked person is
   not good,
  Nor to push aside *and* deprive the
   righteous of justice.
6 A fool's lips bring contention *and* strife,
  And his mouth invites a beating.
7 A fool's mouth is his ruin,
  And his lips are the snare of his soul.
8 The words of a whisperer (gossip) are like
   dainty morsels [to be greedily eaten];
  They go down into the innermost
   chambers of the body [to be
   remembered and mused upon].
9 He who is careless in his work
  Is a brother to him who destroys.
10 The name of the LORD is a strong tower;
  The righteous runs to it and is safe *and*
   set on high [far above evil].
11 The rich man's wealth is his strong city,
  And like a high wall [of protection] in
   his own imagination *and* conceit.

KEYS *to a* Victorious Life *Positive Thoughts and Words*

Our thoughts and words about ourselves are tremendously important. In order to overcome the negative thinking and speaking that have been such a natural part of our lifestyle for so long, we will need to make a conscious effort to think and speak good things about ourselves (see Prov. 18:21).

We need to think and say what the Word of God says about us. Positive confession of the Word of God should be an ingrained habit of every believer. If you have not yet begun to develop this important habit, you can start today. Begin thinking and saying good things about yourself: "I am the righteousness of God in Jesus Christ. I prosper in everything I lay my hand to. I have gifts and talents, and God is using me. I operate in the fruit of the Spirit. I walk in love. Joy flows through me."

The Bible teaches that we can appropriate the blessings of God into our lives by believing and confessing the positive things God has said about us in His Word.

Words are seeds that we sow, and when we sow positive ones, we can expect positive results.

12 Before disaster the heart of a man
is haughty *and* filled with self-
importance,
But humility comes before honor.
13 He who answers before he hears [the
facts]—
It is folly and shame to him. [John 7:51]
14 The spirit of a man sustains him in
sickness,
But as for a broken spirit, who can
bear it?
15 The mind of the prudent [always]
acquires knowledge,
And the ear of the wise [always] seeks
knowledge.
16 A man's gift [given in love or courtesy]
makes room for him
And brings him before great men. [Gen
32:20; 1 Sam 25:27; Prov 17:8; 21:14]
17 The first one to plead his case seems
right,
Until another comes and cross-
examines him.
18 To cast lots puts an end to quarrels
And decides between powerful
contenders.
19 A brother offended *is harder to win* over
than a fortified city,
And contentions [separating families]
are like the bars of a castle.
20 A man's stomach will be satisfied with
the fruit of his mouth;
He will be satisfied with the
consequence of his words.
21 Death and life are in the power of the
tongue,
And those who love it *and* indulge it will
eat its fruit *and* bear the consequences
of their words. [Matt 12:37]
22 He who finds a [true and faithful] wife
finds a good thing
And obtains favor *and* approval from
the Lord. [Prov 19:14; 31:10]

Speak God's Word

*I know that death and life are in the power
of the tongue, and those who love it and
indulge it will eat its fruit and bear the
consequences of their words.*

| adapted from PROVERBS 18:21 |

23 The poor man pleads,
But the rich man answers roughly.
24 The man of *too many* friends [chosen
indiscriminately] will be broken in
pieces *and* come to ruin,
But there is a [true, loving] friend who
[is reliable and] sticks closer than a
brother.

19 BETTER IS a poor man who
walks in his integrity
Than a [rich] man who is
twisted in his speech and is a
[shortsighted] fool.
2 Also it is not good for a person to be
without knowledge,
And he who hurries with his feet [acting
impulsively and proceeding without
caution or analyzing the consequences]
sins (misses the mark).
3 The foolishness of man undermines his
way [ruining whatever he undertakes];
Then his heart is resentful *and* rages
against the Lord [for, being a fool, he
blames the Lord instead of
himself].
4 Wealth makes many friends,
But a poor man is separated from his
friend. [Prov 14:20]
5 A false witness will not go unpunished,
And he who breathes out lies will not
escape. [Ex 23:1; Deut 19:16–19; Prov
6:19; 21:28]
6 Many will seek the favor of a generous
and noble man,
And everyone is a friend to him who
gives gifts.
7 All the brothers of a poor man hate him;
How much more do his friends abandon
him!
He pursues *them with* words, but they
are gone.
8 He who gains wisdom *and* good sense
loves (preserves) his own soul;
He who keeps understanding will find
good *and* prosper.
9 A false witness will not go unpunished,
And he who breathes lies will perish.
10 Luxury is not fitting for a fool;
Much less for a slave to rule over
princes.
11 Good sense *and* discretion make a man
slow to anger,

KEYS *to a* Victorious Life *Wisdom and Patience*

According to Proverbs 19:11 when we use good sense and discretion, we will not be easily angered. Wisdom silently tells us to wait a little while, until our emotions settle down, before we do or say something. Emotions urge us toward haste, pushing us do something and do it right now! Godly wisdom tells us to be patient and wait until we have a clear picture of what we are to do and when we are to do it. I like to say it this way: "Let emotions subside and then decide." We need to be able to step back from our situations and see them from God's perspective. Then we need to make decisions based on what we know rather than on what we feel.

And it is his honor *and* glory to overlook a transgression *or* an offense [without seeking revenge and harboring resentment].

12 The king's wrath *terrifies* like the roaring of a lion,
But his favor is as [refreshing and nourishing as] dew on the grass. [Hos 14:5]

13 A foolish (ungodly) son is destruction to his father,
And the contentions of a [quarrelsome] wife are like a constant dripping [of water].

14 House and wealth are the inheritance from fathers,
But a wise, understanding, *and* sensible wife is [a gift and blessing] from the LORD. [Prov 18:22]

15 Laziness casts one into a deep sleep [unmindful of lost opportunity],
And the idle person will suffer hunger.

16 He who keeps *and* obeys the commandment [of the LORD] keeps (guards) his own life,
But he who is careless of his ways *and* conduct will die. [Prov 13:13; 16:17; Luke 10:28; 11:28]

17 He who is gracious *and* lends a hand to the poor lends to the LORD,
And the LORD will repay him for his good deed. [Prov 28:27; Eccl 11:1; Matt 10:42; 25:40; 2 Cor 9:6–8; Heb 6:10]

18 Discipline *and* teach your son while there is hope,
And do not [indulge your anger or resentment by imposing inappropriate punishment nor] desire his destruction.

19 A *man of* great anger will bear the penalty [for his quick temper and lack of self-control];
For if you rescue him [and do not let him learn from the consequences of his action], you will only have to rescue him over and over again.

20 Listen to counsel, receive instruction, *and* accept correction,
That you may be wise in the time to come.

21 Many plans are in a man's mind,
But it is the LORD's purpose for him that will stand (be carried out). [Job 23:13; Ps 33:10, 11; Is 14:26, 27; 46:10; Acts 5:39; Heb 6:17]

22 That which is desirable in a man is his loyalty *and* unfailing love,
But it is better to be a poor man than a [wealthy] liar.

23 The fear of the LORD *leads* to life,
So that one may sleep satisfied, untouched by evil. [Job 5:19; Ps 91:3; Prov 12:13; Is 46:4; Jer 1:8; Dan 6:27; 2 Tim 4:8]

24 The lazy man buries his hand in the [food] dish,

KEYS *to a*
Victorious
Life *Close the Door to Strife*

Strife is a thief and a robber that we can learn to recognize and deal with quickly. We can control strife before it controls us (see Prov. 20:3).

Strife is defined as "the act or state of fighting or quarreling, especially bitterly; discord." It is bickering, arguing, being involved in a heated disagreement; it can reveal itself as an angry undercurrent. Strife is dangerous. It is a demonic force sent by Satan for the purpose of destruction.

Almost any time someone hurts us or offends us, anger rises up within us. Feeling anger is not sin, but we should not act out the angry feelings in an ungodly manner. We need to resist the temptation to hold a grudge or to fall into bitterness, resentment, or unforgiveness.

A judgmental attitude is an open door to strife, so it's important for us to remember that mercy triumphs over judgment (see James 2:13). Judgment usually leads to gossip. Gossip begins to spread the strife from person to person. Strife hinders us from living in unity and harmony and from enjoying God's blessings.

When we are tempted to think judgmental thoughts toward others, and then to spread our opinion through gossip and backbiting, we should remember this helpful hint: Let the one among us who is without sin throw the first stone (see John 8:7).

Remember that God changes things through prayer and faith, not through strife, judgment, or gossip.

But will not even bring it to his mouth again.
²⁵ Strike a scoffer [for refusing to learn], and the naive may [be warned and] become prudent;
Reprimand one who has understanding *and* a teachable spirit, and he will gain knowledge *and* insight.
²⁶ He who assaults his father and chases away his mother
Is a son who brings shame and disgrace. [1 Tim 5:8]
²⁷ Cease listening, my son, to instruction *and* discipline
And you will stray from the words of knowledge.
²⁸ A wicked *and* worthless witness mocks justice,

And the mouth of the wicked spreads iniquity.
²⁹ Judgments are prepared for scoffers, And beatings for the backs of [thickheaded] fools. [Is 32:6]

20 WINE IS a mocker, strong drink a riotous brawler; And whoever is intoxicated by it is not wise. [Prov 23:29, 30; Is 28:7; Hos 4:11]
² The terror of a king is like the roaring of a lion;
Whoever provokes him to anger forfeits his own life.
³ It is an honor for a man to keep away from strife [by handling situations with thoughtful foresight],

But any fool will [start a] quarrel
    [without regard for the consequences].
⁴The lazy man does not plow when the
    winter [planting] season arrives;
So he begs at the [next] harvest and has
    nothing [to reap].
⁵A plan (motive, wise counsel) in the heart
    of a man is like water in a deep well,
But a man of understanding draws it
    out. [Prov 18:4]
⁶Many a man proclaims his own loyalty
    and goodness,
But who can find a faithful *and*
    trustworthy man?
⁷The righteous man who walks in
    integrity *and* lives life in accord with
    his [godly] beliefs—
How blessed [happy and spiritually
    secure] are his children after him
    [who have his example to follow].
⁸A [discerning] king who sits on the
    throne of judgment
Sifts all evil [like chaff] with his eyes
    [and cannot be easily fooled].
⁹Who can say, "I have cleansed my heart,
    I am pure from my sin?" [1 Kin 8:46;
    2 Chr 6:36; Job 9:30; 14:4; Ps 51:5;
    1 John 1:8]
¹⁰Differing weights [one for buying and
    another for selling] and differing
    measures,
Both of them are detestable *and* offensive
    to the LORD. [Deut 25:13; Mic 6:10, 11]
¹¹Even a boy is known *and* distinguished
    by his acts,
Whether his conduct is pure and right.
¹²The hearing ear and the seeing eye,
    The [omnipotent] LORD has made both
    of them.
¹³Do not love [excessive] sleep, or you will
    become poor;
Open your eyes [so that you can do your
    work] and you will be satisfied with
    bread.
¹⁴"It is [almost] worthless, it is [almost]
    worthless," says the buyer [as he
    negotiates the price];
But when he goes his way, then he boasts
    [about his bargain].
¹⁵There is gold, and an abundance of pearls,
    But the lips of knowledge are a vessel
    of preciousness [the most precious of
    all]. [Job 28:12, 16–19; Prov 3:15; 8:11]

POWERPOINT

Proverbs 20:19 says that we should
not associate with people who gossip
or tell other people's secrets. If a
person tells you someone else's
secret, he or she will likely tell
someone else your secret too. Many of
us have confided in someone only to
find out that he or she told our secret,
and that is a painful experience. Let's
learn to choose our friends wisely and
choose our words wisely.

¹⁶[The judge tells the creditor], "Take
    the clothes of one who is surety for a
    stranger;
And hold him in pledge [when he
    guarantees a loan] for foreigners."
    [Prov 27:13]
¹⁷Food gained by deceit is sweet to a man,
    But afterward his mouth will be filled
    with gravel [just as sin may be sweet at
    first, but later its consequences bring
    despair].
¹⁸Plans are established by counsel;
    So make war [only] with wise guidance.
¹⁹He who goes about as a gossip reveals
    secrets;
Therefore do not associate with a gossip
    [who talks freely or flatters]. [Rom
    16:17, 18]
²⁰Whoever curses his father or his mother,
    His lamp [of life] will be extinguished in
    time of darkness.
²¹An inheritance hastily gained [by
    greedy, unjust means] at the
    beginning
Will not be blessed in the end. [Prov
    28:20; Hab 2:6]
²²Do not say, "I will repay evil";
    Wait [expectantly] for the LORD, and He
    will rescue *and* save you. [Deut 32:35;
    2 Sam 16:12; Rom 12:17–19; 1 Thess
    5:15; 1 Pet 3:9]
²³Differing weights are detestable *and*
    offensive to the LORD,
And fraudulent scales are not good.

24 Man's steps are ordered *and* ordained by the Lord.
How then can a man [fully] understand his way?

25 It is a trap for a man to [speak a vow of consecration and] say rashly, "It is holy!"
And [not until] afterward consider [whether he can fulfill it].

26 A wise king sifts out the wicked [from among the good]
And drives the [threshing] wheel over them [to separate the chaff from the grain].

27 The spirit (conscience) of man is the lamp of the Lord,
Searching *and* examining all the innermost parts of his being. [1 Cor 2:11]

28 Loyalty *and* mercy, truth *and* faithfulness, protect the king,
And he upholds his throne by lovingkindness.

29 The glory of young men is their [physical] strength,
And the honor of aged men is their gray head [representing wisdom and experience].

30 Blows that wound cleanse away evil,
And strokes reach to the innermost parts.

21

THE KING'S heart is like channels of water in the hand of the Lord;
He turns it whichever way He wishes. [Ex 10:1, 2; Ezra 6:22]

2 Every man's way is right in his own eyes,
But the Lord weighs *and* examines the hearts [of people and their motives]. [Prov 24:12; Luke 16:15]

3 To do righteousness and justice
Is more acceptable to the Lord than sacrifice [for wrongs repeatedly committed]. [1 Sam 15:22; Prov 15:8; Is 1:11; Hos 6:6; Mic 6:7, 8]

4 Haughty *and* arrogant eyes and a proud heart,
The lamp of the wicked [their self-centered pride], is sin [in the eyes of God].

5 The plans of the diligent lead surely to abundance *and* advantage,
But everyone who acts in haste comes surely to poverty.

6 Acquiring treasures by a lying tongue
Is a fleeting vapor, the seeking *and* pursuit of death.

7 The violence of the wicked will [return to them and] drag them away [like fish caught in a net],
Because they refuse to act with justice.

8 The way of the guilty is [exceedingly] crooked,
But as for the pure, his conduct is upright.

9 It is better to live in a corner of the housetop [on the flat roof, exposed to the weather]
Than in a house shared with a quarrelsome (contentious) woman.

10 The soul of the wicked desires evil [like an addictive substance];
His neighbor finds no compassion in his eyes. [James 2:16]

11 When the scoffer is punished, the naive [observes the lesson and] becomes wise;
But when the wise *and* teachable person is instructed, he receives knowledge. [Prov 19:25]

12 The righteous one keeps an eye on the house of the wicked—
How the wicked are cast down to ruin.

13 Whoever shuts his ears at the cry of the poor
Will cry out himself and not be answered. [Matt 18:30–34; James 2:13]

14 A gift in secret subdues anger,
And a bribe [hidden] in the pocket, strong wrath.

15 When justice is done, it is a joy to the righteous (the upright, the one in right standing with God),
But to the evildoers it is disaster.

16 A man who wanders from the way of understanding (godly wisdom)
Will remain in the assembly of the dead.

17 He who loves [only selfish] pleasure *will become* a poor man;
He who loves *and* is devoted to wine and [olive] oil will not become rich.

18 The wicked become a ransom for the righteous,
And the treacherous in the place of the upright [for they fall into their own traps].

19 It is better to dwell in a desert land
   Than with a contentious and troublesome woman.
20 There is precious treasure and oil in the house of the wise [who prepare for the future],
   But a short-sighted *and* foolish man swallows it up *and* wastes it.
21 He who earnestly seeks righteousness and loyalty
   Finds life, righteousness, and honor. [Prov 15:9; Matt 5:6]
22 A wise man scales the city [walls] of the mighty
   And brings down the stronghold in which they trust.
23 He who guards his mouth and his tongue
   Guards himself from troubles. [Prov 12:13; 13:3; 18:21; James 3:2]
24 "Proud," "Haughty," "Scoffer," are his names
   Who acts with overbearing *and* insolent pride.
25 The desire of the lazy kills him,
   For his hands refuse to labor;
26 He craves all the day long [and does no work],
   But the righteous [willingly] gives and does not withhold [what he has]. [2 Cor 9:6–10]
27 The sacrifice of the wicked is detestable *and* offensive [to the LORD].
   How much more [unacceptable and insulting can it be] when he brings it with evil intention?
28 A false witness will perish,
   But a man who listens *to the truth* will speak forever *and* go unchallenged.
29 A wicked man puts on a bold face,
   But as for the upright, he considers, directs, *and* establishes his way [with the confidence of integrity].
30 There is no [human] wisdom or understanding
   Or counsel [that can prevail] against the LORD.
31 The horse is prepared for the day of battle,
   But deliverance *and* victory belong to the LORD.

22

A *GOOD* name [earned by honorable behavior, godly wisdom, moral courage, and personal integrity] is more desirable than great riches;
   And favor is better than silver and gold.
2 The rich and poor have a common bond;
   The LORD is the Maker of them all. [Job 31:15; Prov 14:31]
3 A prudent *and* far-sighted *person* sees the evil [of sin] and hides himself [from it],
   But the naive continue on and are punished [by suffering the consequences of sin].
4 The reward of humility [that is, having a realistic view of one's importance] and the [reverent, worshipful] fear of the LORD
   Is riches, honor, and life. [Prov 21:21]
5 Thorns and snares are in the way of the obstinate [for their lack of honor and their wrong-doing traps them];
   He who guards himself [with godly wisdom] will be far from them *and* avoid the consequences they suffer.
6 Train up a child in the way he should go [teaching him to seek God's wisdom and will for his abilities and talents],
   Even when he is old he will not depart from it. [Eph 6:4; 2 Tim 3:15]
7 The rich rules over the poor,
   And the borrower is servant to the lender.
8 He who sows injustice will reap [a harvest of] trouble,
   And the rod of his wrath [with which he oppresses others] will fail.
9 He who is generous will be blessed,
   For he gives some of his food to the poor. [2 Cor 9:6–10]
10 Drive out the scoffer, and contention will go away;
   Even strife and dishonor will cease.
11 He who loves purity of heart
   And whose speech is gracious will have the king as his friend.
12 The eyes of the LORD keep guard over knowledge *and* the one who has it,
   But He overthrows the words of the treacherous.
13 The lazy one [manufactures excuses and] says, "There is a lion outside!

I will be killed in the streets [if I go out
to work]!"
14 The mouth of an immoral woman is a
deep pit [deep and inescapable];
He who is cursed by the LORD [because
of his adulterous sin] will fall into it.
15 Foolishness is bound up in the heart of a
child;
The rod of discipline [correction
administered with godly wisdom and
lovingkindness] will remove it far
from him.
16 He who oppresses or exploits the poor to
get more for himself
Or who gives to the rich [to gain influence
and favor], will only come to poverty.

17 Listen carefully and hear the words of
the wise,
And apply your mind to my knowledge;
18 For it will be pleasant if you keep them
in mind [incorporating them as
guiding principles];
Let them be ready on your lips [to guide
and strengthen yourself and others].
19 So that your trust and reliance and
confidence may be in the LORD,
I have taught these things to you today,
even to you.
20 Have I not written to you excellent things
In counsels and knowledge,
21 To let you know the certainty of the
words of truth,
That you may give a correct answer to
him who sent you? [Luke 1:3, 4]

22 Do not rob the poor because he is poor
[and defenseless],
Nor crush the afflicted [by legal
proceedings] at the gate [where the city
court is held], [Ex 23:6; Job 31:16, 21]
23 For the LORD will plead their case
And take the life of those who rob them.
[Zech 7:10; Mal 3:5]

24 Do not even associate with a man given
to angry outbursts;
Or go [along] with a hot-tempered man,
25 Or you will learn his [undisciplined] ways
And get yourself trapped [in a situation
from which it is hard to escape].

26 Do not be among those who give pledges
[involving themselves in others'
finances],

Or among those who become guarantors
for others' debts.
27 If you have nothing with which to pay
[another's debt when he defaults],
Why should his creditor take your bed
from under you?

28 Do not move the ancient landmark [at
the boundary of the property]
Which your fathers have set.

29 Do you see a man skillful and
experienced in his work?
He will stand [in honor] before kings;
He will not stand before obscure men.

23 WHEN YOU sit down to dine
with a ruler,
Consider carefully what is [set]
before you;
2 For you will put a knife to your throat
If you are a man of great appetite.
3 Do not desire his delicacies,
For it is deceptive food [offered to you
with questionable motives].

4 Do not weary yourself [with the
overwhelming desire] to gain wealth;
Cease from your own understanding of
it. [Prov 28:20; 1 Tim 6:9, 10]
5 When you set your eyes on wealth, it is
[suddenly] gone.
For wealth certainly makes itself wings
Like an eagle that flies to the heavens.

6 Do not eat the bread of a selfish man,
Or desire his delicacies;
7 For as he thinks in his heart, so is he [in
behavior—one who manipulates].
He says to you, "Eat and drink,"
Yet his heart is not with you [but it is
begrudging the cost].
8 The morsel which you have eaten you
will vomit up,
And you will waste your compliments.

9 Do not speak in the ears of a fool,
For he will despise the [godly] wisdom of
your words. [Is 32:6]

Speak God's Word

As I think in my heart, so am I.

[adapted from PROVERBS 23:7]

WINNING THE BATTLES *of the* MIND

Where the Mind Goes, the Man Follows

What we give our energies and attention to will develop in our lives (see Prov. 23:7), or as I like to say, "Where the man goes, the mind follows!" If I think about ice cream long enough, I will probably end up eating some! If we focus only on the negative things in our lives, we become negative people. Everything, including our conversation, becomes negative. We soon lose our joy and live miserable lives—and it all started with our own thinking.

You might be experiencing some problems in life—not realizing that you may be creating them yourself by what you're choosing to think about. You might be discouraged and even depressed and wonder why. Yet if you examine your thought life, you will find that you are feeding the negative emotions you are feeling. Negative thoughts are fuel for discouragement, depression, and many other unpleasant emotions.

We should choose our thoughts carefully. We can think about what is wrong with our lives or about what is right with them. We can think about what is wrong with all the people we are in relationship with or we can see the good and meditate on that. The Bible teaches us to always believe the best. When we do that, it pleases God and makes our own lives happier and more peaceful.

We should always remember that the mind is a battlefield and that our thoughts largely determine our destiny. They aren't just empty words that flow through our mind, so it is very important to decide what we will allow to rest inside our mind. We should also be very aware that our adversary will use what's in our mind in any way he possibly can to trap us.

To put it another way, we can't have a positive life and a negative mind. Our thoughts—our focus—is what determines where we end up. God wants our minds to be filled with positive, beautiful, and healthy thoughts. The more we focus on those things, the more readily we defeat Satan's attacks.

A PRAYER FOR VICTORY

Dear patient and loving God, I ask You to forgive me for focusing my thoughts on things that are not pleasing to You. I pray that You will help me fill my mind with thoughts that are clean and pure and uplifting. In Jesus' name. Amen.

KEYS *to a* Victorious Life *Discipline Has Its Rewards*

Think of an area in your life where you need to refuse to give up and "apply your heart to discipline" (Prov. 23:12). Come up with a goal—one that will require you to be disciplined and overcome some obstacles, but one that also promises great reward. It may be as basic as making your bed each morning or as ambitious as running a marathon. It may be to break free from a fear of public speaking or to overcome an addiction or to get out of debt. Just make sure you and God are in agreement, depend on Him for the strength to do it, and then go after your goal with everything in you.

Be full of holy determination—not some kind of fleshly determination or willpower—but true God-given determination. You do have self-control. It is a fruit of the Spirit, and it is in you—believe it and begin walking in it.

---

10 Do not move the ancient landmark [at the boundary of the property]
And do not go into the fields of the fatherless [to take what is theirs],
[Deut 19:14; 27:17; Prov 22:28]
11 For their Redeemer is strong *and* mighty;
He will plead their case against you.
12 Apply your heart to discipline
And your ears to words of knowledge.

13 Do not withhold discipline from the child;
If you swat him with a *reed-like* rod [applied with godly wisdom], he will not die.
14 You shall swat him with the *reed-like* rod
And rescue his life from Sheol (the nether world, the place of the dead).

15 My son, if your heart is wise,
My heart will also be glad;
16 Yes, my heart will rejoice
When your lips speak right things.

17 Do not let your heart envy sinners [who live godless lives and have no hope of salvation],
But [continue to] live in the [reverent, worshipful] fear of the LORD day by day.

18 Surely there is a future [and a reward],
And your hope *and* expectation will not be cut off.
19 Listen, my son, and be wise,
And direct your heart in the way [of the LORD].
20 Do not associate with heavy drinkers of wine,
Or with gluttonous eaters of meat, [Is 5:22; Luke 21:34; Rom 13:13; Eph 5:18]
21 For the heavy drinker and the glutton will come to poverty,
And the drowsiness [of overindulgence] will clothe one with rags.

22 Listen to your father, who sired you,
And do not despise your mother when she is old.
23 Buy truth, and do not sell it;
Get wisdom and instruction and understanding.

24 The father of the righteous will greatly rejoice,
And he who sires a wise child will have joy in him.
25 Let your father and your mother be glad,
And let her who gave birth to you rejoice [in your wise and godly choices].

26 My son, give me your heart
  And let your eyes delight in my ways,
27 For a prostitute is a deep pit,
  And an immoral woman is a narrow
    well.
28 She lurks *and* lies in wait like a robber
    [who waits for prey],
  And she increases the faithless among
    men.

29 Who has woe? Who has sorrow?
  Who has strife? Who has complaining?
  Who has wounds without cause?
  Whose eyes are red *and* dim?
30 Those who linger long over wine,
  Those who go to taste mixed wine. [Prov
    20:1; Eph 5:18]
31 Do not look at wine when it is red,
  When it sparkles in the glass,
  When it goes down smoothly.
32 At the last it bites like a serpent
  And stings like a viper.
33 Your [drunken] eyes will see strange
    things
  And your mind will utter perverse
    things [untrue things, twisted things].
34 And you will be [as unsteady] as one
    who lies down in the middle of the
    sea,
  And [as vulnerable to disaster] as one
    who lies down on the top of a ship's
    mast, *saying,*
35 "They struck me, but I was not hurt!
  They beat me, but I did not feel it!
  When will I wake up?
  I will seek more wine."

24 DO NOT be envious of evil
    men,
    Nor desire to be with them;
2 For their minds plot violence,
  And their lips talk of trouble [for the
    innocent].

3 Through [skillful and godly] wisdom a
    house [a life, a home, a family] is built,
  And by understanding it is established
    [on a sound and good foundation],
4 And by knowledge its rooms are filled
  With all precious and pleasant riches.

5 A wise man is strong,
  And a man of knowledge strengthens his
    power; [Prov 21:22; Eccl 9:16]

6 For by wise guidance you can wage your
    war,
  And in an abundance of [wise]
    counselors there is victory *and*
    safety.

7 Wisdom is too exalted for a [hardened,
    arrogant] fool;
  He does not open his mouth in the
    gate [where the city's rulers sit in
    judgment].

8 He who plans to do evil
  Will be called a schemer *or* deviser of
    evil.
9 The devising of folly is sin,
  And the scoffer is repulsive to men.

10 If you are slack (careless) in the day of
    distress,
  Your strength is limited.

11 Rescue those who are being taken away
    to death,
  And those who stagger to the slaughter,
    Oh hold them back [from their doom]!
12 If you [claim ignorance and] say, "See,
    we did not know this,"
  Does He not consider it who weighs
    and examines the hearts *and* their
    motives?
  And does He not know it who guards
    your life *and* keeps your soul?
  And will He not repay [you and] every
    man according to his works?

13 My son, eat honey, because it is good,
  And the drippings of the honeycomb are
    sweet to your taste.
14 Know that [skillful and godly] wisdom is
    [so very good] for your life *and* soul;
  If you find wisdom, then there will be a
    future *and* a reward,
  And your hope *and* expectation will not
    be cut off.

15 Do not lie in wait, O wicked man,
    against the dwelling of the righteous;
  Do not destroy his resting place;
16 For a righteous man falls seven times,
    and rises again,
  But the wicked stumble in *time of*
    disaster *and* collapse. [Job 5:19; Ps
    34:19; 37:24; Mic 7:8]

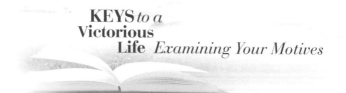

KEYS *to a* Victorious Life *Examining Your Motives*

Our motives—the reasons for doing the things we do—are very important. No matter what we may claim as our motives, we're told that God "weighs and examines the hearts and their motives" and rewards "every man according to his works" (Prov. 24:12).

God wants you to have a pure heart. He wants you to do things because He is leading you to do them or because they are the right things to do. God wants you to be motivated by love. It's important to be able to do what you do because of love—love for God and love for others. It's a good idea to regularly take some time and ask yourself why you are doing the things you do. It is not what you do that impresses God; He is interested in the why behind what you do. Ask God to reveal your motives to you and to change any that are not pure.

---

17 Do not rejoice *and* gloat when your enemy falls,

And do not let your heart be glad [in self-righteousness] when he stumbles,

18 Or the LORD will see your gloating and be displeased,

And turn His anger away from your enemy.

19 Do not get upset because of evildoers,
Or be envious of the wicked,

20 For there will be no future for the evil man;
The lamp of the wicked will be put out.

21 My son, fear the LORD and the king;
And do not associate with those who are given to change [of allegiance, and are revolutionary],

22 For their tragedy will rise suddenly,
And who knows the punishment that both [the LORD and the king] will bring on the rebellious?

23 These also are sayings of the wise:
To show partiality in judgment is not good.

24 He who says to the wicked, "You are righteous,"
Peoples will curse him, nations will denounce him;

25 But to those [honorable judges] who rebuke the *wicked*, it will go well with them *and* they will find delight,
And a good blessing will come upon them.

26 He kisses the lips [and wins the hearts of people]
Who gives a right *and* straightforward answer.

27 Prepare your work outside
And get it ready for yourself in the field;
Afterward build your house *and* establish a home.

28 Do not be a witness against your neighbor without cause,
And do not deceive with your lips [speak neither lies nor half-truths]. [Eph 4:25]

29 Do not say, "I will do to him as he has done to me;
I will pay the man back for his deed." [Prov 20:22; Matt 5:39, 44; Rom 12:17, 19]

30 I went by the field of the lazy man,
And by the vineyard of the man lacking understanding *and* common sense;

31 And, behold, it was all overgrown with thorns,
And nettles were covering its surface,

And its stone wall was broken down.
³²When I saw, I considered it well;
I looked and received instruction.
³³"Yet a little sleep, a little slumber,
A little folding of the hands to rest [and daydream],"
³⁴Then your poverty will come as a robber,
And your want like an armed man.

25 THESE ARE also the proverbs of Solomon, which the men of Hezekiah king of Judah copied: [1 Kin 4:32]

²It is the glory of God to conceal a matter,
But the glory of kings is to search out a matter. [Deut 29:29; Rom 11:33]
³As the heavens for height and the earth for depth,
So the hearts *and* minds of kings are unsearchable.
⁴Take away the dross from the silver,
And there comes out [the pure metal for] a vessel for the silversmith [to shape]. [2 Tim 2:21]
⁵Take away the wicked from before the king,
And his throne will be established in righteousness.
⁶Do not be boastfully ambitious *and* claim honor in the presence of the king,
And do not stand in the place of great men;
⁷For it is better that it be said to you, "Come up here,"

Than for you to be placed lower in the presence of the prince,
Whom your eyes have seen. [Luke 14:8–10]

⁸Do not rush out to argue *your* case [before magistrates or judges];
Otherwise what will you do in the end [when your case is lost and]
When your neighbor (opponent) humiliates you? [Prov 17:14; Matt 5:25]
⁹Argue your case with your neighbor himself [before you go to court];
And do not reveal another's secret, [Matt 18:15]
¹⁰Or he who hears it will shame you
And the rumor about you [and your action in court] will have no end.

¹¹Like apples of gold in settings of silver
Is a word spoken at the right time. [Prov 15:23; Is 50:4]
¹²Like an earring of gold and an ornament of fine gold
Is a wise reprover to an ear that listens *and* learns.
¹³Like the cold of snow [brought from the mountains] in the time of harvest,
So is a faithful messenger to those who send him;
For he refreshes the life of his masters.
¹⁴Like clouds and wind without rain
Is a man who boasts falsely of gifts [he does not give]. [Jude 12]
¹⁵By patience *and* a calm spirit a ruler may be persuaded,

KEYS *to a* **Victorious Life** *God Can Use Your Words*

God has always used people to speak messages to others. Those messages may be extremely important, with the ability to change the course of a nation, a church, a business, an individual, or a family; right words spoken at just the right time are very valuable (see Prov. 25:11).

Whoever you may have an opportunity to speak to, remember that right words at the right time can change a life.

And a soft *and* gentle tongue breaks the bone [of resistance]. [Gen 32:4; 1 Sam 25:24; Prov 15:1; 16:14]

¹⁶ Have you found [pleasure sweet like] honey? Eat only as much as you need,

Otherwise, being filled excessively, you vomit it.

¹⁷ Let your foot seldom be in your neighbor's house,

Or he will become tired of you and hate you.

¹⁸ Like a club and a sword and a piercing arrow

Is a man who testifies falsely against his neighbor (acquaintance).

¹⁹ Like a broken tooth or an unsteady foot

Is confidence in an unfaithful man in time of trouble.

²⁰ Like one who takes off a garment in cold weather, or like [a reactive, useless mixture of] vinegar on soda,

Is he who [thoughtlessly] sings [joyful] songs to a heavy heart. [Dan 6:18; Rom 12:15]

²¹ If your enemy is hungry, give him bread to eat;

And if he is thirsty, give him water to drink; [Matt 5:44; Rom 12:20]

²² For in doing so, you will heap coals of fire upon his head,

And the LORD will reward you.

²³ The north wind brings forth rain,

And a backbiting tongue, an angry countenance.

²⁴ It is better to live in a corner of the housetop [on the flat roof, exposed to the weather]

Than in a house shared with a quarrelsome (contentious) woman. [Prov 21:9]

²⁵ Like cold water to a thirsty soul,

So is good news from a distant land.

²⁶ Like a muddied fountain and a polluted spring

A Prayer To Renew Your Mind

Help me, Lord, to live as a righteous person who does not yield and compromise my integrity before the wicked.

· *adapted from Proverbs 25:26*

POWERPOINT

Exercising self-control is a form of freedom. Not exercising self-control sets a person up for trouble (see Prov. 25:28). You don't have to do what you feel like doing; you're free to do what you know is wise. Discipline and self-control will help you be the person you want to be. Don't ever say, "I just don't have any self-control," because the truth is that you do, but it needs to be exercised in order to be strong. Self-control is a fruit of the new nature God has given each of us as believers in Jesus Christ, and all we need to do is develop it. We develop self-control by using it, just as we develop muscles by using them (see 2 Pet. 1:6).

Is a righteous man who yields *and* compromises his integrity before the wicked.

²⁷ It is not good to eat much honey,

Nor is it glorious to seek one's own glory.

²⁸ Like a city that is broken down and without walls [leaving it unprotected]

Is a man who has no self-control over his spirit [and sets himself up for trouble]. [Prov 16:32]

26 LIKE SNOW in summer and like rain in harvest,

So honor is not fitting for a [shortsighted] fool. [Is 32:6]

² Like the sparrow in her wandering, like the swallow in her flying,

So the curse without cause does not come *and* alight [on the undeserving]. [Num 23:8]

³ A whip for the horse, a bridle for the donkey,

And a rod for the backs of fools [who refuse to learn].

⁴ Do not answer [nor pretend to agree with the frivolous comments of] a [closed-minded] fool according to his folly,

Otherwise you, even you, will be like him.

5 Answer [and correct the erroneous concepts of] a fool according to his folly,

Otherwise he will be wise in his own eyes [if he thinks you agree with him]. [Matt 16:1–4; 21:24–27]

6 He who sends a message by the hand of a fool

Cuts off *his own* feet (sabotages himself) and drinks the violence [it brings on himself as a consequence]. [Prov 13:17]

7 Like the legs which are useless to the lame,

So is a proverb in the mouth of a fool [who cannot learn from its wisdom].

8 Like one who [absurdly] binds a stone in a sling [making it impossible to throw],

So is he who [absurdly] gives honor to a fool.

9 Like a thorn that goes [without being felt] into the hand of a drunken man,

So is a proverb in the mouth of a fool [who remains unaffected by its wisdom].

10 Like a [careless] archer who [shoots arrows wildly and] wounds everyone,

So is he who hires a fool or those who [by chance just] pass by.

11 Like a dog that returns to his vomit Is a fool who repeats his foolishness.

12 Do you see a man [who is unteachable and] wise in his own eyes *and* full of self-conceit?

There is more hope for a fool than for him. [Prov 29:20; Luke 18:11; Rom 12:16; Rev 3:17]

13 The lazy person [who is self-indulgent and relies on lame excuses] says, "There is a lion in the road!

A lion is in the open square [and if I go outside to work I will be killed]!" [Prov 22:13]

14 As the door turns on its hinges, So does the lazy person on his bed [never getting out of it].

15 The lazy person buries his hand in the dish [losing opportunity after opportunity];

It wearies him to bring it back to his mouth. [Prov 19:24]

16 The lazy person is wiser in his own eyes Than seven [sensible] men who can give a discreet answer.

17 Like one who grabs a dog by the ears [and is likely to be bitten]

Is he who, passing by, stops to meddle with a dispute that is none of his business.

18 Like a madman who throws Firebrands, arrows, and death,

19 So is the man who deceives his neighbor (acquaintance, friend)

And then says, "Was I not joking?" [Eph 5:4]

20 For lack of wood the fire goes out, And where there is no whisperer [who gossips], contention quiets down.

21 Like charcoal to hot embers and wood to fire,

So is a contentious man to kindle strife. [Prov 15:18; 29:22]

22 The words of a whisperer (gossip) are like dainty morsels [to be greedily eaten];

They go down into the innermost chambers of the body [to be remembered and mused upon]. [Prov 18:8]

23 Like a [common] clay vessel covered with the silver dross [making it appear silver when it has no real value]

Are burning lips [murmuring manipulative words] and a wicked heart.

24 He who hates, disguises it with his lips, But he stores up deceit in his heart.

25 When he speaks graciously *and* kindly [to conceal his malice], do not trust him,

For seven abominations are in his heart.

26 *Though his* hatred covers itself with guile *and* deceit,

His malevolence will be revealed openly before the assembly.

27 Whoever digs a pit [for another man's feet] will fall into it,

And he who rolls a stone [up a hill to do mischief], it will come back on him. [Ps 7:15, 16; 9:15; 10:2; 57:6; Prov 28:10; Eccl 10:8]

28 A lying tongue hates those it wounds *and* crushes,

And a flattering mouth works ruin.

27

DO NOT boast about tomorrow,
For you do not know what a day may bring. [Luke 12:19, 20; James 4:13]

² Let another praise you, and not your own mouth;

A stranger, and not your own lips.

³ Stone is heavy and the sand weighty,

But a fool's [unreasonable] wrath is heavier *and* more burdensome than both of them.

⁴ Wrath is cruel and anger is an overwhelming flood,

But who is able to endure *and* stand before [the sin of] jealousy?

⁵ Better is an open reprimand [of loving correction]

Than love that is hidden. [Prov 28:23; Gal 2:14]

⁶ Faithful are the wounds of a friend [who corrects out of love and concern],

But the kisses of an enemy are deceitful [because they serve his hidden agenda].

⁷ He who is satisfied loathes honey,

But to the hungry soul any bitter thing is sweet.

⁸ Like a bird that wanders from her nest [with its comfort and safety],

So is a man who wanders from his home.

⁹ Oil and perfume make the heart glad;

So does the sweetness of a friend's counsel that comes from the heart.

¹⁰ Do not abandon your own friend and your father's friend,

And do not go to your brother's house in the day of your disaster.

Better is a neighbor who is near than a brother who is far away.

¹¹ My son, be wise, and make my heart glad,

That I may reply to him who reproaches (reprimands, criticizes) me. [Prov 10:1; 23:15, 24]

¹² A prudent man sees evil and hides himself *and* avoids it,

But the naive [who are easily misled] continue on and are punished [by suffering the consequences of sin]. [Prov 22:3]

¹³ [The judge tells the creditor,] "Take the garment of one who is surety (guarantees a loan) for a stranger;

And hold him in pledge when he is surety for an immoral woman [for it is unlikely the debt will be repaid]." [Prov 20:16]

¹⁴ He who blesses his neighbor with a loud voice early in the morning,

It will be counted as a curse to him [for it will either be annoying or his purpose will be suspect].

¹⁵ A constant dripping on a day of steady rain

And a contentious (quarrelsome) woman are alike; [Prov 19:13]

¹⁶ Whoever attempts to restrain her [criticism] might as well try to stop the wind,

And grasps oil with his right hand.

¹⁷ As iron sharpens iron,

So one man sharpens [and influences] another [through discussion].

¹⁸ He who tends the fig tree will eat its fruit,

And he who faithfully protects *and* cares for his master will be honored. [1 Cor 9:7, 13]

¹⁹ As in water face *reflects* face,

So the heart of man reflects man.

²⁰ Sheol (the place of the dead) and Abaddon (the underworld) are never satisfied;

Nor are the eyes of man ever satisfied. [Prov 30:16; Hab 2:5]

POWERPOINT

Jealousy and envy are negative emotions that torment us (see Prov. 27:4). It is difficult to not be jealous of anyone who looks better than we do or has talents that we don't have. We may want to be happy for that other person, but something in us won't allow it. What God does for you or me may not be what He does for someone else, but we must remember what Jesus said to Peter: Don't be concerned about what I choose to do with someone else—you follow Me (see John 21:22).

21 The refining pot is for silver and the furnace for gold [to separate the impurities of the metal],
    And each is tested by the praise given to him [and his response to it, whether humble or proud].
22 Even though you pound a [hardened, arrogant] fool [who rejects wisdom] in a mortar with a pestle like grain,
    Yet his foolishness will not leave him.

23 Be diligent to know the condition of your flocks,
    And pay attention to your herds;
24 For riches are not forever,
    Nor does a crown *endure* to all generations.
25 When the grass is gone, the new growth is seen,
    And herbs of the mountain are gathered in,
26 The lambs will *supply wool* for your clothing,
    And the goats will bring the price of a field.
27 And *there will be* enough goats' milk for your food,
    For the food of your household,
    And for the maintenance of your maids.

28 THE WICKED flee when no one pursues them,
    But the righteous are as bold as a lion. [Lev 26:17, 36; Ps 53:5]
2 When a land does wrong, it has many princes,
    But when the ruler is a man of understanding and knowledge, its stability endures.
3 A poor man who oppresses *and* exploits the lowly
    Is like a sweeping rain which leaves no food. [Matt 18:28]
4 Those who set aside the law [of God and man] praise the wicked,
    But those who keep the law [of God and man] struggle with them. [Prov 29:18]
5 Evil men do not understand justice,
    But they who long for *and* seek the LORD understand it fully. [John 7:17; 1 Cor 2:15; 1 John 2:20, 27]
6 Better is the poor who walks in his integrity

Than he who is crooked *and* two-faced though he is rich. [Prov 19:1]
7 He who keeps the law [of God and man] is a wise *and* discerning son,
    But he who is a companion of gluttons humiliates his father [and himself].
8 He who increases his wealth by interest and usury (excessive interest)
    Gathers it for him who is gracious to the poor. [Job 27:16, 17; Prov 13:22; Eccl 2:26]
9 He who turns his ear away from listening to the law [of God and man],
    Even his prayer is repulsive [to God]. [Ps 66:18; 109:7; Prov 15:8; Zech 7:11]
10 He who leads the upright astray on an evil path
    Will himself fall into his own pit,
    But the blameless will inherit good.
11 The rich man [who is conceited and relies on his wealth instead of God] is wise in his own eyes,
    But the poor man who has understanding [because he relies on God] is able to see through him.
12 When the righteous triumph, there is great glory *and* celebration;
    But when the wicked rise [to prominence], men hide themselves.
13 He who conceals his transgressions will not prosper,
    But whoever confesses and turns away from his sins will find compassion *and* mercy. [Ps 32:3, 5; 1 John 1:8–10]
14 Blessed *and* favored by God is the man who fears [sin and its consequence] at all times,
    But he who hardens his heart [and is determined to sin] will fall into disaster.
15 Like a roaring lion and a charging bear Is a wicked ruler over a poor people.
16 A leader who is a great oppressor lacks understanding *and* common sense [and his wickedness shortens his days],
    But he who hates unjust gain will [be blessed and] prolong his days.
17 A man who is burdened with the guilt of human blood (murder)
    Will be a fugitive until death; let no one support him *or* give him refuge.
18 He who walks blamelessly *and* uprightly will be kept safe,

KEYS *to a* Victorious Life *Run to God*

One way to maintain peace with God is to never attempt to conceal sin. We should always be honest with God and keep good communication open with Him. God is not surprised by our weaknesses and failures; actually, He knows about our mistakes before we even make them. All we need to do is admit to them and repent of them, and He is faithful to forgive us continually from all sin and to show compassion and mercy (see Prov. 28:13).

It is important to do the best you can out of your love for God. Since none of us is perfect, we will make mistakes. When we do, we can talk openly to our Father about them and maintain a relationship of peace with Him. When you need cleansing, don't ever run from God, run to Him!

But he who is crooked (perverse) will suddenly fall.

19 He who cultivates his land will have plenty of bread,
But he who follows worthless people *and* frivolous pursuits will have plenty of poverty.

20 A faithful (right-minded) man will abound with blessings,
But he who hurries to be rich will not go unpunished. [Prov 13:11; 20:21; 23:4; 1 Tim 6:9]

21 To have regard for one person over another *and* to show favoritism is not good,
Because for a piece of bread a man will transgress.

22 He who has an evil *and* envious eye hurries to be rich
And does not know that poverty will come upon him. [Prov 21:5; 28:20]

23 He who [appropriately] reprimands a [wise] man will afterward find more favor
Than he who flatters with the tongue.

24 He who robs his father or his mother
And says, "This is no sin,"
Is [not only a thief but also] the companion of a man who destroys.

25 An arrogant *and* greedy man stirs up strife,

But he who trusts in the LORD will be blessed *and* prosper.

26 He who trusts confidently in his own heart is a [dull, thickheaded] fool,
But he who walks in [skillful and godly] wisdom will be rescued. [James 1:5]

27 He who gives to the poor will never want,
But he who shuts his eyes [from their need] will have many curses. [Deut 15:7; Prov 19:17; 22:9]

28 When the wicked rise [to power], men hide themselves;
But when the wicked perish, the [consistently] righteous increase *and* become great. [Prov 28:12]

29 HE WHO hardens his neck *and* refuses instruction after being often reproved (corrected, criticized),
Will suddenly be broken beyond repair.

2 When the righteous are in authority *and* become great, the people rejoice;
But when the wicked man rules, the people groan *and* sigh.

3 A man who loves [skillful and godly] wisdom makes his father joyful,
But he who associates with prostitutes wastes his wealth.

4 The king establishes (stabilizes) the land by justice,
But a man who takes bribes overthrows it.

5 A man who flatters his neighbor [with smooth words intending to do harm]
Is spreading a net for his own feet.

6 By his wicked plan an evil man is trapped,
But the righteous man sings and rejoices [for his plan brings good things to him].

7 The righteous man cares for the rights of the poor,
But the wicked man has no interest in such knowledge. [Job 29:16; 31:13; Ps 41:1]

8 Scoffers set a city afire [by stirring up trouble],
But wise men turn away anger [and restore order with their good judgment].

9 If a wise man has a controversy with a foolish *and* arrogant man,
The foolish man [ignores logic and fairness and] only rages or laughs, and there is no peace (rest, agreement).

10 The bloodthirsty hate the blameless [because of his integrity],
But the upright are concerned for his life. [Gen 4:5, 8; 1 John 3:12]

11 A [shortsighted] fool always loses his temper *and* displays his anger,
But a wise man [uses self-control and] holds it back.

12 If a ruler pays attention to lies [and encourages corruption],
All his officials *will become* wicked.

KEYS *to a* Victorious Life *Refuse To Fear*

Fear robs many people of their faith. Fear of failure, fear of man, and fear of rejection are some of the strongest fears that Satan employs to hinder our progress. Proverbs 29:25 says, "The fear of man brings a snare." But no matter what kind of fear the enemy sends against us, the important thing is to overcome it. When we are faced with fear, we should not give in to it. It is imperative to our victory that we determine, "I will not fear!"

The normal reaction to fear is flight (to run). Satan wants us to run; God wants us to stand still and see His deliverance (see 2 Chr. 20:17).

Because of fear, many people do not confront their issues; they spend their lives running away from them. We can learn to stand our ground and face the fear, secure in the knowledge that "we are more than conquerors and gain an overwhelming victory through Him who loved us [so much that He died for us]" (Rom. 8:37).

Fear of failure torments multitudes. We fear what people will think of us if we fail. If we step out and fail, some people may hear about it; but they quickly forget if we forget it and go on. It is better to try something and fail than to try nothing and succeed.

Approach life with boldness. The Spirit of the Lord is in you—so make up your mind not to fear.

13 The poor man and the oppressor have
   this in common:
   The LORD gives light to the eyes of both.
   [Prov 22:2]
14 If a king faithfully *and* truthfully judges
   the poor,
   His throne shall be established forever.
15 The rod and reproof (godly instruction)
   give wisdom,
   But a child who gets his own way brings
   shame to his mother.
16 When the wicked are in authority,
   transgression increases,
   But the righteous will see the downfall
   of the wicked.
17 Correct your son, and he will give you
   comfort;
   Yes, he will delight your soul.
18 Where there is no vision [no revelation
   of God and His word], the people are
   unrestrained;
   But happy *and* blessed is he who keeps
   the law [of God]. [1 Sam 3:1; Amos
   8:11, 12]
19 A servant will not be corrected by words
   alone;
   For though he understands, he will not
   respond [nor pay attention].
20 Do you see a [conceited] man who
   speaks quickly [offering his opinions
   or answering without thinking]?
   There is more hope for a [thickheaded]
   fool than for him.
21 He who pampers his slave from
   childhood
   Will find him to be a son in the end.
22 An angry man stirs up strife,
   And a hot-tempered *and* undisciplined
   man commits many transgressions.
23 A man's pride *and* sense of self-
   importance will bring him down,
   But he who has a humble spirit will obtain
   honor. [Prov 15:33; 18:12; Is 66:2; Dan
   4:30; Matt 23:12; James 4:6, 10; 1 Pet 5:5]
24 Whoever is partner with a thief hates his
   own life;
   He hears the curse [when swearing an
   oath to testify], but discloses nothing
   [and commits perjury by omission].
25 The fear of man brings a snare,
   But whoever trusts in *and* puts his
   confidence in the LORD will be exalted
   and safe.

26 Many seek the ruler's favor,
   But justice for man comes from the LORD.
27 An unjust man is repulsive to the
   righteous,
   And he who is upright in the way [of the
   LORD] is repulsive to the wicked.

30

THE WORDS of Agur the son
of Jakeh, the oracle:
The man says to Ithiel, to Ithiel
and to Ucal:

2 Surely I am more brutish *and* stupid
   than any man,
   And I do not have the understanding of
   a man [for I do not know what I do not
   know].
3 I have not learned [skillful and godly]
   wisdom,
   Nor do I have knowledge of the Holy
   One [who is the source of wisdom].
4 Who has ascended into heaven and
   descended?
   Who has gathered the wind in His fists?
   Who has bound the waters in His
   garment?
   Who has established all the ends of the
   earth?
   What is His name, and what is His Son's
   name?
   Certainly you know! [John 3:13;
   Rev 19:12]

5 Every word of God is tested *and* refined
   [like silver];
   He is a shield to those who trust *and*
   take refuge in Him. [Ps 18:30; 84:11;
   115:9–11]
6 Do not add to His words,
   Or He will reprove you, and you will be
   found a liar.

7 Two things I have asked of You;
   Do not deny them to me before I die:
8 Keep deception and lies far from me;
   Give me neither poverty nor riches;
   Feed me with the food that is my
   portion,
9 So that I will not be full and deny You
   and say, "Who is the LORD?"
   Or that I will not be poor and steal,
   And so profane the name of my God.
   [Deut 8:12, 14, 17; Neh 9:25, 26; Job
   31:24; Hos 13:6]

10 Do not slander *or* malign a servant
    before his master [stay out of another's
    personal life],
    Or he will curse you [for your
        interference], and you will be found
        guilty.

11 There is a generation (class of people)
    that curses its father
    And does not bless its mother.
12 There is a generation (class of people)
    that is pure in its own eyes,
    Yet is not washed from its filthiness.
13 There is a generation (class of
    people)—oh, how lofty are their eyes!
    And their eyelids are raised *in
    arrogance.*
14 There is a generation (class of people)
    whose teeth are like swords
    And whose jaw teeth are like knives,
    To devour the afflicted from the earth
    And the needy from among men.

15 The leech has two daughters,
    "Give, give!"
    There are three things that are never
        satisfied,
    Four that do not say, "It is enough":
16 Sheol, and the barren womb,
    Earth that is never satisfied with water,
    And fire that never says, "It is enough."
17 The eye that mocks a father
    And scorns a mother,
    The ravens of the valley will pick it
        out,
    And the young vultures will devour it.
    [Lev 20:9; Prov 20:20; 23:22]

18 There are three things which are
    too astounding *and* unexpectedly
    wonderful for me,
    Four which I do not understand:
19 The way of an eagle in the air,
    The way of a serpent on a rock,
    The way of a ship in the middle of the
        sea,
    And the way of a man with a maid.
20 This is the way of an adulterous woman:
    She eats and wipes her mouth
    And says, "I have done no wrong."

21 Under three things the earth is
    disquieted *and* quakes,
    And under four it cannot bear up:
22 Under a servant when he reigns,

Under a [spiritually blind] fool when he
    is filled with food,
23 Under an unloved woman when she gets
    married,
    And *under* a maidservant when she
        supplants her mistress.

24 There are four things that are small on
    the earth,
    But they are exceedingly wise:
25 The ants are not a strong people,
    Yet they prepare their food in the
        summer; [Prov 6:6]
26 The shephanim are not a mighty folk,
    Yet they make their houses in the rocks;
    [Ps 104:18]
27 The locusts have no king,
    Yet all of them go out in groups;
28 You may grasp the lizard with your
    hands,
    Yet it is in kings' palaces.

29 There are three things which are stately
    in step,
    Even four which are stately in their
        stride:
30 The lion, which is mighty among beasts
    And does not turn back before any;
31 The strutting rooster, the male goat also,
    And the king *when his* army is with him.

32 If you have foolishly exalted yourself,
    Or if you have plotted *evil, put your*
        hand on your mouth. [Job 21:5; 40:4]
33 Surely the churning of milk produces
    butter,
    And wringing the nose produces blood;
    So the churning of anger produces strife.

31 THE WORDS of King Lemuel,
    the oracle, which his mother
    taught him:

2 What, O my son?
    And what, O son of my womb?
    And what [shall I advise you], O son of
        my vows?
3 Do not give your [generative] strength
    to women [neither foreign wives
    in marriages of alliances, nor
    concubines],
    Nor your ways to that which destroys
        kings.
4 It is not for kings, O Lemuel,
    It is not for kings to drink wine,

A Prayer To Renew Your Mind

YOU CAN PRAY THIS PRAYER FOR YOURSELF
OR FOR A WOMAN YOU KNOW.

*Lord, I pray that I will be an excellent
woman, one who is spiritual, capable,
intelligent, and virtuous. I am more
precious than jewels and my worth is
far above rubies or pearls. I pray that
the heart of my husband will trust in
me with confidence, and he will have
no lack of gain. Help me to comfort,
encourage, and do him good, not evil,
all the days of my life.*

· *adapted from Proverbs 31:10–12*

Or for rulers to desire strong drink, [Eccl 10:17; Hos 4:11]

5 Otherwise they drink and forget the law *and* its decrees,

And pervert the rights *and* justice of all the afflicted.

6 Give strong drink [as medicine] to him who is ready to pass away,

And wine to him whose life is bitter.

7 Let him drink and forget his poverty

And no longer remember his trouble.

8 Open your mouth for the mute,

For the rights of all who are unfortunate *and* defenseless; [1 Sam 19:4; Esth 4:16; Job 29:15, 16]

9 Open your mouth, judge righteously,

And administer justice for the afflicted and needy. [Lev 19:15; Deut 1:16; Job 29:12; Is 1:17; Jer 22:16]

10 An excellent woman [one who is spiritual, capable, intelligent, and virtuous], who is he who can find her?

Her value is more precious than jewels *and* her worth is far above rubies *or* pearls. [Prov 12:4; 18:22; 19:14]

11 The heart of her husband trusts in her [with secure confidence],

And he will have no lack of gain.

12 She comforts, encourages, *and* does him only good and not evil

All the days of her life.

13 She looks for wool and flax

And works with willing hands in delight.

14 She is like the merchant ships [abounding with treasure];

She brings her [household's] food from far away.

15 She rises also while it is still night

And gives food to her household

And assigns tasks to her maids. [Job 23:12]

16 She considers a field before she buys *or* accepts it [expanding her business prudently];

With her profits she plants fruitful vines in her vineyard.

17 She equips herself with strength [spiritual, mental, and physical fitness for her God-given task]

And makes her arms strong.

18 She sees that her gain is good;

Her lamp does not go out, but it burns continually through the night [she is prepared for whatever lies ahead].

19 She stretches out her hands to the distaff,

And her hands hold the spindle [as she spins wool into thread for clothing].

20 She opens *and* extends her hand to the poor,

And she reaches out her filled hands to the needy.

21 She does not fear the snow for her household,

For all in her household are clothed in [expensive] scarlet [wool]. [Josh 2:18, 19; Heb 9:19–22]

22 She makes for herself coverlets, cushions, *and* rugs of tapestry.

Her clothing is linen, pure *and* fine, and purple [wool]. [Is 61:10; 1 Tim 2:9; Rev 3:5; 19:8, 14]

23 Her husband is known in the [city's] gates,

When he sits among the elders of the land. [Prov 12:4]

24 She makes [fine] linen garments and sells them;

And supplies sashes to the merchants.

25 Strength and dignity are her clothing *and* her position is strong and secure;

And she smiles at the future [knowing that she and her family are prepared].

26 She opens her mouth in [skillful and godly] wisdom,

And the teaching of kindness is on her tongue [giving counsel and instruction].

WINNING THE BATTLES *of the* MIND
Kindness on Your Tongue

For years I was angry and spoke harshly as a result of being mistreated and abused as a child. I ended up with a harsh, hard spirit; therefore, all the words I spoke were harsh and hard. As a young adult, I determined that no one would ever hurt me again, and that attitude permeated my thoughts and influenced my speech.

Though I tried to say things that were right and pleasing to others, once those comments had passed through my soul (my mind, my will, and my emotions) and picked up the hardness and bitterness hidden there, they came out sounding angry and impatient.

No matter how right people's hearts may be before the Lord, if they have pride, anger, or resentment in their soul, they cannot open their mouths without somehow expressing that negativity. They may not even recognize the harshness in their tone of voice, but others will.

Jesus said that the reason we cannot keep our thoughts and emotions from influencing our words is this: "For the mouth speaks out of that which fills the heart" (Matt. 12:34). Whatever is in us will come out in our words.

Because I spent years as a harsh, angry person, the Lord had to do quite a work in order for me to develop gentleness. Part of what God revealed to me in His Word concerning this issue was Proverbs 31:26. When I read it, I thought, *Oh, Lord, I need help!* I felt that whenever I opened my mouth, out came a hammer.

Maybe you can relate to what I experienced. You may have been mistreated and abused as a young person as I was, and you are now filled with hatred, resentment, distrust, anger, and hostility. Instead of kindness, you express harshness and hardness, even when you do not want to.

Spending time in God's Word and in fellowship with Him, letting Him heal the hurts of your past, seeking counseling if you need it, and working to overcome the negativity you have grown up with are worth the effort. When the law of kindness is on your tongue, not only will the people around you benefit, you will also feel better about yourself and be more able to enjoy your life.

A PRAYER FOR VICTORY

Lord, whatever it takes for You to heal me and help me to learn to speak kindly and gently, I ask You to do it in my life. I don't want to speak words that sound harsh, but words that bless and encourage the people around me. In Jesus' name. Amen.

²⁷ She looks well to how things go in her
  household,
  And does not eat the bread of idleness.
  [1 Tim 5:14; Titus 2:5]
²⁸ Her children rise up and call her blessed
  (happy, prosperous, to be admired);
  Her husband also, and he praises her,
  saying,
²⁹ "Many daughters have done nobly, *and*
  well [with the strength of character
  that is steadfast in goodness],

But you excel them all."
³⁰ Charm *and* grace are deceptive, and
  [superficial] beauty is vain,
  But a woman who fears the LORD
  [reverently worshiping, obeying,
  serving, and trusting Him with awe-
  filled respect], she shall be praised.
³¹ Give her of the product of her
  hands,
  And let her own works praise her in the
  gates [of the city]. [Phil 4:8]

How To Have a Real Relationship with Jesus

God loves you! He created you as a special,
unique, one-of-a-kind individual, and He has a specific
purpose and plan for your life. He wants you to live in
victory. Through a personal relationship with your
Creator—God—you can discover a way of life
that will truly satisfy your soul.

No matter who you are, what you've done, or where you are in your life right now, God's love and grace are greater than your sin (your mistakes). Jesus willingly gave His life so you can receive forgiveness from God and have new life in Him. He's just waiting for you to invite Him to be your Savior and Lord.

If you are ready to commit your life to Jesus and follow Him, all you have to do is ask Him to forgive your sins and give you a fresh start in the life you are meant to live. You can begin right now by praying this prayer:

Lord Jesus, thank You for giving Your life for me and forgiving me of my sins so I can have a personal relationship with You. I am sincerely sorry for the mistakes I've made, and I know I need You to help me live right. Your Word says in Romans 10:9, "if you acknowledge and confess with your mouth that Jesus is Lord [recognizing His power, authority, and majesty as God], and believe in your heart that God raised Him from the dead, you will be saved." I believe You are the Son of God, and I confess You as my Savior and Lord. Take me just as I am, and work in my heart, making me the person You want me to be. I want to live for You, Jesus, and I am so grateful to You for giving me a fresh start in my new life with You today.
I love you, Jesus! Amen.

It's amazing to know that God loves us so much! He wants to have a deep, intimate relationship with us that grows every day as we spend time with Him in prayer and Bible study.

For more about your new life in Christ, visit www.joycemeyer.org/salvation to request at no cost the book *A New Way of Living*. At joycemeyer.org, you can also find other free resources to help you take your next steps toward everything God has for you.

Congratulations on your fresh start
in your life in Christ!

MY VICTORIES
on the BATTLEFIELD
of the MIND

I believe that the only way to win the battle of the mind is to read, study, and live according to the Word of God. That's why I want to provide you with the following pages as a place for you to record the victories God gives you on the battlefield of the mind. Feel free to write your prayer requests and answered prayers, to make a list of the mental challenges you are overcoming, to jot down what you are learning about living as a victorious believer, and to make notes about how you are learning to recognize and resist the enemy when he comes against you. Just as *Battlefield of the Mind Psalms and Proverbs* is a compilation of many years of life lessons I've learned about how to better think as God thinks, I hope you will use these pages to write about all the lessons God is teaching you and the victorious experiences you are having with Him during this time in your life.

Joyce Meyer

MY VICTORIES *on the* BATTLEFIELD *of the* MIND